The Shooting Gallery

Julian's Private Scrapbook

Book 3

The Shooting Gallery

Special Edition

a summer frolic
by
Eldot

Kravitz & Sons
INNOVATORS IN PUBLISHING, MARKETING AND ADVERTISING

To WGH

In cooperation with Diphra Enterprises, this Special Edition of Poker Club is a production of Kravitz and Sons.

Kravitz and Sons LLC
204 E Arlington Blvd. Suite B
Greenville, NC 27858

Published by Kravitz and Sons LLC.

ISBN: 979-8-89639-447-1 (sc)
ISBN: 979-8-89639-446-4 (e)

The Shooting Gallery:
Julian's Private Scrapbook, Book 3

Eldot

Reviewed January, 2019

Quality Review Service

In part three of Julian's private scrapbook, 15 year-old Julian Forrest's odyssey continues. As suggested by the extended title, it is indeed a homoerotic fantasia, with a crucial difference. It is set within the detailed context of Camp Walker, a boy scout camp, with simple, exhilarating, all-male joys. Swimming naked, canoeing, archery, hiking, forestry; earning merit badges and enjoying the camaraderie of buddies, with a noteworthy absence of toxic pissing contests. Like similar, benign, men-only communities, they do inspections and dutifully make their beds, cook for each other, and plan funny skits. They help each other with skills sets like holding a bow properly, how to navigate a canoe across a lake, adjusting their uniforms just so, and plenty of banter and unabashed sharing to boot. They giggle and shake hands and josh and fart as if nothing could be more hilarious. It's really very touching, maybe because they can be themselves, without girls to impress. (Hey, I can't get the hang of this life vest. - No worries, man, it's easy-peasy. Here.) Eldot has a vivid feel for the energy and chemistry of guys enjoying the company of guys. And, yes, sometimes impulsively engaging with other blokes to appease a spontaneous boner.

Julian is crushing pretty hard on Scoutmaster Mark Schaefer, but he's too sweet and deferential to push or be inappropriate. Mark is well aware of Julian's attempts to catch a glimpse of him naked, and takes it all in stride. After all, many boys, straight or gay, are curious about other guys, and Mark gets it. Right away Mark realizes the extent of Julian's naïvete, and insists that they share his cabin, lest Julian fall prey. Mark genuinely cares for Julian, and would never exploit Julian's feelings. He addresses Julian as a scoutmaster and a friend, answering his questions honestly. Keeping him safe, while encouraging him. Mark understands boys and men, and never shames Julian for his curiosity or intrepid desire to understand his burgeoning sexuality. When he gives Julian a talk about using careful judgment in certain circumstances, Julian gets the gravitas while feeling empowered to learn and grow. None of this, or anything else in Eldot's novels, is tongue in cheek. Not really. He never indulges in the winking, or salacious nudging so common in queer erotica.

And Eldot doesn't neglect the supporting cast. Nick and Tom discover unexpected intimacy in their sexual capers. Sid and Julian catch Doug and Paul getting oral underwater and decide to try it themselves. On land. A small group of the guys sit on the dock and answer the urgent call for a quick circle jerk. Sid, adorable but skinny, and Kurt the muscle guy, find impulsive joy by experimenting on each other. Eldot introduces Geoff Staples, a beautiful Hawaiian boy, who is not at all shy (though discreet) when it comes to his desires and demonstrating formidable skill. In a delightful episode, Andy and Tony catch up with Tom on the trail and engage in some gorgeous, adventurous ways of sparking ecstasy. Throughout all of this, Julian brings such utter kindness and unpretentiousness, that he earns the affection and respect of all the guys. His impulsive bravado gets them jazzed; fills them with sublime glee. It's important to note here, the friendly, playful group dynamic that Eldot creates. It is a sad fact that when The Barr Meadow series is set (the early 60's) intolerance and persecution of the Gay Community was prevalent. Ruined lives wasn't the worst of it. It's also a disgrace that though it's gotten better, ignorance and abuse persist to this day. Eldot's halcyon gathering, where straight and gay chaps rock their mutual sexuality in't far off the mark. It's not exactly front page news that teenage guys have rampant libidos. Even after the age of majority, many men, given the right circumstances (often the absence of women) have no problem with same gender sexuality. Wherever they take it, they can move ahead without shame.

Eldot embraces the unspoken truth that guys can explore each other's eroticism without humiliation or self-loathing, if they know how; especially when surrounded by enlightened buddies. Eldot's prose is measured and down-to-earth, without the purple, hyperbolic descriptions that too often define man to man queer erotic literature. We go inside the character's heads and learn about their boldness, their reasoning, their graciousness, their insecurities, their eagerness to find the sybaritic realm of pleasuring. The encounters are plain-spoken and enjoyable, set within a plausible context, and not too formal to discuss the first time you connect, with amazing results. The Shooting Gallery culminates in a funny, randy, circle jerk competition; fifteen guys, glorying in bouncing erections, go off like rockets, if you'll excuse a flight of fancy.

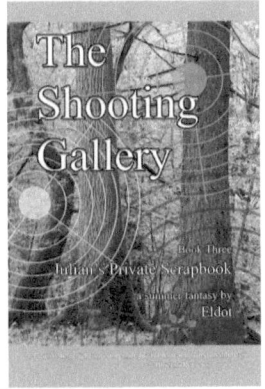

QRS Highest recommendation

QUALITY REVIEW SERVICE

The Shooting Gallery: Julian's Private Scrapbook Part Three
Eldot
Xlibris, 287 pages, (paperback) $15.99, 978-1-4771-4986-7
(Reviewed: April 2014)

The Shooting Gallery is the third in Eldot's five-part series: "Julian's Private Scrapbook."We find ourselves in a Boy Scout Camp, where our pubescent hero, Julian Forrest,comes of age in June 1962.

Julian is a prodigy when it comes to drawing, a talent that garners many accolades. As we might expect, there are other skills to be mastered at camp: swimming, canoeing, archery, cooking — and, in this case, sex. In *Barr's Meadow* (Part 1) readers came to appreciate Julian's beauty, exuberance, affability and guilelessness. There, Eldot laid out the rituals and routines of scout camp: inspection and clean-up, naked swimming and campfire sing-alongs. In the midst of this cheery beehive, Julian had his first sexual experience with another scout; another encounter involved two older, more experienced boys.

In *The Shooting Gallery*, the author again presents the everyday activities we might expect, but now, sexual behavior is more frequent. While this kind of intimacy is often explored in fiction, it's much rarer to find it imbued with positive, canny eroticism, as it is here. In *The Shooting Gallery*, the tone is somewhat Utopian; the characters are not influenced by the usual shame or taboos society places on sex between males. Boy Scout Camp becomes a refuge where characters freely (though conscientiously) experiment with same-gender eroticism.

Eldot not only examines male-only sexual episodes, he anchors them in verisimilitude. Unlike more fantasy-driven erotica that sets up outlandish, compulsive scenarios, the sex here arises organically from the plot. The author goes inside the heads of the characters, so that we understand their bashfulness, their longing or curiosity. There is a nonchalant, playful tone that removes the stigma of queer intimacy that easily might have tormented teenaged American men in 1962.

All in all, *The Shooting Gallery* is a satisfying, intelligent story, notable for its warmth and credibility. It's perfect for those who appreciate homoerotic content without the usual overblown raunch so common to the genre.

Also available in hardcover and ebook.

Publisher's Note:

This book is written for a mature audience. Though LBGT romance fiction has become popular, the subject remains controversial and sensitive to many. It is not written to serve or encourage prurient interests; it contains no pornography or graphic language, but there are several intimate male/male passages. Readers who are offended by that should be prepared to skip over a few scenes. For the convenience of new readers, the prefatory note from the first book is included at the back of the book. It addresses the social rationale that underlies the series.

The placement of this story in a scout camp has not been made with permission. The story is not about any organization or its activities, goals, or personnel. It is about fictional characters and what is happening in their lives outside of the scouting domain. Presumably much of what the characters do would not be approved or condoned by any scout organization, and nowhere is such a thing suggested or inferred. But in the time and place that this story takes place, as in much of the developed world, the scouting enterprise was so universal and ubiquitous that scout camp was nearly generic. It is a logical setting in which to focus on these characters' lives. The scout organization in this story, entirely fictional as well, is depicted with respect and admiration whenever and wherever it is mentioned.

Though its origin is a response to true-life experience, *Julian's Private Scrapbook* is a work of fiction. Similarities to actual persons and places have been modified to eliminate any basis for recognition. Some of the places exist, but are used fictitiously.

For a deeper look the technical side of this book, extensive essays are available at the series website (diphra.com)

Table of Contents

Back of the book extras

Key to Symbols

	Title page
	Segment End, Non Text
	Camp Day Teaser Synopsis End
	Jump Forward in Time
	Chapter end
	Jump to Concurrent Event or Viewpoint
	Flashback Segment
	Scene Continued in a Following Chapter
	Day end

Julian's Private Scrapbook

Barr's Meadow

The Poker Club

The Shooting Gallery

Thunder and Lightning

The Champions

first... a note from the author

The Shooting Gallery is out of the ordinary: readers deserve an alert about two things: the special challenge of starting a story in the middle of things, and secondly, the unique purpose of the Julian's Private Scrapbook series.

the number three son...

How to alert a reader to the peculiar challenge he confronts when beginning a third-in-a-series? An analogy comes to mind—the "family constellation." The third son is the rebel, the one who needs to strike out on his own so as to not be overshadowed by the older siblings.

The Shooting Gallery is similar; some of the episodes are bolder and independent of the first two books. But the main story thread of Julian, the protagonist, remains at the center. The alert, then, is to warn the reader that much of what happens is ongoing, and if something was missed or forgotten, it may be hard to follow or understand what a character is doing—especially when there are so many. The synopsis of the first two books and the descriptive index of characters at the end of the book are provided to help new readers get up to speed.

the series

Until recently, the subject of Julian's Private Scrapbook has been taboo in mainstream fiction. It is nearly commonplace for a young person to develop a crush on a coach, teacher, scoutmaster, priest—or a relative, cousin, or neighbor. The object of affection does not need to be in a position of authority, but he or she often is. What has remained largely in the dark and unaddressed is the adolescent's perspective in a coming of age story that involves this social taboo.

The Julian's Private Scrapbook series takes an unusual approach to confronting this social quandary: it is a romantic comedy. Lets put villains, bullies and prejudices aside for a while and take a fresh look. Maybe if we look at life without the standard assumptions and societal dressings we can learn something; maybe we can get beyond this unpleasant and hostile defect in our culture. Let's rediscover what is beautiful and natural, and fun.

It is not possible of course to please everyone. There are wildly diverging tastes and interests. To accommodate them all is impossible. There are those that regard bare ankles as obscene—others find them arousing; they are neither to most people. But this series has no special agenda other than to help, and to inform by looking at that taboo head on. It does so by using comedy and everyday foibles, and it tries always to be honest as well as entertaining. That means it walks a fine line somewhere between the bare ankle and the style of sock fashioned to cover it.

The reader will have to decide whether or not to skip a passage—if it's too much, they should. After all, exaggeration and surprise are standard items in comedy. Everyone has his own line, ultimately. If it isn't to your liking, skip to the next scene.

The Preface to the first edition has been included in the supplementary materials at the back of the book. There is already way too much up front.

Above all, have fun with this book.

· Eldot

Fonts:

Times New Roman: all narrative and character content, all third person point of view is in standard Times, sentences are capitalized; all first person is in *italics,* sentences are not capitalized.

Optima: sound effects, noise, anything heard that isn't or can't be identified by quotation marks; these are placed between arrow brackets:

>> squipp-squipp... << and >> *whack!* <<

Bradley Hand Bold: Handwritten letters home.

Chalkboard is used to convey information from the author about the setting and story.

Friday

Sixth Day

The scouts of Troop Nine have been in camp nearly a week. Their schedules and routines are well established. As in the previous two books, **Julian** remains our protagonist. He is on a secret personal mission to learn about love and sex in ways that will prepare him for his Life Quest: **Mark**. We take time to focus on a few secondary characters for a while. Some of these we have met in earlier scenes, others are in the spotlight for the first time.

Friday begins in high spirits. The annual troop barbecue and songfest last night was a huge success, but it creates a wakeup surprise for some. **Max's** baked beans and **Brad's** onions have been fermenting overnight.

Developments in the domestic life of the Flaming Arrow Patrol have stretched the limits of discretion. **Nick** and **Tom** have set up sleeping accommodations in the supply tent. **Julian** is fearful that Scoutmaster **Mark** will discover what is going on. By day's end, stability is assured.

Introducing **Kurt** Davis, a member of the Zebra patrol. Circumstances bring him into Julian's circle of friends, Jeremy, Sid and Justin. He has a grudge against Tom that he can't talk about directly.

Introducing **Andy** Ashbaugh and **Tony** Johnson. They are close friends that, unlike most in Troop Nine, want to have more to do with **Tom**. Lots more.

On Tuesday the sophisticated **Geoff** induced Tom to join his poker club; Tom's enthusiasm led Nick, Robin and Casey to join in the next game. Geoff was intrigued by **Nick**, and decides to get better acquainted. Geoff and Nick become friends; Nick gets a glimpse of the outside world.

Sid's snorkel led to an adventure with Julian on Wednesday. It comes in handy again. **Kurt** wants to learn how it works. He gives Sid his first canoe ride.

Julian's conferences with **Mark** continue; he learns about the need for discretion.

Barr's Meadow

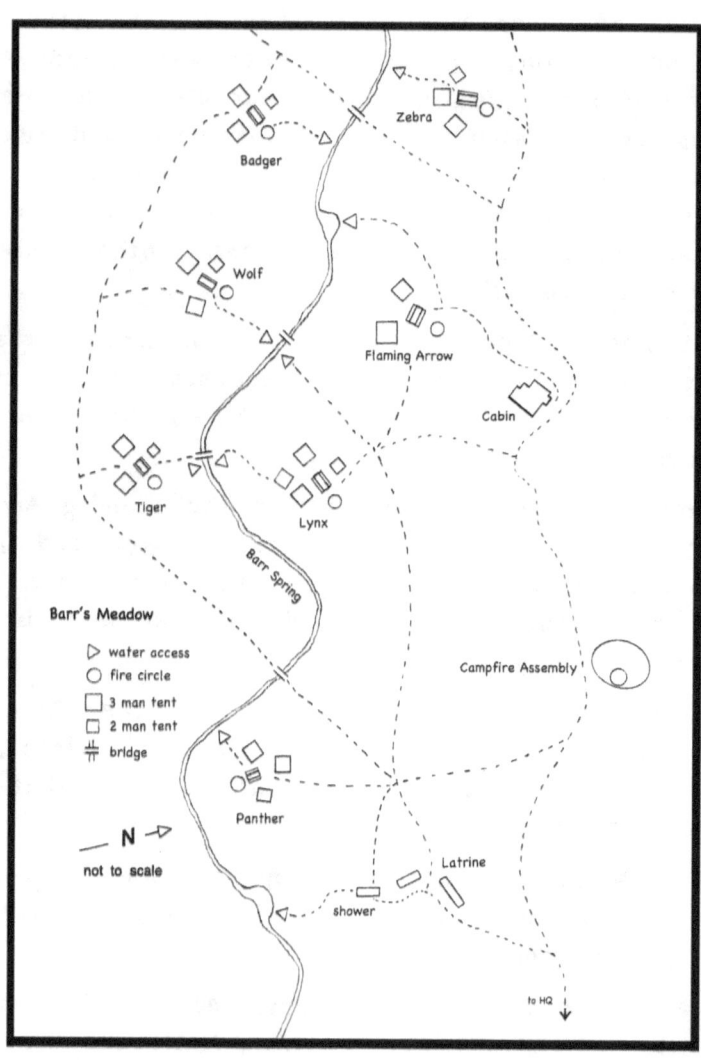

1 *voices of the morning*

Danny awoke suddenly: he felt pressure below. He rolled to the right and lifted his left leg slightly.

>> ***braaap!*** <<

wow... bigger than I expected. He pressed the top of his sleeping bag tight against his chest... too late. He twisted his nose. *of course... it's Max's beans.* He flapped the bag open and closed... *maybe I can fan it away or something.* He got a good whiff... it wasn't too bad... *someone told me once that the loud ones aren't as stinky as the soft ones.* He wiggled his butt briefly. It felt sort of good... the mild stinging sensation reminded him of Geoff, actually... Geoff's wonderful "lessons." He reached over to the lid of the footlocker and checked his watch. *hmm... fifteen minutes before Julian will be here to help fix breakfast for the patrol.* Thinking of Geoff made him realize he was due for a little relief on the front side... *I'm ready... should I do it before I have to run down the hill? oop... another announcement is on the way... interesting, how they suddenly bubble up like this.*

>>bwu—***EET!*** <<

why do they feel better when I lift one leg and push? lucky Tom and Nick are in the other tent... mm. better head down the hill to the latrine. the next one might produce more than noise.

—∿—

Julian wrinkled his nose... he smelled something... *gosh! I must have cut one in my sleep.* He looked across the room... *Mark's still asleep.* He held down the top of his bag. *maybe I can stop more from escaping… maybe it will fade away before Mark wakes up. how far can these things drift, anyway?*

that song must be right. At the campfire last night Max led everyone in the musical fruit song. What a great time… *just about the most fun I've had in scouts, and that's saying something.*

Julian was not used to cutting farts, because his mother was extremely upset by them for some reason. She inherited her aversion from his grandma. She always took care to serve food that didn't lead to such an outcome. Personally, Julian found them amusing. Once in a while at school someone let one go, and it usually caused a fuss of some kind. All the girls hated them, though.

He sat up again to look at the clock… it was turned at an angle, so he couldn't tell if it was about to go off or not. The light coming through splits in the curtains told him it was plenty light outside. *might as well get up… I'll be quiet so Mark can sleep some more.* He flipped back the sleeping bag and sat on the edge of the cot. *eee! this floor is always so cold in the morning!*

He went to the footlocker to get a pair of socks—*it's a put-on-clean-socks day.* His mom had it all planned—*every other day I'm supposed to put on fresh socks and undies.* She wanted it to be every day, but he told her his pack couldn't hold all that. It probably could have, but he had to head off Sid's wisecracks. He could just imagine Sid's commentary as he watched a pack stuffed with underwear and socks being emptied.

Mark had been aware of a nether drift for a while… *must have been a silent one.* Obviously, last night's menu had worked its way through the pipes. He sensed a little pressure in his lower abdomen. Clearly, he had one on the way—a major one. *I hear Julian doing something, so he's awake… I'd better make an announcement.* Last night he had told Julian that a good roommate always gave a warning.

"Purple cloud—" Mark bent his left knee and pushed.

>> bwuump! <<

Julian lost his balance and almost fell over laughing. He'd just slipped on fresh underwear. "Purple cloud!" He looked at Mark. "I never heard that one!" He was tickled by that term.

"That's what we always called them." Mark laughed. "We used to have contests to see who could fart the longest." He chuckled. "Some of the guys got pretty good." *I never mastered it myself.*

Julian sat on the edge of his cot. "Who won?" Fart contests! That's one thing Julian had not imagined. *maybe it would be okay if it was outside.*

"I don't know. Nobody kept track, as far as I know. A guy named Terry Nelson was real good." Mark laughed. "He had an advantage, though. He was real heavy, and he trapped it between his buns and released it gradually. It was hard to tell when it had actually been cut—it sort of went putt-putt-putt forever."

Julian roared. He pictured Bruce in his mind... his torn paper hat in hand, inching daintily forward. He couldn't believe Mark was talking about this!

Mark had a big one on the way. *I almost forgot how much fun these are...* he was too used to behaving himself. "This is fair warning... you have to choose whether to plug your nose or your ears—" He lifted up his far knee and pushed...

> > *bwooo-ooomm!* < <

Julian was in hysterics.

—⁓—

Nick wondered if there was a merit badge group working on birds this year. He was curious about what kind of birds were making all that racket out there. A convention or something was going on in the birch trees; *how can they possibly understand each other?   they're all chirping at the same time. maybe if there was an expert around I could find out. not that it would help any. a BB gun might.*

Thanks to the birds—and to the **unfriendly** floor in this tent—he didn't have to rely on his alarm clock this morning. He'd set it anyway, of course. Danny got them awake just in time yesterday—he didn't have a plan worked out yet on how to handle Julian. *it's only a matter of time before he figures out what's going on with Tom and me.* Nick figured that Julian could probably be convinced to keep it a secret, if it was approached just right. *but he's so much younger... no way can I expect Julian to understand. I'll deal with it when we work on the scrapbook article.* The sketch of Max should be done by then... *maybe I can figure out what to say by then, too. it's essential that Mark not find out about our special bedroom.* It wouldn't be allowed... What would Mark do if he found out? *wouldn't be fun, that's certain.* Three nights already... *how long can our luck hold out?*

"Mmm-hmmm," Tom hummed in his sleep. He scratched his crotch briefly, and nuzzled Nick's shoulder.

Nick looked down at Tom's face—his eyes were twitching. *what's he dreaming about? must be something agreeable.* He resisted the temptation to stroke Tom's hair... *no need to wake him yet.* Nick had almost learned how to deal with this new sleeping phenomenon; he was getting used to it, but it had an odd aspect... *every time I roll over to get a little room, Tom follows... in his sleep! it gets so warm I have to throw off the cover all the time... what the dickens will we do when camp is over? we haven't begun to think about that one.* He did not understand why Tom wanted to be cradled all the time. He was a stand up macho jock during the day. *not that I'm complaining...* A revolution—one that he welcomed. But he needed to understand it so that he didn't foul up somehow.

oh-oh. the beast has awakened—Nick had learned how to tell when Tom was conscious. *ha! I knew it!* A hand was creeping across his leg. *I'm being checked on... I won't disappoint.*

Tom had grown quite fond of Nick's cock. *it's a good size.* He understood better now the disadvantage of having to tote around gigantus all the time. Subtleties were impossible. *with Nick there's so much I can do! he's good at both ends! he doesn't always wake up hard, either... yeah! today he is!* He zoomed down: "Yeowm!" He gobbled it into his mouth in a single move.

Nick chuckled. He wasn't sure if Tom was being playful or horny... could be either, or both. He stroked the top of Tom's head as it bobbed up and down. He checked his watch on the other wrist. *borderline.* He pushed his hips up gently. "We've only got ten minutes."

Tom pulled off and moved up to Nick's face. "I just felt like saying good morning like I really meant it." He smiled and kissed Nick. He poked his tongue into Nick's mouth and swished it across the tongue.

He sat back, enormously pleased with himself. "How do you taste, this morning?"

Nick broke up; he bonked his forehead against Tom's. "Same old, same old?"

"No, no! You're supposed to say 'dee-licious!' You're supposed to say, 'I want a second helping!'"

good: it's playtime, not sex time. Nick started the underarm tickles. Tom would win that one big. *we can scoot over to the crew tent in a minute.*

The wrestling around had an unexpected effect—sort of like shaking up a bottle of soda pop. Nick had to cut one. "Better hold your nose: musical fruit time..." He pushed.

> > *br-uump.* < <

It was muffled because he was on his back... *probably a rosy one, from the way it felt—very warm.*

Tom lifted the cover up mischievously. He inhaled deeply. Nothing. "I heard it... so where's the... *hoo!"* He pulled the cover tight again. **"Bad!"**

"I warned you..." Nick laughed. He lifted his right leg and cut another one.

"Man!" Tom was impressed, actually... *hah!* He had one now—a big one. He turned his butt against Nick' side and pressed.

> > *pwohmm!* < <

"Take that!" That felt good! He wiggled his buns as if to rub it in.

"C'mon." Nick threw off the cover and stood up. "Maybe we can get over to the other tent and escape the cloud." It would be good to get over there in plenty of time for a change. Danny had to get them up the last two days. Besides, the effect of filling this tent with butt breath from two guys wasn't something he wanted to research. The beans from last night's barbecue would likely produce more before the day was very far along.

Julian skipped happily up the path on his way to help Danny with breakfast; he started giggling again when he passed the Farting Post. Mark had let a couple of really big ones this morning. *they're so funny.* Julian didn't have very many for some reason. *didn't eat enough beans probably; next time I'll eat more.* He didn't have much experience with farts. Grandpa Oscar did though. He just remembered one time when grandma scolded him good. Her voice screeched: "Oscar Mattson, you know better than to pass gas in this house! OUT!" She made him go out on the porch. Julian laughed. He'd forgotten all about that until now. He'd almost forgotten all about grandma and grandpa, actually. That's too bad. But he was only five when they passed on. He always liked to sit on Grandpa Oscar's lap and listen to him read stories. He chuckled; Grandpa had winked at him on his way to the porch.

oh! Danny's fixing the coffee already. Julian glanced over to the crew tent. Nick and Tom were there this morning, sitting on the edge of their cots. *shucks.* He wanted to get a peek of them asleep in the supply tent again. *oh well.* He joined Danny at the stove.

"Hey, Julian. Guess what?"

Julian never knew how to answer that question. He envied Sid's ability to fire back an instant wisecrack at times like this. He hiked his shoulders and made a "dunno" gesture.

"French toast today! Get the mixing bowl and tools."

"Wow!" What a surprise. *I love French toast. Mom only makes it on special occasions, like Easter Sunday.* Julian hopped to; *assisting Danny during breakfast is fun—I always learn something new.* He peeked into the supply tent as he got the mixing bowl and stirring spoon. No way to tell for sure... *I bet Nick and Tom spent the night in there again.* It was unusual for them to be up this early. *they're pretty good actors, luckily.*

Danny was in his element. Breakfasts were his specialty, and this one was a favorite. He set about assembling the ingredients. *hmm. this bread is a little too fresh. Dad says that to be really good, the bread should be old and tough.* "Help me spread it out on the table, Julian. This needs to dry out a little." *maybe that will help. soggy French toast is a no-no.*

Was there anything Danny didn't know how to fix? It was easy, actually. Julian dabbed a square of French toast in the puddle of syrup. *I'll surprise Mom and fix this one day.   mmm, this is good.   maybe a little messy, but...* Julian saw Mark tense suddenly. *oh no—*

Mark stood up rapidly and held up his right forefinger. He had a big one. "Be right back." He ran down to the farting post and elevated his left foot a few inches. It was a very big one:

> > braa-aa-A-A-P! < <

Laughter and applause from the Flaming Arrow table.

Mark bowed gratefully.

Julian blushed even though he was delighted... the Zebra Patrol was standing at their table applauding too! The whole meadow must have heard that one.

"Almost a T.A.," Mark remarked to himself quietly as he sat down. He squirmed unconsciously on his canvas stool, seeking to soothe the minor stinging sensation—the aftereffect of his achievement did not come as a surprise. He speared a link sausage and casually delivered it up to his mouth. He saw four pair of eyes fixed on him. "What?!"

There was a brief silence. Nick leaned forward with their question: "What's a T.A.?"

Mark blushed slightly; he hadn't intended to say that audibly. He had to make a fast decision... *well, there's no way I can keep this to myself, now.   telling a group isn't a very bright thing to do, but...* he could see they were waiting. He shrugged and put down his fork. He took a sip of coffee.

"When I was a scout we had a little jingle that described the varieties of farts that could be cut. I forget if it was Terry that made it up, or if he just heard it somewhere. Terry was our resident expert on farts. T.A. was short for "tear-ass," the ones that almost hurt because they have such force."

The Flaming Arrows roared with laughter. Mark's fart was a masterpiece and was fun enough—but they were not expecting such candor about this subject from the scoutmaster. The shared humanity was wonderful. The pause created an opportunity to have another bite or two, between chuckles.

Tom had to ask the next question. "So, what were the other kinds?"

The others all turned to look at Mark. Would he actually tell this?

Mark looked at the group. *hmm.* He wanted to share this, but it was risky… he needed to be mindful of his position. He wished it were an audience of only one—Julian, probably. But that option was not available now.

"Okay—but you have to swear that you won't tell where you heard this." He was certain that it would spread through the troop before the day was out. That was fine with him; he just didn't want the credit. He looked at them with a straight face. He saw smiles and eager nods.

"No go. You have to swear." He raised his right arm into the Scout Sign.

They all raised their hands and swore.

Their eager sparkling eyes were irresistible… he tried to remember the jingle. *man, it has to be ten years since I've heard it.* He closed his eyes and tried to mimic Terry's jolly performance. He raised his arms above the table and swung them back and forth in a mock dance cadence:

> There's the fizz, there's the fuzz;
> There's the fizzy-fuzz.
> There's the rip, the snort, the tear-ass,
> And there's some that go poo…

On the last line Mark tried to imitate Terry's soft slow suggestion of a silent fart. The patrol nearly fell off the benches with laughter.

Mark was pleased with himself, actually… *I may have forgotten part of the jingle, now that I think about it… it might have been a line or two longer.*

"Aaagh!" Shouts and laughter from the Badger camp. Julian could see Bruce staggering away from their table, fanning his butt. They were all spreading out. *he must have let a really bad one.*

By the time breakfast was over, everyone in the Arrow had made a successful visit to the farting post. Julian's was very modest... *well, I'm new at this, after all. I should have kept track.* Tom was better than everyone... he'd had more beans, probably. Occasional cheers and cries could be heard from other camps. Julian looked at Mark. *smiling... he enjoys all this. he sure laughed at Bruce!* Julian saw another side of him now. *he's fun as well as cool.*

After KP Julian and Danny had the job of inspecting the individual patrol camps. Today they were going along as usual: very boring, because everyone was perfect. *whoa—* Julian did a double take: Doug was sitting at the table in the Panther camp. *so, he's a Panther!* He looked around to see if Paul was anywhere... *no; he's probably in another patrol, come to think about it.* Paul and Doug have that stopwatch; Julian and Sid had seen them timing themselves sucking off in the lake. Funny—but hot, all the same. He followed Danny with the inspection checklist poised. This patrol was always flawless, but they had to be checked anyway; Mark wouldn't hear of anything else. Julian glanced down at Doug's lap as they passed the table: did that big bended down one bulge a little? *nope. scout shorts are pretty good at hiding things if you're sitting down... oh well.*

He nudged Danny when they left the camp. "Do you know him?"

Danny looked over his shoulder. "You mean Doug? Sure. Not very well, but sure. Why?"

Julian didn't know if he should tell Danny about the stopwatch contest he and Sid had seen at the lake. He was sort of hoping he could try out Doug's method on Danny sometime... after inspection one day, maybe. He was curious whether Danny's would taste like Sid's. Waking Danny up yesterday morning kept popping into his mind—it was fun watching him get hard. *I wasn't in the mood then...* But the more he followed along behind Danny today on the inspection route, the more he noticed those choice buns. It had been a few days since he applied that sun cream… he imagined kneading them as he sucked away doing Doug's technique. *I'm not sure if Danny wants to do anything like that though.*

"I saw him using a stopwatch the other day. I just wondered if I should ask to borrow it one day." He had chickened out of telling Danny for some reason. He wasn't quite ready to be that bold. *maybe if Danny makes a suggestion or something I will. I'll stay alert for a chance.*

"Dunno why not," Danny stopped. "Want to go back and ask?"

"Maybe not." Julian wasn't sure. "Maybe later."

"So what do you need a stopwatch for, anyway?"

"I'm trying to learn how to stay under longer. You know, when I swim. I never can tell for sure if I'm doing better or not."

"Oh." Danny thought for a minute. "Maybe they check them out at the HQ or something. You could find out at lunch."

"Oh yeah; thanks Danny." That might be a better idea, in fact. He looked at Danny: something told him Danny wasn't in the mood to play around this morning. He was tending to business today. *that's okay too.*

2 *the appointment*

Nick sat on the boardwalk edge watching the water polo team being briefed; the pipe running along the edge of the boardwalk made an ideal footrest. Mark was giving them some kind of instruction. Nick had not meant to, but he had found a superb place to sit, just in front of the tower. He had undressed as usual and was about to swim out to the platform to wait for Geoff—but when he saw the teams assemble along the boat dock, he stopped to watch. *if only they allowed cameras at this part of the camp—easy to understand why they don't.* Tom was standing in the front, one leg straight as usual, the other to the side with the knee bent. *what a masterpiece. to think that I get to sleep with that at night!*

Nick was at the lake to keep his appointment with Geoff. He made it yesterday out on the platform after their very interesting conversation. Geoff had found a way to make him tell all about his "first time" with Tom; in return, Geoff promised to tell his story today. He was curious whether Geoff would follow through. At first, Nick felt intimidated—*he's so clever and amusing and outgoing. but I held my own yesterday.* Nick felt more self confident now... *still, I need to pay attention... no telling what Geoff is likely to say or do next.*

He looked around to see if he was approaching... no sign yet. Nick was early because he'd come in with Tom and Mark. Their water polo team was in the first match this morning. His attention shifted to Mark, standing on the left, gesturing; a wide sweep with his right arm illustrated a special technique... must have something to do with how to hit the ball just right. *hmm. there they are again. I noticed Mark's buns yesterday, too. strange... why do they look so sexy now? I've seen them before at camp—this is my third year. I just never really looked at them before, evidently. of course, now they're uncovered... that always helps.*

Nick let his eye rove over the rest of Mark's body. *huh.* A sense of being out of bounds crowded his mind suddenly—he just now realized: *this is a treat. boy, he looks good! it isn't just his buns... his manner is different... more animated, or something.* Nick couldn't put his finger on it. Mark didn't seem to be so remote, so above, so on the pedestal or something. *hmm...*

Silently, without a word, let alone a flourish, Geoff slipped into place at Nick's right. "You must be looking at what I am," he quipped; he gave a friendly nudge with his left thigh. *oh-h, yes, he is! look at the pink cheeks appear!*

"Good morning."

"Tell me no lies: who is that Apollo, anyway?"

Nick turned to look him square in the face. "That is forbidden territory: that is our scoutmaster." He raised his eyebrows. He had just won the "top this if you can" contest before it even began.

Waterfront

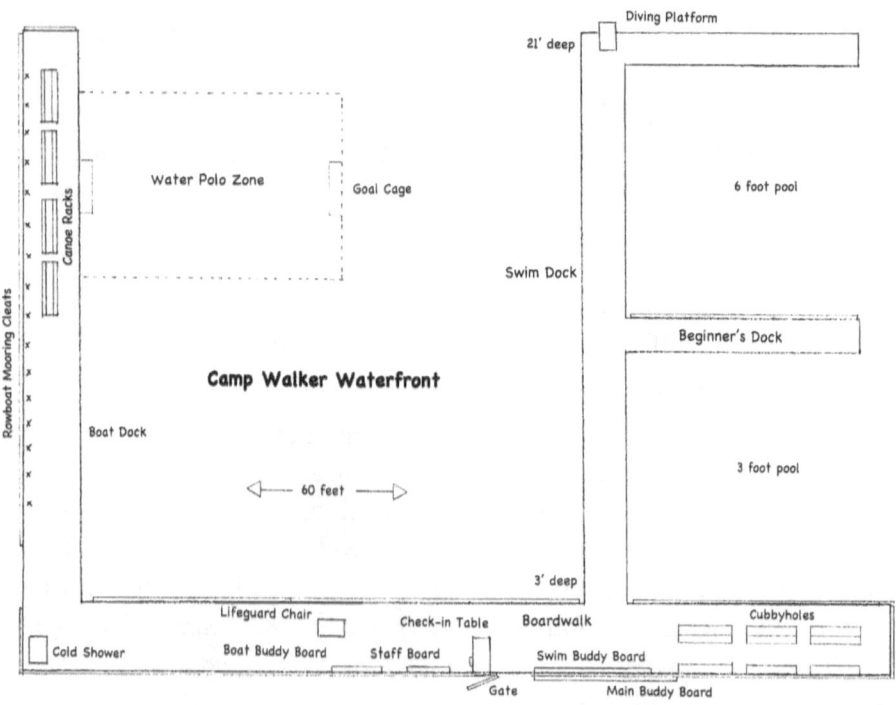

"Mercy!" Geoff studied Mark's movements. "Thighs of doom! How old is he?"

"Twenty six? seven? Around that, I think. He set some kind of record when he started as scoutmaster. He was only twenty one or so."

Geoff looked at Mark's buns. "I'm afraid to think what wonder dwells on the other side of those." *hmm... hardly noticed him yesterday at the tryouts... he was sitting with the other coaches. I was looking at Tom anyway, of course.*

"I'd say about two thirds of Tom's. I haven't looked closely."

"I intend to arrive at a more accurate measurement." Geoff licked his lips. "Doesn't he ever turn around!?"

Nick was amused... *Geoff isn't serious. he's probably trying to delay delivering on his promise. I'll be patient; there's plenty of time. besides, I like the view myself.* They watched in silence. Nick wondered, in fact, if **Mark would** turn around. His curiosity about this had been awakened. *oho!* Mark just drew Tom into a one-on-one private consultation, and there they stood, side by side, facing the boardwalk head on. Mark had his arm over Tom's shoulder. Nick heard Geoff gasp.

"I've gone to heaven!"

They watched the entire conference. It was wonderful. It wasn't nearly long enough. Just as they were through talking, Tom noticed them sitting there; he smiled and gave a small wave. They small waved back. They watched the entire team line up along the edge. The other team stood farther down the dock, just next to the goal cage. They were preparing to dive in, all at the same time.

"Mmmmm!" Geoff whined.

"Shhh!" Nick hissed, nudging sharply with his elbow.

On a whistle command, the teams dove in and raced to their positions in the water polo playing zone. Mark swam along the boardwalk side and the other coach swam on the lake side. A rowboat with a referee/lifeguard was poised on each side halfway between the goal cage and the center of the playing zone. The ref on the far side tossed the ball into the water, and the game was on.

Nick and Geoff savored the moment.

Geoff fanned his legs happily. "We must do this every day, you know."

"What's that?" Nick enjoyed playing along.

"See the boys off, of course. It's our patriotic duty."

"Right. I wonder who won?"

"We did!" Geoff nudged Nick in the ribs.

"Right!" Nick chuckled. "That show was unexpected... fourteen of Scoutdom's finest. And we were here!"

They looked at each other and laughed. At some point, they had both crossed their arms over their laps. It was the only way to shield what they could not stop from happening. At this point, they looked down at each other's erections to confirm what they knew their situation to be. They looked left and right to see if it was clear. It wasn't.

"Ideas?"

"Nope." Nick blushed. *I've never had this happen on the boardwalk.* He glanced around to see if anyone had noticed.

"What did you do for Leonard, by the way?"

"Do? What do you mean?"

"When I signed in as your Buddy just now he gave me the impression that you were his number one favorite." Geoff nudged Nick in the ribs. "He approved highly of my Buddy choice."

"Huh. You've got me." Nick pondered. "I was friendly, as always. I mentioned that you would be along, of course. That's it." *well, it doesn't hurt to be in good with Leonard. he's one of the power people around here.*

They sat a while longer... maybe the short wait had taken care of their problem? They looked again.

"You could start telling the story here."

"No, I couldn't!" Geoff laughed. "That would make it worse."

They looked back and forth again. It was thinning out some, but there were still too many around.

"I know," Nick had an idea. "We'll just plop in... you know, sort of suddenly, in a cannonball. Once in, we can swim out to the cold water. How's that for a plan?"

16

"I have nothing better."

They plunked into the water the second they could see that no one was facing their way. They swam out around the end of the water polo game toward the platform. Geoff stopped suddenly and held up his hand.

"Occupied."

"That figures." Nick treaded water, looking around. He looked at the small group on the platform... no way to tell if they would be out there a long time or not. They needed a secure spot, probably, which the platform was not. The west end of the F fork? Bad idea... that would probably attract attention. "You okay for surface travel yet?" They could use Geoff's tent, if nothing else.

Geoff checked himself: "Halfway, yeah. I'll be okay by the time we swim back."

"Me too. Let's get dressed and figure a plan B."

They headed for the boardwalk doing a slow crawl. They dressed, pulled the badges from the Buddy Board, and walked up to Leonard.

what is it with these two? Leonard knew Nick and Tom were an item. He didn't know where Geoff fit in. *this is the second day now they've been Buddies. is Geoff up to no good? hmm.*

"Hi Leonard," Geoff came up to the table. He had Leonard in his sights. He wasn't sure when or how yet; he knew it was achievable. He could see it in Leonard's eyes. His predatory talents rarely failed to identify likely prospects.

"Leaving us so soon today?" Leonard drew a line on his clipboard. *Geoff's eyes are dangerous: I must not look at them directly.*

"We're sorry, really," Geoff paused, expecting Leonard to look him in the eye. "We have to tend to something. We'll be back again," he added brightly. When Leonard looked up Geoff gave a knowing wink.

Leonard blanched.

Geoff reached out and touched his arm briefly. "Really. We're all good friends." He tried to be reassuring, comforting. He didn't want to spook Leonard. The wink was crude and clumsy... *a mistake I won't make again. I understand Leonard's problem; his secret is safe.*

Leonard looked at Nick. He saw a friendly smile there. He felt reassured, but he didn't know why. He watched them walk out the gate and go up the trail. *hmm... they don't seem to be about to horse around. they aren't in a hurry at all. strange...* he felt confused at best. He shook his head and turned back toward the lake.

Nick and Geoff walked a few yards up the slope toward HQ. They stopped to plan.

"Your camp is closest; do you have a safe place?" Geoff knew he did; he'd been there with Danny.

"Well, sort of. It should be safe..." *I have to head this off.* "But there's always a chance we'll be seen by somebody. The trail there is so wide open." Nick did not want to use his new "bedroom," actually. Hawk Camp was a longer walk, but the space was nearly identical. He only knew of one hideaway in the forest—Tom's special clearing. *isn't much closer.* "What about yours?"

"I thought you'd never ask," Geoff gestured an invitation.

"You promise to behave?"

"Never."

"Good. Then I'll come along." Nick elbowed Geoff as he stepped forward. "But you have to tell all first."

"Promise." Geoff did a skip and took the lead.

Nick hurried to catch up. *why did I say that? is my self-confidence being a bit too adventurous?* Being this daring was new... felt good.

3   *circle on the platform*

Justin folded his arms across his chest. The frown on his face was subtle—only a close, careful look would have enabled anyone to discern that he was, in fact, entirely displeased. It was generally his custom to mask his feelings; he didn't expect that anyone would notice that he was out of sorts. He always sought to avoid drawing attention to himself. He had learned from experience that it was safest that way. His sister, in particular, had taught him that; he was vulnerable to her nags and teasing when he was visibly upset. She was skilled at doubling his misery, given the opportunity.

The cause today was the sudden appreciation of his standing at the ropeyard: zero. The numbers here were large again this morning. Too large. All the stations were taken, and no one seemed inclined to include him in one of the projects. That wasn't unusual, of course. Justin had never been inclined to assert himself. But it was clear that today the only thing he'd be able to do is stand around and watch. Again. He came to a most unusual decision: *I have stood here watching long enough. this is a waste of my time.* He turned around and left the ropeyard.

I'm going to swim today instead of play with those ropes. He had grown bored with that, anyway. All they were doing now was lashings. *I don't want to build a tower.* He was just fine on the ground. He didn't want to build a bridge, either. He didn't have to, anyway—he wasn't working on the Pioneering Badge: he doubted if he would now, in fact. *Julian's been pestering me about spending some time at the lake.* He had not been to the lake since the first day. *maybe it isn't so crowded now.* He glanced over his shoulder as the ropeyard was swallowed by the forest—he was now out of sight. No one noticed that he had left, evidently. *good. it's a quick walk to the lake from here…*

As he passed the bank of latrine booths, he could see a few scouts sitting on the grassy slope... *if I'm lucky, I can catch Julian before he goes through the gate; he said he usually goes swimming in the morning free time.* Justin didn't want to go in there all by himself, especially. Swimming was something he was very good at—he didn't need any assistance or pats on the head. He chuckled briefly... Bob's wisecrack about him being part fish came to mind; Bob was the head lifeguard at the pool. Bob always relied on Justin to pitch in if one of the beginners needed help.

He stopped about halfway down the slope to look over the swim area—just as he expected: lots of swimmers. Still, he'd seen it worse at the pool. This was about six times the area. He checked the hillside to see if he knew anyone—he didn't see Julian, but Sid was sitting on the grassy slope. *Sid's one of Julian's friends... he'll know what to advise. they're in the same patrol—or used to be.*

"Hi."

"Well, fancy meeting you here!" Sid had an automatic affection for anyone else that wore glasses. *it's Julian's protégé, the brainy kid.*

Justin sat down and smiled. *lucky I spotted Sid.* He'd forgotten that Sid was so friendly; he didn't like to impose.

"I see you're all equipped." Sid gave the elastic strap holding his glasses a small tug.

"Yeah. I'd be a goner without that." He looked out at the lake. "Oh! That must be the water polo." The players were swimming fast toward the east goal cage.

"Yeah. You can have it." Sid was grumpy because the game had supplanted the water sport he wanted to spectate. He couldn't tell from this distance if Doug and Paul were in a new spot. He had brought along the viewing equipment just in case. On Wednesday he'd lent Julian the snorkel and missed the chance to see their underwater "contest." *maybe today I'll get a good look-see of my own.* He glanced at Justin. *Julian likes him, so he must be okay, even if he is a Zebra.* "So, do you want to go swimming, or just sit here and watch?"

Justin blushed. "I didn't get a Buddy. I forgot about that."

"Well, you're in luck. I'll go in with you. I was waiting around for Julian, but he hasn't shown up." Sid stood up. "I'm tired of waiting. Let's get wet." He led Justin to the Buddy Board.

Justin was quite relieved. *I'll stick with Sid. he knows all the right things to do.* He watched Sid grab his badge from the Buddy Board. *hum. where's mine?* He wasn't sure where he had hung it on the board.

"What's the problem?"

"I can't find my badge." Justin bent down to read the names.

"Well, where did you hang it? Nobody's supposed to touch it except you, you know." He stepped back to help look.

hum. Justin had forgotten exactly where. Everything was so confusing that day, with hundreds of scouts all over the place. "I was only here on the first day." He felt bad for holding Sid up. He scanned the bottom row. *nope.* Next to the bottom... *nope, not there either.* Next row... *darn! I'll find it if it takes all... aha!* "I found it!" He grabbed it off the hook. *yep, it's my name.* He showed it to Sid with a big grin.

"Good work, Sherlock. Now we have to check in."

Justin smiled gratefully and followed Sid to the gate. He glanced back over his shoulder at the Buddy Board. "Is that my reserved space?" *I don't remember hanging it there. somebody must have moved it.*

"Nah. When we check out, put it on any hook you want. Just try to remember where next time." Sid looked at Justin... *about as tender as any tenderfoot he had seen; it's hard to believe he's a First Class already.*

well... Jack Sprat has found a new mate, has he? Leonard remembered that Sid had come in with Julian yesterday. Julian's troop was always well represented at the lake, but this one was new. He looked at Justin's badge. "Hello. I don't know you."

Justin blushed. "I'm Justin. This is my first time since I qualified."

Leonard knew this; he had the badge and he had a photographic memory; he recognized everyone who came through the gate. "Well, I'm glad you could come today, Justin." *what a charming tender little thing you are...* "Sid here can show you the ropes. He knows what to do.

Have a good swim." He handed Justin back his badge. *the blue is colored in... I didn't expect that.*

Sid led Justin over to the swimming Buddy Board. "Hang your badge here with mine. When you hear the whistle, you find me, wherever I am. We raise our hands together until the whistle blows again... then we can swim some more. What are you going to do, by the way?"

"Gosh, I don't know. I don't have anything special in mind." He thought a minute. *nope... whatever Sid's going to do is fine.*

oo dear... Sid didn't plan on having a tagalong—especially a S.Y.I.T. like Justin. *what if I find some hot viewing, what then?* "I'm going to play with my snorkel some, then I'll practice some distances, probably. I'm keeping an eye out for Julian, too." *please don't ask about the snorkel, please.*

Justin felt the distance at once. He knew how to tell when he was extra, which was most of the time. *well, now that I'm here, I might as well practice my speed... might as well get the first section of the outer ring colored in on my Buddy Badge... I don't want to be a pest.* "I'll just swim some lengths, I guess. Is it okay to swim from the boardwalk to the platform and back?"

Sid's eyes went blank. "Sure." *what a stupid question: why wouldn't it be?* He looked at Justin... *hmm. cut him some slack, Sid, c'mon. he's not stupid, just new.* He found a good slot in the cubbyhole unit for his clothes. "Pick any open slot." He pointed to a good one, sensing that Justin might take a while to choose; he wanted to get wet without further delay. "Okay... just don't swim across the lake or anything like that without touching base with me first." Sid figured Justin would stay near the dock; *he'll be easy to spot with those glasses on.* He checked his own elastic band and stepped to the edge of the boardwalk.

His attention was drawn by a fuss over at the water polo game. A sizeable bunch on the boat dock was yelling at the ones in the water. Sid wasn't a sports fan at home, and he wasn't likely to become one here. The polo boys would have to do without his advice. *other than them, it isn't too crowded out in the lake today... plenty of room to splash around. where should I get in?* A path was open about six or eight feet out from the dock; *I can swim out to the end of the F and back, for openers.   Mother always pesters me about improving in the water, so I better get some kind of practice in.   I might even swim out to that platform again. wasn't that hard... I did it on the first day—'course, I rested up for a few hours afterward.   Sid chuckled to himself: Justin seems to think it's no big deal—well, he's enthusiastic, at least.*

Sid hopped off the edge. He dipped the mask into the water and put on the snorkel. He looked back to the gate to see if Julian had shown up yet... *nope.   I'll keep on the lookout for him anyway.   I might even run into the stopwatch boys' new location.   if they aren't here, maybe I'll come across somebody else playing around.*   He submerged and moved out along the F dock... *plenty open today.   the sights down here remind me a little of the other day... too bad I let Julian hog this thing. he made up for it in the cabin afterwards!   I can't get that out of my mind—I want to do that again.   I have to figure a way to get him to ask... he probably won't.   he moves in pretty high circles these days... usually with the Flaming Arrow bigwigs.   but he wants to improve his swimming—so I'll just hang around, mess with my snorkel some.   he has to show up sooner or later, doesn't he?*   Sid rose up to the surface; he needed to clear the pipe again.

—ɯ—

Julian was doing something different today: testing his time, only without swimming. He ducked down with his nose pinched shut, and counted for as long as he could. *I made it to 38 seconds yesterday... maybe I can go longer just staying put.*   He stayed close to the corner by the boat dock rinse shower where it wasn't busy. His first try wasn't so hot—only 28. His goal was a full minute. *take deeper breaths...   stop trying to look at buns...   see if that helps.   pointless to look without Sid's goggles, anyway.*

He did this several times, but it was boring. Luckily, he was taking a breath of air when the Buddy whistle blew, so he heard it. He jumped up to check on Bruce... *yep; there he is, way over there in the F.*   He waved and pointed until the lifeguard nodded. While he waited, he pondered about his lack of progress. *practicing this is probably stupid. for one thing, I need a stopwatch to tell if I'm really improving... I keep losing count... my mind wanders all the time.   I need a partner.   if only*

I had something, maybe just a regular watch that could go under water. He looked around… didn't see anybody he knew. hard to recognize anyone out here. I was sort of hoping to catch Nick again… *but I hate to be a pest. Tom's over in the water polo game. better stay clear of that…* Julian didn't know if he could look at Mark and not get into trouble.

>> ***BLEET-BLEET*** << the all clear whistle sounded.

He ducked back under; determined, he held his breath once again. He got up to 25… or was it 24? *hmm. lost count already! this is silly, Julian. smarter to hang it up and try some distance practice for a while.* He looked past the polo game. *there's only a couple of guys on the platform. I'll swim out there and back a couple of times. do a good arm workout before going to archery. I can work on holding my breath this afternoon.*

He swam around the end of the water polo cage and headed into the open water. His stroke was strong today; at least that was going well… *whoa!* A speed racer just swam past going like mad! *I've never seen anyone go that fast! what rating is he going for?* He'd only gone a few yards when the same guy raced by again, returning to the Boardwalk. *wow—he's a small guy, too… look at him go!*

okay… Julian reached the platform in good shape—even if it was at turtle speed. He grabbed the ladder rail and looked back: *man alive! that kid's almost at the Boardwalk already!* He went up, content with himself, anyway. *hey! Jeremy and Kurt! haven't seen them for a long time…* He grinned wide.

"It's Julian!" Jeremy looked at Kurt. "He useta be in my patrol. Hi, Julian."

"Hi! How's Wolf's Lair doin'?" He knew, but wanted to be sociable. He sat down next to Jeremy. He didn't know Kurt at all. He always seemed sort of standoffish for some reason. *maybe he's just shy.*

"No complaints." Actually, he missed Julian. *I get all Sid's wisecracks now.* "Stu is thinking of picking Barney to take your spot. Know him?"

Julian thought for a minute… *not sure.* "No, I don't think so."

"He's the kid who moved in from Nashville just after Christmas. You know, red hair and freckles everywhere—a good runner."

"Oh, yeah. I never had a class with him. I know who you mean; sounds good." Julian was startled… the idea that he was being replaced in the Wolf Patrol… he hadn't thought about that before. It was a little sad. Being promoted to the Flaming Arrow Patrol had its downside.

"This is cool, out here. We never came out here before."

"Really? How come? I come most every day. Twice, sometimes."

"'Cause Kurt and I spend a lot of time working on the Canoeing merit badge. We're on the lake over an hour a day as it is."

"Is that a hard one?" *Kurt's quite muscular. hmm. he didn't used to be.*

"Hard enough, let me tell you," Jeremy pressed on his meager left bicep with a resigned expression.

"I bet it's a breeze for you." Julian looked at Kurt's biceps and pecs and opened his eyes wide, grinning.

"S'pose, yeah…" Kurt blushed at the unexpected compliment.

"How did you get all those muscles, anyway?" *maybe Kurt wants to become a Beefcake, like that other guy.*

"I started a program at JB Sullivan's Gym a year ago."

"Wow." Julian wanted to ask why, but thought better of it.

"It was either that or karate, and that was too much money."

"Oh." Julian wasn't attracted to that stuff, himself.

"Gotta be able to defend yourself, y'know."

Julian looked at him, genuinely curious. *defend against what?* Maybe Kurt would say. He looked at Jeremy. He didn't seem to know what the big danger was either. Julian followed his usual policy of not asking stupid questions. *I'll ask Mark later.* He smiled, as if he agreed.

"Don't believe me, huh? Well, I hope for your sake, you're lucky. You never know when somebody bigger'n you might jump ya; what'll ya do then, huh?"

Julian shrugged. He didn't know, in fact. The matter had never come up, as far as he knew. *there aren't any bears around here, either, are there?*

"I've seen ya goin' around on those inspections, mornings."

"Yeah; Mark appointed me to help Danny with that… it's kinda stupid, if you ask me." They had never found an unmade bed, even once.

Their heads nodded in agreement.

"Everybody's always perfect. We asked Mark, but he said we had to do it anyway. Something about overall troop points or some such thing." Julian shrugged. *nothing I can do about it.*

"What else do you guys do over there?" Kurt wanted to know what Tom did, actually. He wasn't about to come right out and ask, though.

"I work with Nick on the Newsletter and Scrapbook. I help Danny fix breakfast and do dishes. That's all I do. I spend most the time drawing stuff for the scrapbook, I guess."

He saw that they expected more. "Mark runs a meeting every morning when they plan everything out. I don't pay that much attention. That's for Tom and Nick, mostly—and Danny too. I usually work on the scrapbook then. Yesterday they were doing that vote on what skit to do at the last assembly." *something is bothering Kurt.* Julian couldn't figure what it might be… *maybe he'll say something.* "Either of you guys have a stopwatch?"

Jeremy shook his head no. "What for?"

"I've been practicing holding my breath under water. I'm trying to work up to a full minute; it's real hard."

"Can you use those under water?" Jeremy was doubtful.

"Must be; I saw a couple of guys using one the other day, over there where they're playing water polo." Julian did not mention what use was being made of it, of course. He had no plans along that line anyway.

Suddenly, splashes at the ladder: Sid's snorkel appeared first.

"You were right!" Sid called out to Justin, who was just swimming up. "Hi, Julian." He slapped himself and the snorkel down next to Kurt and smiled wide, catching his breath.

"That's Sid," Jeremy explained to Kurt. "He's in my tent over at Wolf Patrol."

Sid glanced at Kurt and nodded a brief hello.

Kurt looked at Sid; *I've seen him around.* So far, he had no opinion… *none of these guys look very ferocious or wolf like, though. patrol mascots never did make much sense. here comes Justin. like me, he's supposed to be a Zebra. who came up with that idea, anyway? better than Badger, I guess.*

Justin climbed up onto the platform. *I hope it's okay... there's plenty of room.* He nodded at Kurt; he was a fellow Zebra. He waved at Julian and sat down between him and Sid. He sat cross-legged and smiled at everyone. *Julian's the only one I knew very well. I passed him a little while ago practicing my speed laps.*

Julian smiled wide at the sight of Justin. He gave a wink and a thumbs up. *he's come to the lake at last. lucky it isn't so crowded today.*

"So what's going on, anyway?" Sid nudged Julian with his foot. "You takin' a break from your Olympic training again? You'll never make it at this rate, y'know." He winked at Jeremy. They used to enjoy poking fun at Julian when he was a Wolf.

"Worry not," Julian said grandly. He held out his arms wide. "After ten trips out here and back, I decided to let that speed demon use my lane for a while." He looked over his shoulder to see if he was still racing away.

Jeremy and Sid hooted at that.

Justin blushed. *he doesn't know it was me that raced by!*

"See anything interesting, lately?" Julian gave the snorkel a prod.

Sid blushed slightly. He had not shared this with Jeremy or anyone... "No. Everyone is behaving today." He wasn't ready to deflect Julian's misstep.

Julian grimaced... *I shouldn't have asked that.*

Sid realized too late that he had put that **exactly** the wrong way: three sets of eyes had gone wide and were aimed straight at his. *Julian's going to get it for this... I have to tell all about it now. except for the follow up session, naturally. I'll make Julian help out.*

"Okay... gather in a circle you guys, and I'll tell about it. This is something I don't want to talk about **too loud**." He looked over his shoulder to see if there was anyone else swimming up to the platform. "Be sure to tell me if you see anybody coming, okay?" He placed his snorkel directly in front of his lap.

They nodded. They sensed a good scandal, and didn't want to miss a word; they scooted so close in that their knees almost touched.

Julian looked forward to what he would do with this... *Sid's a genius at making things funny.*

Sid began by explaining the limited yet unique advantages of the snorkel. Next, he explained how he had come across the two bobbing up and down in the water by accident, and how he needed a pretext for getting a closer look.

When he mentioned the detail about a stopwatch, Jeremy and Kurt looked at Julian instantly. Julian caught their look and shrugged. Without thinking, he bounced his eyebrows up and down a couple of times.

"So, I was on my way to get a close up look-see, when I ran across this cub reporter here," Sid gave a skewering look across at Julian. "He borrowed my little implement and scooped me, first thing!" Sid was pleased with himself. He had just passed the ball to Julian. He'd much prefer to be a listener than a teller of this part... mainly because he so badly wanted to do it again himself. He was afraid he might give himself away... twice already he had gotten a stiff one just thinking about it.

Kurt was intrigued by this: he had a pretty good idea who must have been having that contest. When he was a Panther he'd declined an offer by Doug to engage in something similar; he'd always been sort of sorry, too. It was amusing to be sitting here with this bunch of green kids. *they're all a year younger... obviously had no encounters of their own yet. a little advance notice would be good for them. sure wished I'd had one.* That little trip to Hayden Park still pissed him off, and it had been over a year ago. *good thing he hasn't tried that again here at camp. Tom's still older and bigger, but I have enough know-how to make him pay if he tries anything.*

Jeremy was amazed. He was really glad to be in the company of friends right now. He was a little bothered about being so clueless all the time. *I'll pretend to know what they're talking about, like always. maybe I will know after this.*

Justin thought he had seen it all when he was with Julian the other day in Forestry. Those two guys "doing the dog" still scared him—*what if we'd been caught spying?* He stifled a shudder... *now it looks like I'm about to learn a whole lot more.* He felt very lucky all of a sudden. He would never have been able to find out about this stuff on his own.

Julian had the ball. *boy, how do I do this? I don't want to get anybody in trouble.* He took a second to figure out a way. Tom and Nick came to mind. *maybe Doug and that other guy, Paul—are like them, or something.*

"Okay... But first you guys have to understand one thing, okay?"

They looked at him seriously, and nodded their heads.

"No names. I'll tell everything I saw, but I won't tell any names."

"Why not?"

"Well, it wouldn't be right, Jeremy. I mean, what if you did something, maybe silly or stupid, or even a little against the rules— would you want everybody in the world talking about it?"

"I guess not." That sounded right... Jeremy couldn't think of what he might do...

Julian was more serious than usual. "Listen, you guys: when you talk about someone, without their permission, or knowledge, you are hurting them. Somebody might tell and get them in trouble. You have no right to hurt anybody. If you do, then you deserve to be hurt back. You don't want that, so don't ask for it, okay?"

They were very silent and respectful... some remembered having violated that rule, and they were sorry now. They knew they couldn't take it back, either. Suddenly, they had a great trust in Julian. And they were grateful for having a rule to guide them in the future, too.

Julian decided to go all out on this. He described the entire event, beginning with the test run; he picked up the snorkel and showed how he had worn it. The only thing he would omit would be the names of the participants. He told how he had snuck up in stages... how having to surface for air complicated things.

"The very first thing I saw looked weird at first," Julian held his hands out in front and spread out his fingers, imitating the way Doug had been holding Paul's buns. "There were these buns, y'see, and..."

>> *BLEET-BLEET-BLEET!* <<

The Buddy whistle blew. Four loud groans of frustration erupted from the circle, and four hands went into the air instantly.

Julian had to stand up and look for Bruce in the F intermediate practice space. There! He raised his arm and waved—he told Bruce he might come out here. Bruce waved back and pointed. Julian pointed as well and stood in place, waiting for the whistle.

Sid was worried. Having only one arm to cover what was going on in his lap was awkward... he hoped no one had noticed; he had the dubious advantage of knowing what was about to be disclosed. Slowly, he inched the arm over into the center of his lap. *it's going to get worse... much worse. what will I do?*

Kurt felt a strong glow begin in his groin. He had a real good idea about what was coming. He smiled at his unspoken pun. It made things a little worse. He slowly moved his free arm back a little to cover himself. "Do they always take this long?" He'd forgotten that the Buddy Whistle was so annoying.

"It depends on how many guys are out in the water." Julian shrugged. "Maybe the polo is slowing things up, or something."

Justin looked over at Jeremy. He felt sort of a kinship; Jeremy looked about his age. *how much does he know about this stuff? maybe I'll ask Julian about him tomorrow at Forestry.* Jeremy smiled back. That helped; it gave him courage.

The whistle blew at last.

"Where was I?" Julian sat back down.

"Buns!" Kurt and Sid said in unison. They looked at each other in surprise.

"Oh, yeah. I remember." Julian reached forward again. "I came in too fast, and I about ran into these jiggling buns! Fingers were grabbing them on both sides, doing this!" He flexed the fingertips in a mock kneading motion. "I turned real quick and swam to the side just in time. Boy, did I see something around front!"

Julian described in detail the length and particular qualities of the cocks. Watching their amazed expressions as he described the one that bent down was fun. He put his hands on Jeremy's thigh, which was right next to his. Slowly, he stretched his hands apart, as if he were showing it grow hard—he illustrated the contour of the bend carefully. *hmm... Jeremy's skin feels nice.* He exaggerated the size just a little... he described how it was a little darker on the lower part, and got light just past the bend. He grabbed Jeremy's thigh with both sets of fingertips and pulsed them, mimicking the action on the buns that he had seen.

Jeremy felt a strange sensation at Julian's touch... it was a new feeling. It tickled right behind his balls all of a sudden. He stared wide eyed at Julian's fingers... the hand sliding up his leg felt very warm... he blushed a little; he thought he might be going to get a stiffy. *the pulsing fingertips! wow.* He was very glad when Julian took his hands away. Getting a stiffy in front of everyone was a scary thought.

Kurt watched this performance intently. He had seen that very cock himself, he was certain. The memory of it was one he used from time to time... it caused him to swell some more. He wasn't conscious of that until he noticed that Julian's demonstration was having a similar effect on Jeremy. That made it impossible for him to stop what was happening in his lap. He had to cross his arms... *oh-oh. I've never been able to stop after it got this far up.*

Julian turned to Justin, sitting on his right. He traced the outline of the other cock on Justin's leg with his fingertip.

Justin's mouth dropped open: he stared at Julian's finger...

Julian showed how it curved up perfectly, starting at the base of the top side, up to the tip, around and down the shaft to the base at the bottom, and the balls hanging down below. He thought it must have been pretty good sized too... probably seven and a half or eight inches. He couldn't be too sure, because he only saw it out of the other guy's mouth a couple of times; most of the time, the other guy had his mouth clear down to the balls.

"I don't know how he could get it all the way down his throat like that." Julian shook his head. He kneaded Justin's knee to illustrate how he had seen the balls being massaged. He drew his hand slowly up Justin's thigh to show how the foreskin had been pulled tight. He may have exaggerated the length a little.

Justin's cock swelled rapidly. The impact of the story, augmented by the electric effect of Julian's touch, was inevitable... he could feel the blush on his cheeks and temples... *it will be all the way up soon.* He wasn't embarrassed because he couldn't stop looking at what had happened in Kurt's lap. The tip of the cock peeked over the top of Kurt's arm. It pulsed involuntarily while he watched... it reminded him of what he and Julian had seen. Kurt was about the same size as the guy who gave the spiral hand job. Remembering that that took him up to full hard.

Julian was having so much fun with this! He looked at Sid eagerly, expecting to be agreed with. "They were too far away for us to hear if they were making any noise or anything. You remember, Sid, how that second one lifted his shoulders and shook all over? He must have just had the best one ever!" He laughed merrily and slapped his own thigh. *Sid hugged me so hard when that happened.*

His audience was silent. They were trying to avoid looking at each other's laps—an impossibly difficult task; none were successful.

"Yeah..." Sid had to answer; he was very nervous, because of the condition down below. "I liked the first one a little better, though. It looked just as intense. And when he spit out at the end..."

Julian laughed, "Yeah! This perfect arc: swissshhh... plonk!" Julian traced the arc in the air with his fingertip from his mouth to the floor in the center of the circle. He paused and glanced at Sid, who was sitting opposite, between Justin and Kurt. He would guard their little secret, of course. "To tell you the truth, it looked like those guys were enjoying it so much, I kinda thought about trying it out myself. But I can't hold my breath near long enough, for one thing. Besides, we didn't have a stopwatch."

Everyone laughed, nervously. No one said anything for a minute.

is something wrong? Julian looked at Sid, questioning. Then at Justin: he was smiling strangely. He looked at Jeremy—*he's blushing! what's going on here?* He looked at Kurt. Kurt gave him an 'aw, shucks' look and raised his arms up: his huge hard-on wagged proudly. The others raised their arms too. Julian's jaw dropped. *everybody's hard!*

"Wow!" Julian looked down at his limp one. *I don't get this at all.* He looked around for somebody, anybody to say something.

"You tell some story, Julian," Kurt applauded briefly. "Congratulations. You've got everybody ready for a circle jerk."

Everyone gave him a puzzled look.

"Oh, I see." *I should have guessed.* "You guys don't know what that is? It's pretty basic. You sit in a circle like this, and everybody jacks off. It's a race to see who can get off first. No prizes... just brags." The Panthers did that on campouts whenever they could get away with it.

They all looked at each other. Tentative smiles. They all wanted to do this. Nobody was about to start, though.

"Well, if limpdick there will get with it, we can just about do it by lunch, okay?" Kurt grabbed his cock and started to stroke. He'd been here before... more than once.

Seeing that was all Julian needed. He stroked too, and became hard real fast.

They got down to business. They alternated between pleasuring themselves and stealing furtive glances at each other's equipment.

Sid was quite intrigued by Kurt's. *has to be six and a half or seven inches, anyway. he has a lot of hair, too.* He looked at Julian's... he had a special memory of that one. *ummm.*

Justin was amazed and thrilled... *looks like Jeremy is the smallest, followed by Julian. Sid's is pretty big, but Kurt's the prizewinner... and his big muscles flexing as he strokes...* he never imagined ever seeing such a thing. It was strangely thrilling.

Jeremy looked at Kurt and Sid. He was around these guys a lot and had never even thought about what they were like down there. He was glad about this. Somehow it made them more connected. He felt a new sense of belonging. *who will come in first? might as well look for some pointers...* He had only learned about doing this a few months ago. *I didn't think Sid or Julian even knew about this.*

Kurt gave a glance at each of them at one time or another. None were particularly interesting. A couple barely knew what to do. He closed his eyes and thought about that wonderful bent cock of Doug's. That had to be one of the two Julian was talking about. The other could be any one of a half dozen guys. He didn't know them that well himself, but he knew that they played around quite a bit. He thought back to that campout, and Doug. This fantasy was an old friend... he started to get there real soon thinking about that. *I'm more ready for this than I thought...* He made some swipes with his tongue around his lips. *oh, yeah...*

Julian watched Kurt closely... *some new things... ways of holding himself I've never tried.* Julian tested a few as he watched... *spit in the palm, that's a winner! ooo, yes.* He saw the closed eyes... what could Kurt be thinking about? *he sure moves his butt a lot. ooo: he must be getting close.* Julian caught Sid's eye and nodded in Kurt's direction.

Sid was glued too; he nudged Justin and alerted him. Jeremy had been paying attention right along. Soon everyone was beating hard, watching Kurt's ecstasy. Suddenly they saw him stiffen, and OOOF!

Kurt shot a presentable wad in a high spurt, probably three and a half feet, and it went splat! right in the center of the circle. He pumped out three more, then sat back. He opened his eyes and saw the hard-working audience. He smiled wide, victorious: he had shot first. He wasn't too surprised. He looked around to see who was going to be second... *looks like Sid, probably.*

"Nnn-nn!" Jeremy suddenly shot a slivery stream straight ahead, about a foot and a half. He was as surprised as anyone.

Kurt nodded congrats, and patted him on the shoulder.

Julian wiped saliva on his palm and got serious. Sid and Justin saw him and followed his example. It looked like they were in sync with each other. They worked for a while. It felt pretty good, all right.

Jeremy sat up suddenly. "Hurry up, you guys!"

"Oh-oh!" Kurt saw them too. "You have about ten seconds! A couple of guys are swimming out here!"

That spurred them on—*whoof!* Sid went first, followed by Julian. Justin went just a second later.

"Everybody jump off, quick." Kurt stood and tried to smear the evidence around. "Head for the shore!"

Tony and Andy weren't racing to the platform, so Andy deferred. He let Tony go up the ladder first... he wanted to deliver a little goose. Tony slowed on purpose to see whether Andy would do a good one this time.

"Thanks. I needed that." Tony sat down and wiggled his butt appreciatively.

"Glad to oblige." Andy sat down next to him and bumped legs.

"Who was that bunch that just took off in a hurry, anyway?"

"Dunno. I wasn't paying any attention." Andy bumped his leg against Tony again. *I'm needy this morning.*

"Right here? In front of everybody?" Tony smiled. "I thought I was the horny one." *usually Andy is the one telling me to cool it.*

"I know. It's just that we never seem to find a place. How long to lunch, anyway?" He was bored, actually.

"Can't be that long… five, ten minutes probably, max."

"Hmm." Andy looked over at the water polo game. They couldn't see it any better from here. "I can't figure it out. He's never alone. He should have jumped one of us by now." He was really hungry for that log.

"Yeah. You s'pose he's tired of us?" Tony wanted it too. He reached over and fondled Andy briefly. *hmm; he is horny, at that.*

"Probably not." He reached over and handled Tony. "He's just got too many guys to keep happy." *Tony has the limpies.*

They laughed at that. But it could be true. They played on with each other, though they knew it wasn't going anywhere.

"Have you talked to Nick lately?" Andy didn't know Nick too well. "He seems to know what's going on better than anyone." He squeezed a little, waiting for a pulsation or two. He got them.

"No, he's always with that Julian kid. They're always writing stuff." Tony licked his palm. *might as well up things a degree or two.*

Andy had an idea. "You think we might be able to trap him someplace? We could trade off, you know?" He licked his palm too. Tony was making him seriously hard. *lucky nobody's out here.*

"I hate doing this left handed." Tony's arm complained. "You think I dare turn around?" He was surprised he'd gotten this far.

"Too risky. Somebody would figure it out. Anyway, it feels fine."

The whistle blew. They looked at each other and shrugged. They could pick up later on. They dove into the cold water. It wouldn't take long to shrink up.

4 *Geoff's story*

Nick glanced around the Hawk Camp supply tent. *shade… nice. tents in the meadow turn into ovens by this time of the day.* He sat down in the center to wait. Geoff had gone to his personal tent for something. It was hard to believe that he and Tom had been here just two days ago in that wild poker game. He was glad there were no traces. Those were in his head, permanently… no reminders needed. He just realized that he was vulnerable, to a degree. Having been so exclusively Tom's had left him completely unprepared for any other appeal to his sexual appetite. It was an unknown quantity. Tom had unwittingly opened that door. Nick did not know, honestly, how to handle that knowledge. Was it a threat? Or was it an opportunity? Or was it something else entirely that he did not know about or suspect? He wasn't afraid… he was wary, though. That's why he had let Geoff bring him here: something inside said he could be trusted. His curiosity was in charge more than anything. *Geoff is so witty and entertaining; this has to be fun, at least.*

"Here we are…" Geoff carried in a small canteen and a daypack. "I never leave anything behind here. I wouldn't want the wrong person to discover things; you know what I mean." He chuckled briefly and looked at Nick. This was a rare event. *I'm not going to do my usual campy showoff stuff. Nick probably wouldn't put up with it anyway.* He wasn't sure just how to begin a straightforward conversation. "Let's spread this out, first of all," he pulled a small throw from his daypack. "We don't want to sit on the bare ground, now, do we?"

Nick stood and brushed the dust off his backside. He watched Geoff fluff out the small blanket. He didn't envy Geoff's situation, having to start cold like this. He had to be gracious. Besides, he was truly curious about this fascinating guy… *why not be friends, too?* He lay down and propped himself up on one elbow. It was Geoff's turn to tell about his first time. *I told about mine yesterday out on the platform.* He resisted the urge to stare... *Geoff is so exotic in appearance.* He gave Geoff the opening line he needed:

"Once upon a time there was a cute little boy scout named Geoff..."

"Thank you." Geoff paused. "You are the sweet one. I'm sure Tom has no idea. Well, we'll talk of that later." He sat down cross-legged. "What you see before you is an unfortunate transplant from the far, far west. Have you ever been to California?"

Nick shook his head. "St. Louis is as far as I have ever been."

Geoff wasn't surprised. "Well I hope you have seen something on television or on the big screen, because I doubt that I can do it justice alone." He pondered a second. "You know what a surfer is, surely?"

Nick nodded.

"I'm so glad. My first one was a surfer god named Ronnie." Geoff gave Nick one of his crafty looks... he couldn't help himself. "You may have to be patient with me. Telling about him is going to be such a delight... I will be in grave danger of developing hungers and cravings; you may not be entirely safe." He flashed his eyes. "This will be your only warning, by the way."

Nick was delighted to have a bit of the Geoff he had seen before back again. He licked his lips just to be a tease.

"Ooo!" Geoff was delighted. "Here goes." He wiggled slightly to improve his comfort—*too bad I didn't bring a cushion. looks like Nick is comfortable enough.* "We lived in this swanky set of apartments just north of Burbank—you don't know where Burbank is, do you?"

"Sorry."

"Well it's the new movie and TV center for several studios and networks, for one thing—lots more posh than Culver City. It's north of Hollywood... one of the scads of cities in Los Angeles. You know, La-La land, and all that. My father is a TV exec, and his station plopped us there when we got in from Hawaii. He seems to move to a new station about every five years or so. He's working miracles in Atlanta now. Who knows where we'll go next.

"So anyway... these apartments were owned by some movie studio mogul who has just tons of money. He has this son named Ronnie, and Ronnie had his own private apartment right there alongside ours. His was the really swanky one. It had its own pool and sauna and rec room. The other apartments had to share a central set.

"This is four years ago, remember. I'm just a squirrelly little kid at the time. However: this happens to be one squirrelly kid who figured out what he wanted at a very young age." Geoff smiled slyly. "By the time we moved to Burbank, I had been playing with surfers in Hawaii for three or four years already. Beach parties, luaus, the works—when you're little and cute and know how to be quiet and tuck yourself away into little hiding places, you can learn a whole bunch, you know."

Nick was mesmerized... exotic wasn't the half of it. He had no idea what most of these things were. *so Geoff is Hawaiian! I'd never have thought of that.*

"Let me tell you about Ronnie." Geoff squirmed again. "You have to sit up like me, and close your eyes. I want you to picture this in your mind."

Nick followed instructions... he squirmed to get comfy too; *the diffused light in here is nice.* He closed his eyes... *I feel like a Buddha or something.*

"Six feet three inches... one hundred seventy eight pounds... blue eyes, set very deep. Eyebrows are bleached almost white from the sun... skin complexion, velvet smooth; skin color: caramel tan with areas of burnished brown, where the sun has had its way... especially on the forehead and along the top of the shoulders. The small of his back and bun tops are darker too." He closed his eyes—he needed to picture this precisely. "His nose is straight and fine, with distinctive nostrils... the very tip is slightly flat with a teeny small cleft at the very end. Stunning cheekbones... perfect white teeth. Hair: blond and wavy, also bleached to near white in places... by the sun—no peroxide, no chemicals..." He paused and said slowly, "his hair was three and a half feet long."

Geoff reached across and put his right forefinger at the top of Nick's forehead.

Nick's eyes popped open, and he watched Geoff continue. This narrative was hypnotic and thrilling.

"If he were here, this is where you would see those silky golden threads hang." Geoff traced his finger slowly, sensually, across Nick's forehead down the side of the left temple to his ear; he followed the imaginary edge of the locks he was describing.

"He preferred to have his ears show." Geoff ran his finger around behind Nick's ear. He remembered doing this very thing once when he was in Ronnie's lap... Nick was merely sitting in on a cherished memory. He continued down Nick's neck, and then brought up his other hand.

Nick found the effect of this touch entirely pleasant. *a good thing we're dressed. the reverence in Geoff's voice... wow... he must really love this guy.*

"At the shoulder, a large lock spilled down his front, and crossed over his nipple, just so." Geoff traced this line with his left hand, and stopped right on the nipple button—he could feel it through Nick's t-shirt. He held that in place as he went back to narrating the movement of his other hand. "The rest of his mane flowed back behind... it fanned out where the natural waves took it." He sat up so he could reach around behind Nick's left side. He spread his fingers and in a gentle wave, traced them down Nick's back until they rested on top of his left bun cheek, just below the scout belt. He kept them in place while he returned to the hand in front.

Nick was stunned by this—mostly because of what he saw in Geoff's eyes and face. This was incredibly sexy and was turning him on, but not because that's what Geoff was trying to do. He could see that Geoff was in another place, seeing in his mind what he was describing. Did Geoff realize this? Probably not... Nick felt like he was watching a private movie... the thrill was, he was being put into it.

"From the nipple, the front lock waved its way down, gently back and forth, to his waist, where it spread in two parts to become a perfect frame for his incredible eight and a half inch staff."

Nick felt Geoff's fingers trace that wavy line down from his nipple to his navel, where Geoff spread the fingers so that they came down on either side of his fly, which was just now beginning to swell. Nick was almost sorry Geoff's fingers were pressing on his shorts instead of directly on what was becoming a ready instrument.

Geoff pulled his hands back into his own lap, where they rested on his own recently developed hard-on. He looked at Nick's lap, then at his.

He smiled humbly. "He always did that to me." He shrugged. "Sorry about that."

"Not at all." Nick took a much needed breath. "Do continue." He was turned on, but wanted to hear more.

"It's funny, you know. The hair never covered him in front, limp or hard. I don't know why. Oh: one last thing about his looks, before I forget... You remember this morning, when Tom and... what's his name?"

"You mean Mark? Our scoutmaster?"

"Yes!" Geoff's eyes flashed. "He almost has Ronnie's exact body! I couldn't believe my eyes. You guys may need to put a guard around him. Same pecs, same buns, same thighs! Grrr-mmpf!"

Nick understood that; he was having trouble not looking at Mark lately himself.

"I've gotten sidetracked... sorry. So anyway, we moved in there... the place looked like a Spanish hacienda—balconies everywhere, lawns, tile roofs, fountains and pools. The very first afternoon I was busy exploring the place, and I just happened to be on the south balcony— that's the one that looked out over the central path. I was admiring the way it wove through the palms to the parking area. That's when I saw him. He'd just closed the door of his MG—fire engine red! He was headed up the path in my direction." Geoff paused briefly and patted his heart lightly as if to calm himself. "My eyes were locked on him from the first second—" Geoff reached forward and touched Nick's knee. "He was wearing a turquoise bikini!" Geoff exhaled and nodded his head. "The long beach towel draped over his right shoulder swung back and forth—it masked his backside; his canvas shoulder bag hung on the left shoulder. His sunglasses were unique... probably one of a kind. I watched him walk all the way up the path. When he was directly across from our apartment he glanced up and noticed me, and smiled. I was in love instantly, of course. He signaled me to come down... I raced."

Geoff touched Nick's knee and whispered an aside: "he **always** wears a bikini!" Geoff glanced briefly at Nick and smiled. The rapt expression was wonderful; *I'm so glad I agreed to tell this story.* Remembering Ronnie was always a pleasure.

"He wanted to meet me because I was a new tenant, mostly. I don't know if he had to look out for things because his father was the owner or not; I think he was just curious about who the new occupants were. He invited me to walk along with him to his pool, where he was headed to spend a little time relaxing.

"We sat at one of the round tables he had there. He asked me what I'd like to drink. He offered a coke, lemonade, whatever I wanted... he was going to have some iced tea, of all things. Lemonade sounded good... he rang a little brass bell that was on the table: a servant came out in seconds. You won't believe this: the servant, undoubtedly a Mexican, was as hot a number as you have ever seen. He was anywhere from sixteen to nineteen, I'm not sure; there were three of them, I discovered later! What do you think the uniform was?

Nick had no idea. He looked back blankly.

"A bikini! Yes! His was nearly a thong, actually."

Nick was puzzled. Thong he did not know.

"You've never seen a thong?"

Nick shook his head no.

"Of course not; silly me... that's not likely around here." Let's see... what else can I compare... of course. "A thong is like a G-string."

"That either." Nick shook his head again.

"Okay. This you need to know. Stand, please."

Nick stood. His erection had pretty well gone down, at least. So had Geoff's. They still had healthy bulges though.

"It's a matter of covering as little as possible. A bikini is like this." Geoff traced the line of a bikini from under Nick's crotch, around the left side of his thigh to his waist, then down across his bun and back under to the back of his scrotum. "See? There is a front and a back—skimpy, but there, right?"

"Yeah," Nick had seen those; the lifeguard's Speedos came close to being a bikini. He was glad—or was he—that he still had his clothes on. This demonstration would be deadly if they were undressed like yesterday out on the platform.

"Okay. A G-string only has a pouch." Geoff put his thumbs and forefingers together around Nick's cock and balls and drew them tight together into a triangle, making the bulge point straight out. "It's held in place by a string. The string attaches on each side at the top of the pouch in front," he paused. "Spread your legs apart."

Nick enjoyed this a lot. He spread his legs wide.

Geoff released his hold and stepped around behind. "Another connects right in the center behind the balls." Geoff placed a finger behind Nick's scrotum and nudged gently. "That string comes straight up the butt crack to the waist, where it attaches to the other two strings from the front." He traced the line around both sides and stopped his fingertips right where he could feel the top of Nick's cock. He gave a friendly gentle push from both fingers. He noticed that it was considerably larger there now... *well, sometimes these things can't be helped.*

Nick was amazed; he couldn't imagine a use for such a thing. His erection had returned; he didn't mind.

"A thong," Geoff stepped back in front, "is a cross between the two. It's a bikini in front, and a G-string in back." Surely Nick understood. He saw a blank look. "No?"

"I'm just wondering why, I guess." Nick was genuinely puzzled by this garb.

Geoff sat back down. "Believe me, Nick: if you're sitting at a table by a swimming pool, and a waiter comes to the table dressed like that, you will know why in an instant. Freely working cheeks are such fun to watch. I could do it all day... I have, actually." He giggled naughtily, and patted Nick's right calf, now resting across from him again. Geoff doubted if Nick would ever see such a sight. *pity.*

"How was the lemonade?"

Geoff laughed. "I think it was probably good. Ronnie always had the best of everything. Well, we talked and he found out all about me, where I was from, who my folks were, all that kind of thing. What I didn't know then was... he was actually cruising me." *I was still a beginner then, after all.*

Nick looked at him blankly again.

Geoff tilted his head. "How old are you?"

"Sixteen."

Geoff was amazed. He had been cruising for four years when he turned sixteen. *hmm... Nick and his troop must be small town folk... I'll be kind. I don't want Nick to be embarrassed. maybe I can help him get an edge on things when he gets back home.*

"Cruising is when you're scoping out, you know, seeing who is there, what they have, whether you might want any of it, whether you want to put out anything yourself." Geoff paused to see if this made any sense to Nick.

"Wow. I never thought about doing that." He had never felt the need.

"Never?" Geoff was nonplussed. "You never look at other guys?"

Nick thought about it. *I never do, really.* He shook his head no. "Just Tom."

Geoff understood at once. He was astounded by the simple understatement. He said nothing. Nick had just been placed into his Department of People I Care About. He was sure that Tom had no idea of what he had. He decided to continue his story, but with some care. *I didn't expect to be holding school today; I'm the perfect one to fill the vacuum.*

"Well, I discovered after a while that Ronnie was humoring me most of all, because I was so young: I was twelve at the time."

"Yeah, I was just past that when Tom got me, actually." That seemed perfectly normal to Nick... *just about everyone I know started about then. Except maybe Julian—I figure Julian's still a year away from things.*

"What really amused Ronnie was discovering that I was cruising him!"

"How long did that take?"

"About five minutes!" Geoff laughed. "I was not cool about it at all. Seeing that waiter tipped the scale, probably. I had a hard-on early, just before we sat down. Ronnie was so hot—I couldn't stop it. It had gone down after we talked a little. But when that kid came back with the refreshment tray and wagged his butt at us, I lost my cool. I grinned wide and looked at Ronnie. He knew at once, and grinned back. He reached over to my lap and found out exactly where I was."

"'Geoff, my boy, we must get better acquainted,' he said. He asked when I was expected back home. It so happened that I had about two hours free just then." Geoff paused... *it's so nice to remember this.* It had helped define him, after all. It had proven to him he'd discovered where he was supposed to go with his life. He had never doubted it for a minute.

Nick sensed that the getting acquainted line was the entry point to the nitty gritty. He tried not to be suggestive as he made a slight adjustment.

Geoff grinned, and looked at Nick directly. He saw the desire reflected there and was startled for a minute. He looked down and saw Nick's condition. Then he looked at himself and saw his own. He looked back at Nick. "Oops."

"Very oops."

"But I haven't finished telling it yet!"

"How much is left?" Nick pleaded.

"Hours!" Geoff exaggerated for effect. "Two hours!"

An excruciating quandary: they were both ready to go this minute, and they knew it... but Geoff had just begun his story, really.

Nick realized it was his call... he looked at his watch. They didn't have two hours: they had about fifty minutes. He looked at Geoff. "Ummm..."

Geoff just knew he was about to get a break in the narrative. He raised his eyebrows, not innocently.

"How about a little break, now... you know, for a sip from your canteen, and... well, whatever else we need to take care of... then you can tell what happened next on that patio." Nick grinned proudly; he had spun an excuse.

"What a good idea!" Geoff reached for the canteen. He had decided what else he wanted Nick to get a sip of some time back. He was confident that thirst was there, too. He took a sip and passed it across to Nick. While Nick guzzled he stood and took off his clothes. *that's better.*

Geoff understood something suddenly: Nick had said "only Tom." *wow. Nick knows only the one thing. I'm looking at a fellow bottom boy! I need to help this lad out in a major way.* The fun he had planned just got better: *I'm going to teach Nick how to do a truly ultimate blow job...* He knew exactly what had happened at the card game, because he had programmed it on that card. *I'll bet that that was a first and only time—unless Tom allowed it along the line some other time.*

"That's enough, kiddo. We may want some later." Nick was gulping it down. *I don't want too full a bladder to interfere.*

"Sorry... guess I was thirsty." Nick looked at Geoff expectantly. He had no clue of what to say or how. He knew he had given permission was all. He was ready. *oh... I'm the only one here with clothes on.* "Umm... you're quite right. It is getting a little too warm in here." He looked at Geoff. *what a nice smile!* He disrobed silently and sat back down. *this feels ever so much better.*

Geoff reached over and traced a circle around Nick's left kneecap. "How many times have you sucked someone off?" *there... come right to it.*

Nick blushed. He had not expected this question. He held up a single finger.

"And that was just the other day, right here. Wasn't it?"

Nick nodded yes.

"How did it go?"

Nick thought about that. He wasn't sure. "Well... he didn't complain, so it must have been okay."

Geoff waited. He knew there was more.

"It wasn't that good. It couldn't have been. I had no idea what to do. Tom would never let me, until yesterday." Nick blushed. Tom had insisted, which blew his mind. He looked up suddenly. "No! That's two now, isn't it?"

"Yeah, it is. Was the second one good?" So he had blown Tom yesterday?

"Hmm." Nick paused. "I don't know. It went too fast. He was so hot he came in a second; it wasn't because of anything I did—with my mouth, anyway."

Geoff was thunderstruck! Tom went bottom? *whoa! things are starting to fall into place.* He stared at Nick hard... he wanted him to elaborate.

"You see, something different is going on lately... I mean, really different. You gotta promise to keep this to yourself. Okay?" At this point, Nick didn't feel real sure about how open he ought to be about Tom and himself.

Geoff reached out and held Nick by the shoulders. "Nick, please. You can trust me. More than you can understand right now. **You** are the only person I have ever told about Ronnie... and I'm planning to tell you a whole lot more. You have my word that I will talk to no one else. Even Tom. Especially Tom, come to think about it... unless you **tell** me to. I won't even ask—you'll have to tell me. Right?"

Nick relaxed suddenly. A huge load had just been lifted... he hadn't even known it was there. He looked at Geoff... he didn't know how to thank him. Maybe Geoff would be able to sense his gratitude somehow... he nodded his head and continued.

"All he wants now is for me to do him... it's just the opposite of what it's always been. It's really **strange**... because before, he would never let me even try. Now, he seems to **crave** it."

"So what are you doing that's so right, do you think?" Geoff thought he knew.

"You see, last winter I read this novel. It was really wild. I came across it by accident. Anyway, it had this scene that described in detail a really fabulous fuck—way better than anything Tom had done to me. So I planned for a long time to get him to try it out with me. But I could never work up the courage to talk about it. He always thought he was the great pleasure giver—making suggestions was never a good idea. So I came up with a fallback idea, and I pulled it off the second night here. I got him at just the right time—he was so desperate and horny I was able to trick him into letting me try it on him. He didn't really want to, but for some reason he gave in. I still don't know why." Nick shook his head.

"And now, that's all he wants to do! So I guess the book was right. It seemed right, as I read it... I remember that." Nick paused momentarily and reflected on how he had followed the book's instructions to the letter. "So far he hasn't done it to me yet, though... like that." Nick was stumped, in fact.

Now it was clear to Geoff: that's why Tom had been so good. "Nick, I owe you. Tom did it to me the next day at the poker game. I tricked him into that." He paused. "I had seen him sitting in that lifeguard chair. When he stood up, I knew I had to have that one put in me, somehow." Geoff had been unable to think about anything else for twelve hours, in fact. "Let me tell you: it is fabulous. I'm talking about your technique. Combined with his dimensions?" Geoff wiggled his butt naughtily. "He owes it to you once, at least."

"Huh." Nick still didn't understand it all. *surely that isn't what made Tom say he loved me... I'm not ready to talk about that part.*

"I'm sure he'll want to, eventually. Be patient. In the meantime, however..." he looked down. My word, what's happened to us? We've gone all limp!"

"Yeah. Now you can tell what happened!"

"Yes! That will fix us real quick, I have to warn you." He raised his eyebrows as if seeking permission,

"Go, go!" Nick laughed.

"Let's see..."

5   *class time, think time*

Today, Jeremy was especially glad he was the front position in the canoe. The event on the platform this morning was still so strong in his mind that he didn't want to look at Kurt in the face just yet. That whole event was so… *I just didn't expect any of that.* His best friends were there and all… plus two other guys, one that he barely knew, even. *doing that in a circle was sort of fun, now that I look back on it…* Jeremy was amazed that he was able to join in. *probably because Julian was there… otherwise I'd have been too scared.* But watching Kurt was so amazing. *I had no idea about any of these things before now. especially the stuff Julian was talking about. maybe sometime I could talk to Julian about it without anybody else around. it's amazing that he knows so much about these things. how long has Julian been… we've been best friends since way back in Cubs, and nothing like this ever came up. hmm…* Jeremy frowned; same thing with Sid.

"Hey, Jeremy… I'm gonna head over to that inlet." Kurt had to take a whiz. He should have hit the latrine before class, but didn't feel the urge. He'd been lagging behind on purpose. *we're way too far out to go back… no way can I hold it until the end of class. I don't dare go in the lake—Mr. Brady is out of sight, but I can still see a couple of the canoes….*

"Uh… okay…" *why is he doing that? today we're supposed to…*

"I'm gonna need you to stand guard for a minute or two." Kurt didn't usually break the rules like this, *but if ya gotta go, ya gotta go.*

It sounded like Kurt had to take a leak. Jeremy didn't approve, but there was no point in saying anything. *I want to keep on his good side.* Jeremy looked back toward the lake. The other canoes were pretty far away… maybe they wouldn't pay any attention. *I lost track of Norman and Don a long time back.*

"Anyway, we can use the practice. We need to know how to go ashore at a natural bank as well as a dock." Kurt was forming an explanation, just in case.

"Okay…" *I don't have to get out too, do I? will we be able to catch up with the class?* Jeremy looked back—the others were pulling away pretty fast.

Kurt steered the canoe toward a likely passage—there were several of these along the bank; *this one looks like it goes in far enough… trees are fairly close to the bank along here… plenty of cover.*

Kurt braked with a backstroke as they moved into the irregular passage… *gotta take it slow… no telling what we'll run into. we don't need to hit a snag or scrape bottom. Mr. Brady hasn't exactly made exploring inlets a part of the class.* They inched forward cautiously.

Jeremy grimaced… *I sure hope Kurt knows what to do here.* He looked over the side. The bottom was becoming visible… *looks muddy.*

"I'm gonna take it as close to the bank as I can." Kurt slowed the canoe to a near stop. "Do a pivot sweep, Jeremy… let my end nose in first."

They did a double sweep and reversed the canoe's direction.

Kurt drawstroked with all his strength; his end was aimed directly at the bank. He watched the stern nudge into the silt… *easy as pie.* "Steady it, Jeremy…" Kurt dug the tip of his paddle into the mud and pulled hard. It moved forward several inches. *hmm. still a foot from the bank… can I step over there without… nope.* He turned around and sat on the stern seat. "I gotta take off my shoes." *too bad we don't have room to do a parallel landing.*

Jeremy nodded. They learned how to stabilize and exit the day before yesterday. He dipped his paddle in and held it tight against the gunwale.

Kurt peeled off his socks as fast as he could… *man, I'm about to wet my pants!* "Here goes…" He held onto the prow and stepped into the water. *at least I have on short pants… ug. cold and squishy…* he stepped onto the grassy bank. "Be right back." He hopped gingerly through the grass toward the nearest tree.

—⟋⟍—

Sid was pleased with himself today. He was the fastest in his group to do the triangle bandage on a sprained ankle. He sat back and watched some of the others... *how could anyone have trouble with this? well... gives me time to think about other things. the next one is probably harder—a sprained knee.* He looked forward to Mr. Soames proving his claim about the universal triangle bandage. I can hardly wait for broken arms and legs. *at least we're finished with all the poisonous bites and stings, and skin rashes. if anybody ever has blisters or slivers to fix, I'm ready.*

His mind wandered to the morning free swim... he chuckled to himself—the fast exit they had to make off the platform this morning. What a surprise that circle thing was! He was amazed that Jeremy knew what to do. *I never thought that Jeremy ever had a boner, even. well, that's stupid... I thought the same thing about Julian until the day before yesterday. the three of us have been best friends for a long time. somehow we discovered sex by ourselves and kept it a secret. still, I don't think that playing around with Jeremy would be a good idea. obviously he's just a beginner... not likely to be as good at things as Julian.*

tonight after lights out will be interesting... Jeremy never beats off at night—I would have heard something. I'm fairly sure he's never heard me do it... but now, after today, he might be listening. I'd better be careful.

nope... playing around with Jeremy would be a bad idea. I'd just as soon he didn't think I was a total sex fiend, even if I am. besides, this sex craze is a temporary problem. I figure by the end of summer I'll have it under control... well, by Christmas for sure.

say, now: what about the other Wolves? they're all a year or even two years older... I bet some of those guys are exercising in their sleeping bags at night. Norman for sure... Stuart is such a goody-goody type, he might not be. oop: better get my mind back on First Aid—a slight twinge was starting in down there again. Having a boner would not be good right now... he was about to have his ankle "triangled."

—⟋⟍—

"You're on a roll today, Julian!" Cory was proud of Julian's progress. *the small bow is perfect for him. he hit the target five out of the last six.*

Julian glowed at the praise; it was a long time coming. Cory had stopped the wisecracks about confusing his nocks and cocks. The joke was getting too old, anyway. He'd mastered his nocks at last, and he hadn't scraped his forearm today even once. "Thanks to your coaching!" He looked at Cory gratefully... *maybe there's something I can do in return.* "How's swimming going? Maybe I could help you some with that."

Cory looked at Julian... *that would be handy, in fact.* "Maybe so. I qualified this morning, just barely. I'm supposed to repeat it two more times before they'll give me the rating." *it would be nice to have somebody I know along...* he still didn't like to swim, but he had to admit that it was a good thing to know. And advancing in rank was essential. Every one of his friends was heading for their Life patch already.

"I buddy with Bruce sometimes while he's working on that... I could do that if you want." *oo... wait.* "I can't this afternoon, though." *Nick talked to me at lunch; he's gonna give me another one-on-one swim lesson—with a stopwatch! finally I'll know exactly how I'm doing.*

"Yeah, Bruce qualified this morning too." In fact, Bruce had done so well that Cory was almost shamed into getting his rating. It was hard to admit that Bruce was a better swimmer... a better anything. "How about Sunday?" *I have plans for the ropeyard tomorrow.*

"Sure." Julian had no plans for Sunday—and the free swim would be longer, because there were no classes. "Your turn," Julian gestured. The whistle had blown, signaling that it was time to "loose the next end." Julian smirked: he still had fun with these silly Archery words. He stood back and gave Cory plenty of room. *hmm. Cory's buns are okay... not choice like Danny's, but okay. maybe I'll ask Nick's opinion about that this afternoon. I've been so busy lately I haven't been looking at buns all that much.*

6   *waylaying Tom*

Another boring afternoon swim. Andy had walked out to the end of the F dock with Tony, but declined his challenge to race across to the boat dock. He watched Tony speed across. *sure is a good swimmer... why isn't he on the swim team? oh yeah... paper route, that's right.* Andy wasn't in the mood to swim this afternoon. His latest Reptile class had made him just a little more fond of dry land. Alligators were not something he wanted to risk. They would never be found up at this altitude, of course, so there was no real danger. They were supposed to have a live one tomorrow. The pictures were enough for Andy. *he's almost to the other dock already... later maybe I'll swim out to the platform with him and hang out.* He started back toward the boardwalk.

Tony touched the boat dock. He had just finished a speed lap from the end of the F. No reason, he just liked to stretch his ability from time to time. He'd watched a few of the water polo guys this morning; *I'm just as fast as most of them—or faster.* Being on a team wasn't his thing. He paused briefly to catch his breath. He was about to swim back over and rejoin Andy when he noticed Nick checking in at Leonard's table; *he's with that blond that drops by every morning—the one with the incredible eyes—his buddy this afternoon, evidently. oh that's right— they're both putting out the newsletter now. must be doing an article about the lake.* Tony hiked himself up onto the boat dock and focused on his dive; he wanted to improve his time on the return to the F dock. *then I'll see if Andy wants to go out to the platform... not a whole lot of scenic interest around here today.*

Halfway up the slope Tom watched Nick and Julian sign in as Buddies. At lunch Nick told him about his plan to get Julian up to speed about the sleeping situation—a very good idea. *Nick is good at things like that. he can get Julian to work with Danny to be our cover. the morning tent hopping is really a drag. Nick can fix that with this little talk. so... I'm on my own this afternoon... no duties.* He didn't want to hover. *Nick probably wants to spend the whole period with Julian. don't see any poker club guys around... fine with me. I'm not in the mood for them, anyway.*

He wandered up the trail toward the merit badge work areas. He had some good memories about these places. Some were pretty hot ones too! He chuckled. He was a different person now. That amazed him even more. He sort of welcomed the quiet out here. The badge sessions were all done for the day, so he didn't expect to run into anyone. *I'll hike up to Cooper's Rock... maybe to the forest boundary, then double back to camp in time to help Nick fix supper.*

Andy walked aimlessly, still without ideas about what to do today. He'd made it all the way to the east end of the boardwalk already. He turned around and was on the way back, when he noticed Tom at the top of the grassy slope. *whoa!* He did a double take: *he's alone!* He ran over to the east side of the tower and looked carefully through the ladder rungs. *yep! oh boy—where's Tony?* He scanned the lake where Tony was doing his speed thing... *ha! just pulled himself up onto the F Dock.* Andy waved his arms wide and gestured for him to come over, quick! He kept an eye on Tom—*he's moving off to the west... he's not going to swim this afternoon!*

Tony saw Andy's frantic waving; *he's excited about something.* Tony dove back in and swam directly through the center. He drew a few startled glances and had a near collision. He splashed to a stop at the edge of the boardwalk. "What's up?"

"Look who's wandering off there, all by himself!" He pointed to Tom's back, now about forty feet off.

Tony hiked himself up onto the boardwalk and ran over to the tower. He looked where Andy was pointing. "Wow! This is it!" Tony pointed back along his swim path: "Nick's over there, working with that blond kid!" He headed for his cubbyhole at once.

Andy was right behind. They dressed rapidly, waved perfunctorily at Leonard, and hustled to put their badges away. They had a plan ready for such an opportunity.

Andy couldn't believe their luck—Tom was walking slowly for some reason. They were about to catch up when he bent down to pick something up. They slowed to a stop. Their plan called for sneaking up and surprising him from behind. They froze… Tom was examining something. He started walking again, slowly. In long silent strides they closed the gap.

Tom examined the blue heron feather he had just discovered. This was a much better sample than the old tattered one they had at the junior college. A couple of years ago, when he was a Second Class, he worked there on the Bird Study merit badge; theirs looked like it had been rescued from a bird fight or something. He poked it into his shirt pocket; *I'll pass it on to Mark later. kind of lucky, this close to the camp… herons are usually way off to the west end of the lake where people are scarce. they spook pretty easy. nobody could just walk up to one.*

Tom was about to pick up his pace when he had a nice surprise from behind. *who can it be?* A warm palm rested on each of his buns. He stopped at once.

Now there was a hand over each of his eyes… *it's two guys!* Obviously they wanted to play a guessing game. The hands on his buns moved off and took hold of his hands. He heard giggles. One took his right hand and pulled it down to hold it against—of course! A very nice shapely butt. The other one did the same with his left hand. *this is fun.* He rubbed them all over.

"Mmmm… very nice set, yes." He patted the one on the right. "Ohyeah…" He ran his hand down low between the legs of the one on his left. *I should be able to identify these… they're familiar.* "Do I get any hints?"

Andy was ready: "May 24, 4:40 pm."

Tom blushed. *I know that voice, all right.* "And the other one?"

"May second, 7:30 pm," Tony boasted.

Camp Walker

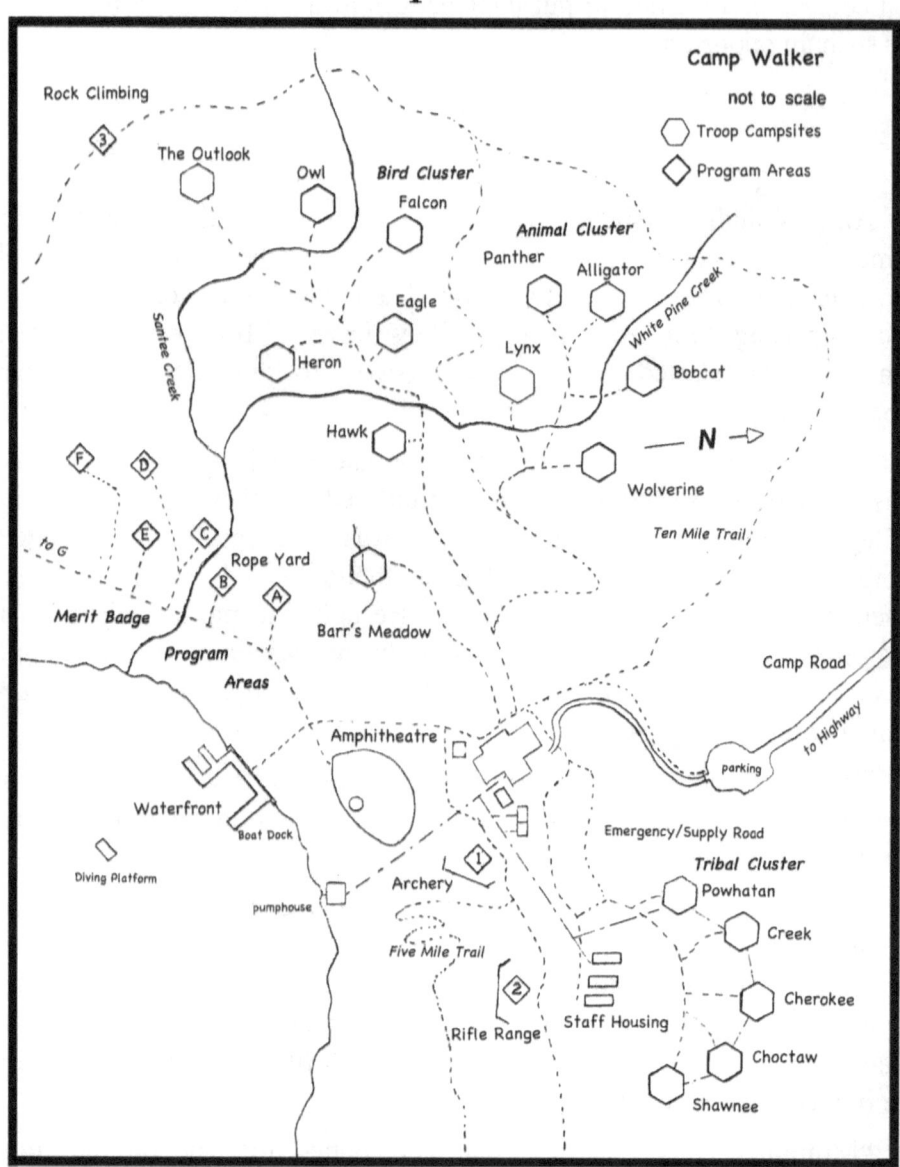

They wagged their butts vigorously and uncovered his eyes. They had a good laugh. Tom was flattered and completely surprised.

Andy pointed at Tom's bulge. "See? I told you he needed us around!"

"So, where have you been all week?" Tony pushed Tom playfully.

Tom blushed again. It was true... under his old ways he'd have jumped both of these guys by now, at least once. "Kind of hard to explain." *that was lame...* He was at a loss to tell them the real reason. He had to protect Nick.

Andy and Tony had decided that Tom was not going to get away without a little action of some kind. Andy reached over and rubbed the bulge lightly... *it's on the way!* "We know, the bigwig Junior Assistant has been real busy. Well, your old friends are here to provide a little R&R. I bet you know a handy little hideaway along here somewhere? You, who wrote the manual on quickies in the woods?"

Tom was a little surprised; he was getting horny... he looked around to get his bearings. "I know just the place. F is a nice hidden area... and it's even furnished!"

"I knew it!" Tony grabbed Tom's hand and started the run up trail.

Tom brought them to an abrupt halt when they came to the Forestry Merit Badge entrance. "Shh!" He spoke softly. "We have to make sure no one's here." He led them in slowly... Scoutmaster Henderson often spent extra time here getting set up for the next day's session. They came into the clearing; several easels were set up along one side, a row of numbered footlockers on the other. The tables in the pavilion were bare, and no one was around. Tom marched over to the far table proudly. "Boys," he turned and opened his arms in a wide welcome.

Andy and Tony skipped over and began to disrobe him at once. He watched, mildly amused, as they methodically removed what little he had on. As they started to undress themselves, he realized that there was something new here. "How are we going to do this?" He had always been a one at a time person.

"We have it all planned. We had a special drawing earlier, and I won!" Tony danced in a circle briefly, and bent over right in front of Tom and bumped his butt into him playfully. He was ready.

Tom laughed. Tony's butt did look awfully good. "I don't have any..."

"But I do," Andy stepped forward with the tube he had just plucked from his pocket over on the bench. He removed the cap and handed the tube to Tom. He raised his eyebrows several times and grinned.

"You guys!" Tom was delighted... *but how can I make this fun all the way around?* He surveyed the space. "Okay, we have a big table—three tables actually, benches, a lot of ground... what are you gonna do, Andy? Just watch?" It had been a month or more since he'd played with either one—*they're both excellent.*

"Oh no. I'm going to be a free agent until it's my turn. I'll do a little of this, a little of that... then I get to trade places. No fair going all the way: you have to finish with me!" He and Tony had it all planned.

Tom was hot now: *I've never had a three way.* Obviously his boys had it all figured out—*they do look mighty good. I'll do what they want. maybe I'll go a second round, even.* That's one thing the second poker game had shown him he could do. He squeezed some KY into his right palm. *not only that: these guys don't know about Nick's special... are they ever in for a good time!*

"So you want back door, then?" Tony was still backed up to him, waiting.

"Mm-hmm, yes please." Tony wagged his butt impatiently.

Tom spread the lube over his very hard cock, and covered his first three fingers. "Boys, I have a nice surprise for you." He handed the tube back to Andy and slowly pushed his forefinger into Tony's awaiting back door. He worked it back and forth a bit at a time, then started the rotation. He connected with the prostate about ten seconds in.

"Ooo!" Tony was pleased as could be.

Andy watched carefully. This was not the usual blunt force poke at all! He watched Tom work in the second finger. *look at his face! I've never seen him concentrate like this. this is so hot!* Tony twisted with pleasure again! ooo! Usually the good part was a lot farther down the line! A third finger! Andy's jaw fell open: *look at that opening!* Tony was writhing and twisting in obvious pleasure, and Tom hadn't even put it in yet!

"Ohhhmm..." Tony felt Tom slip in... full length on the first thrust... slowly, smoothly. He felt Tom hold him by his sides; he moved in response, and Tom massaged his lower stomach in time. Tom caught the rhythm almost at once, and they were a unit.

Andy shook his head in wonder. He went around in front and presented himself to Tony, as planned... he had to nudge.

ooop! Tony opened his eyes and mouth quickly...he was having such pleasure that he had forgotten all about Andy. *yum! this is going to be one for the record book! I'm busy at both ends! please let's do this all day!* He had never felt so good and so full at the same time. *Andy tastes fine today.* He reached up with his right hand and worked Andy's balls lightly. *it's hot to feel them sway back and forth.*

yes! Andy caught the sway and joined in the same rhythm. *oh, this is nice... very nice.* He looked over Tony's back—Tom going in and out! *how hot can this get! look at that monster! oh! I can hardly wait for my turn. ooo... nice tongue, Tony.*

I owe Nick big for this... Tom's old standard way of doing things had been transformed by that opening routine. This was a whole new experience. He opened his eyes for a minute... wow! His eyes went wide: Andy had just entered Tony's mouth! He'd never seen a hot thing like that... *while I'm doing this? incredible.* He had to watch that a sec... *unn! Tony's doing good things too... how long can we go without getting too close... I want to draw this one out.* He slowed the pace... *concentrate on feeling the entire length, and what it's touching.* He reached around under Tony with his left hand and grasped... *yes! still hard... another benefit of Nick's method! no more limpies!* He pulled up the foreskin... Tony's sphincter grabbed... *uhmm, that's good! too much of that and I lose control... never when my tip is there—that's for the very end.*

Andy was too far along... *Tony's tongue is magic today... so are his tight lips. I'm tempted to go all the way... it would be a real good one.* He pulled out. *hoo!* Just in time. Time to swap around. He looked at Tom. It took a second to catch his eye. He smiled, and gestured 'time,' by tapping his left wrist, as if he were wearing a watch.

Tom saw the signal. *I don't want to stop, but I'd better.* One last push: he drove all the way in and held briefly... on the way out he pulled on Tony's foreskin... *ooo, yess... nice tight exit.* He did it slowly. *oh that was nice!*

Tony was not happy... but he knew it had to be. He stood and turned around to look at Tom. He did not know how to say what he wanted to.

"Nice, eh?" Tom enjoyed Tony's amazed expression.

"Oh, yeah! That is..." Words failed him. "Where did you **learn** that?"

"Trade secret. I'm glad you like it. It's too bad to stop midway, though. The finish is **really** good."

They took a break. They had gone more than half way. They stood in a rough circle, admiring each other's erections. Finally, the involuntary pulsing stopped. Andy was closer to the brink than the others. They sensed this and waited for him to give the signal. They looked at each other with lustful smiles. No words were needed.

Andy stepped over to the spot Tony had occupied and bent over. It was a familiar position; watching Tony get pumped had made him more than ready. He only hoped it didn't go too fast.

Tom chuckled. He stepped over to the bench and picked up the two towels. He spread one out directly behind Andy. "Here's another trade secret. You have to lay down on your back."

Andy turned around. "What?" He saw the towel. He looked up at Tom.

"Trust me." Tom gestured to the ground.

Andy looked at Tony; they shrugged... *why not?* Andy got down onto his back. *it isn't quite a blanket, but it will do.*

"Spread wide." Tom spread out the other towel between Andy's legs, and kneeled down. *this is more like it.*

Tony watched this, amazed. *how am I going to do my bit? Andy's facing the wrong direction. oh! the tube!* He fetched it from the bench and handed it to Tom.

"This one's called the front door." *they'll like it as much as I do.* Tom raised Andy's knees.

Tony watched Tom begin his preparation routine: he greased three fingers … *so that's what he did! I'll just remember this… yes indeedy.* He watched Tom's entire procedure… this was all new. After the first finger, Tom lifted Andy's right leg and put it over his shoulder. *hot!* The second finger… Tom pulled Andy's foreskin… *I remember that! why did… ooo… it caused a pucker—ah! the grab. of course. that's worth knowing… the third finger. look at that! the circular bit, that's what he was doing! ooo-oo!* Andy flinched. Tony sure knew what that meant: magic button time!

He watched Tom lift Andy's other leg and slide in. *what a sight!* Tom went in and out slowly—all the way, and pulled back out right to the tip. *what a monster… I just had that in me minutes ago. this is so hot!*

okay… time to figure this out, Tony—you don't want to be a spectator. how can I do this? can I just back in there? ah… if Andy grabs when I'm down far enough… just might work. oh! a pillow— Tony grabbed the other towels from the table and folded them into a small square. *there…* he ran over and slipped the improvised pillow under Andy's head. "Coming in!" He kneeled down above Andy's head and inched back.

Andy lifted his left arm to guide Tony in. *this is going to work!* He looked up and watched the hanging balls inch down past his eyes, then the shaft. *if Tom weren't being so incredible, this sight alone would turn me on! there. Tony's in just the right spot.* Andy pinched Tony's thigh and took his cock with his other hand. He slid it into his mouth. *delicious! I can taste the pre-cum already.* "mmmm."

Tom really enjoyed this—it reminded him of the session with Geoff. And now, another sight! *Tony's butt inching toward me!* Tom moved his hands up to make room for Tony's legs. He pressed Andy's knees down briefly as he pumped away. Soon, Tony's legs were right there, alongside Andy's torso. He watched Andy massage Tony's thighs as he began to pump. Looking at Tony's balls swing was a bit of fun. *hey. here's something I haven't thought about before:* he watched Tony's anus flex and pucker as he pumped. *hot hot hot!* It made him drive in just a little harder. **"Mmmmm!"** He reached out and massaged Tony's calves for a minute. He enjoyed how they felt when Tony flexed them as he moved in and out. It was a little awkward, so he brought his hands back up to Andy's thighs.

Andy had this wonderful dilemma: pay attention to Tom's pole driving into him, or to what his tongue and suction could do for Tony? He alternated for a time... he began, eventually, to focus on both. This couldn't last too long... every time Tom pulled out he rubbed against the prostate; a few more of those, and he'd be over the edge, like it or not. "Mmmmm" He squeezed his lips a little harder. He wanted to feel that swell from Tony happen again.

Tom turned things up a notch. He lowered his hands to Andy's upper thighs and pulled him back as he drove in. He made his drives slower, farther in... pause... then another pause when his head was just at the door on the way out. He did this several times. His torso stiffened... he was pretty close.

Tony sensed that Andy was getting close because he squeezed his lips harder each time he pulled out. *it's time:* he slowed and savored every centimeter. He'd be there in another three or four pushes.

Andy could tell Tom was on the home stretch. He reached down and took hold of himself... he stroked in time with Tom's thrusts. He knew what that was doing... he was in perfect sync. He felt Tom stiffen and fire. He gave a small thrust as he sprayed his first shot.

Tony felt the splash of hot juice from Andy hit his butt. That did it! Into the mouth he went!

Somehow, these three jets alternated perfectly. Tom had six. Andy had five, Tony had five. They held briefly. This was a really good one.

"Whoo!" Tony pulled out and flopped over onto his back.

"Mmmm." Tom pulled out. He lowered Andy's feet to the ground and sat back on his heels.

"Wow." Andy stayed right where he was.

They were quiet for a while, catching their breath. They savored the memory of what they had just done.

Tom focused his eyes at last. He looked down at himself... *still two thirds up.* He wasn't surprised. Tony was half way soft; Andy was nearly hard. "Boys, I have another surprise for you." *the looks on their faces! I love this.* "The nice thing about round two," he paused. He wanted to see it register in their minds. He watched their eyes go wide. "It takes a little longer."

Andy and Tony looked at each other in disbelief. They turned back to Tom. They would do whatever he said.

"First, you have to trade places. Andy, you'll have to stand up, since you are now a back door." He smiled wide, and stood. He was up full already.

Andy giggled and stood up. He looked at Tony and shrugged. He turned around and bent over.

7   *Nick coaches Julian*

Nick held the stopwatch this time. Indulging Julian by helping him practice his time under water was a good idea; his own time remained a solid forty-eight seconds, and Julian had worked his way up to a true thirty-seven seconds—his count without a watch was a little too generous. Julian needed another year or two of physical development before his lung capacity could do much more; his distance endurance above water had come a long way, too.

Julian was forced to surface before he was ready—a forest of legs suddenly appeared in front of him, and there was no way through. He turned around and swam back.

"Those guys! Where did they come from all of a sudden?" Julian came to a stop and stood next to Nick in the shallows.

"I'll tell Tom about them. It's a bunch from the other water polo team doing a practice of some kind." It wasn't the whole team—he saw four. "Are you about ready to call it a day on this?"

"I s'pose." Julian didn't want to push his luck; obviously Nick was ready to quit.

"Let's head in. I want to get caught up on the newsletter." They had a little more than half an hour left, which should be just about right. Nick had been going over things in his mind; he had it figured out, pretty much. *if only I had a little more confidence.*

Julian felt really good today. Nick's help had made a huge difference. *boy, having a real watch is something: a second is a long time! I'm tired...* It was a happy tired. He went to his cubbyhole while Nick returned the stopwatch to Leonard. *boy am I lucky to know Nick... I have a new sketch to show him. will he like it? it's a little different. he'll probly guess what it is real quick.* Julian wrapped his towel around his neck and took his Buddy Badge off the swim hook. He stepped over to Leonard's desk to wait.

"Do you have to sit there all day?" Leonard must get pretty bored.

"It must seem that way. Only during the free swimming periods." Leonard looked at Julian fondly. *what a gem. they'll be chasing after this one soon.* "Thanks for asking." He noticed the sketch tablet. "Can I peek at your work?"

"Sure!" Julian was delighted that Leonard was interested. He handed the sketch tablet over. *I like Leonard's face. hmm. yes...* he formed a picture in his mind... *I'd like to draw that face... distinctive nose; lips sharply defined.*

"My, Julian..." Leonard was impressed. "What are these for, may I ask?"

"The Troop 9 Scrapbook, mostly. Maybe the newsletter, I'm not too sure yet about that... if Nick wants to use any." Leonard's positive reaction gave him a nice feeling. He was the first person to see these.

Nick dried himself off systematically, but roughly... he was eager to get going. The wild morning with Geoff was threatening to intrude into his thoughts again... that he did not need. He had to get this matter of Julian's cooperation taken care of. He wouldn't get a better shot at it than now. He had been trying all afternoon to figure out how to get started. *how much information can Julian handle? he's barely into puberty, to look at him. here goes; I'll figure something out on the way.*

"What do you think of my Assistant Scribe's work?" He patted Julian's shoulder.

Leonard looked up. "I have to say I've never seen its equal." Leonard closed the tablet and handed it back. "I hope you'll let me look at these again, Julian. I'm quite impressed."

Julian blushed. "Sure." *maybe next free swim. hmm. that way I can figure a way to put Leonard in one, too. narrow wrists, elongated. interesting.*

"See you later." Nick held the gate open. "We're off to an editorial meeting."

Julian followed Nick out and turned to look at Leonard with a smile; he waved as he hung his badge on the inactive Buddy Board. He did a skip and trotted on ahead. Leonard had given him quite a boost!

Leonard watched them walk up the trail… moments like this made his job the best in the world.

Nick walked a few steps behind Julian… *whoo! look at those little buns! why do they look sexier in the shorts? I didn't even notice when he was on the boardwalk. at least they're safe from Tom, now.* He had to wonder just a little, though… who, if anyone, might get in there first? He scurried to catch up... *those thoughts are not helping any. besides, that's a long way off. and beside the point.* Nick went over everything he wanted to say as he and Julian hiked up the trail. Soon, the cabin was in view. "You want to grab the scrapbook and meet me over at the table?" Nick didn't want to meet in the cabin, especially. He had to cut off the discussion when he saw Tom coming.

"Sure! Be right there." Julian hurried over to the cabin. He was glad Nick wanted to meet at the camp. *I can stow my towel and go potty.* He'd had a few warnings from Mother Nature… she needed to be kept happy.

He hung his towel up and looked in the mirror. "There's that lucky kid again. Why is your hair all messed up every time I see you?" He made a face. "Because I can't keep that silly Julian out of the lake." He reached for his comb. "He did a good job today, so be nice." He combed quickly... it's still a little wet. "Happy now?" "Yep." He bent close to the mirror and checked his chin, then his upper lip… *none yet. oh well.*

He relieved himself quickly, grateful that he had a bathroom instead of a latrine booth. He fanned the door to bring in some fresh air. As he felt the air rush by he happened to glance at the chair—*of course!* He stepped out to get it. It nearly filled the little room, but he turned its back to the open door and stood on the seat. He faced the door and twisted his head around to look: at last he had a full view of his backside.

hmm. what's the big deal? "I don't get it." Nothing looked special at all. *what makes them choice?* After the talk with Mark he understood why they were called choice. But he still couldn't see whatever it was that made his so special. Both Nick and Mark were emphatic about it, too. *all I see is a regular butt. aha!* He pulled down his pants and looked again. *maybe… eew… looks kind of small. dents are okay...* he turned back and forth. He'd seen a lot of bare butts the last few days, and this one looked pretty much like the others.

So after days of study and worry about this, what had he learned? He got off the chair and looked at himself in the mirror. "Just be glad they don't look like Bruce's, okay?" He nodded at himself. For the time being, the matter of figuring out about Choice Buns was taken off the active list. *at least they don't look goofy or weird.* He pulled up his pants and returned the chair to the table.

He grabbed the scrapbook and notepad on the way out. "Hurry, hurry, hurry," he quoted the Tigers, and hustled to meet Nick at the Flaming Arrow table.

8   *Sid and Kurt*

"S-D-H." Sid muttered between his teeth... he watched Julian leaving the lake with Nick. He'd hung around all swim period hoping to get Julian off to the side. *after this morning's performance out on the platform, it's fair to assume Julian is just as hot to go as I am... I even brought along this blasted snorkel. how am I going to get Julian to do the "D/P" again?* That was his new nickname for it. *I'm not that choosy, whether it's the Doug or the Paul style, at this point... either one, any time. besides... I have to have a little more practice before I can make a final evaluation, don't I?*

He had to hang around now anyway... he'd come in with Bruce, who was slaving away over in the F. *there's always tomorrow; maybe I should link up with Julian in the morning when he stops by for the inspection. why did I just now think of doing that? sometimes I just don't seem to be all there these days.* He swam along the dock for a while, practicing the snorkel. *maybe I'll come across something interesting— !!*

A muscular chest appeared suddenly in front of his mask. He was forced to surface. He nearly gulped a mouthful.

"That thing really work?" Kurt was amused at having made Sid lose his momentum. He'd made up his mind to check into this, finally. He'd been watching Sid off and on for half an hour. Jeremy was over by the chair, a safe distance.

"Oh! Hi. It's you!" *I remember him, all right. wow. the shot he produced into the center of the circle was excellent.* "Yeah, pretty good." wow. *this is a surprise.* "You want to try it out?"

"Yeah, kinda." Kurt was only partly interested in that. He remembered how Sid's face looked when Julian was talking about Doug and whoever. This was a kid who wanted some. Kurt wouldn't mind some himself. That story had primed him pretty good; the quick one on the platform wasn't anywhere close to satisfying. This looked like a pretty fair chance. "So, show me."

Sid demonstrated the snorkel and gave it to Kurt to try out. Kurt's backside broke the surface as he jumped upward and swam off. *what I wouldn't give to have cheeks like those!* There were times that Sid really hated his scrawny, stringy body. *say... maybe Kurt could tell me how I could build myself up some.*

Kurt swam carefully and looked through the lens. *hmm... I expected to see farther.* He glanced back and forth. It was clear, better than the naked eye. He thought a little about Sid. He didn't know how to manage this kind of thing... he'd always allowed somebody else to invite him, not the other way around. He wasn't the conquering kind, like Tom. He liked to give somebody permission, at least... *that's what I did once with Doug.* He preferred to be invited to somebody else's party. *this kid is a little younger... probably isn't savvy enough to be in charge. but he's old enough to play—I saw that for myself.*

He turned around to swim back. *not much point in this rig, actually.* When he got there, he noticed through the lens that Sid was wagging one at half-mast... *hmm.* He surfaced. "How far can you see with this, really?" Sid's condition looked promising.

"Depends on the water. Real far, if it's clear"

"Did you really see those guys?" Kurt was curious about what Sid actually thought. *is he interested in playing around?*

"Yeah!" Sid grinned. He was delighted that Kurt had brought it up... his mind began to detect a possibility. "Not as good as Julian, maybe. I just saw them with my eyes, not this." He tapped the snorkel mask. "And I didn't have my glasses on, either, like today." *even so, I saw enough to know what was going on.*

"Wow. So how close did you get?" Sid had some kind of strap that held his regular glasses onto his head.

"Well…" Sid sensed that he just might have a chance here. "About two feet. I was swimming underwater and came across them by accident. I couldn't hang around, you know. I didn't want to get caught."

Kurt's eyes grew larger. "Two feet!" He held his hands two feet apart. "You could have reached out and…" this kid had been up close!

"I never thought about that! But you're right. I was really surprised. After I swam off, I thought some about it. That's why I went after the snorkel." Sid looked around briefly to check if anyone was listening. "It was pretty hot, if you wanna know."

Kurt took the snorkel off and handed it back to Sid. "I take it those guys aren't around now?"

"Nah. I haven't seen 'em since that day. It could be because the water polo bunch took over the space." Sid remembered the two finishes… and his own. Boy, did they make him feel needy right now. "I bet they're doin' it someplace, though."

Kurt could see the hunger in Sid's expression. He was starting to feel real receptive, himself. "Why do you say that?"

"Man, if you could have seen the expressions on their faces! Who wouldn't want to do that again?" He looked at Kurt in the face. "I'm telling you: if I could ever figure a way…" *oop… maybe I went too far. I better cool it, here.*

Kurt decided. "Well…" he looked down to see if the half mast was still there. "You guys sure make a case for trying it out, at least." He kept his head down and looked up to see Sid's reaction… *yep.* Sid just licked around his mouth.

"But I don't see doing it underwater. I can barely stay down for a minute. Not even that, actually." Sid wasn't about to let on that he knew another way just yet. *Kurt's older; he probably has some good ideas—if he's really thinking about it like I hope he is.* The thought was causing his problem down below to grow.

"Me either; I doubt if it was the lake that made it feel so good, anyway." It hit Kurt like a slap on the butt: *I can take this kid to that inlet I found!*

"Exactly!" *why didn't I think of that?!* He looked straight at Kurt. Something told him that Kurt had an idea.

"Ever been out in a canoe?"

"No." *what difference does that make?*

\>> ***BLEET-BLEET-BLEET!*** <<

"I hate that thing!" Sid turned around and searched for Bruce. *there...* they waved at each other and pointed.

Kurt scanned the area around the Boardwalk for Jeremy. *there he is...* they raised their arms; Kurt beckoned to Jeremy to swim over. *the spot I found during canoe class today is perfect... we'll be there in five minutes. what time is it, anyway? this can't wait.* "You won't hate it for long."

"Huh?"

Jeremy worked his way over doing a slow walk; he wasn't supposed to swim until the whistle blew again.

The whistle blew and Jeremy swam up. "Hi, Sid."

Sid blushed. "Hi." He looked at Kurt. *including Jeremy isn't a good idea, at all. how can I say that without—*

"I've got a job for ya, Jeremy."

"Sure." Kurt was super in Jeremy's book.

"I'm gonna take Sid here for a run in the canoe. I need you to keep Bruce company for the Buddy Whistle."

"Bruce? I haven't seen him around."

"He's over there in the F." Sid pointed. "He has to swim there until he can get qualified for his blue half."

"Oh. I've never been over there." Jeremy jumped up to see over the dock. Bruce was resting against the bottom fork of the F. "There! I see him now." He grinned. *I don't know Bruce, but...*

"Good. Sid will go tell him while I go tell the Counselor at the gate." Kurt had it mapped out now. "I'll move the badges around, too, just in case we don't make it back before the swim time is over."

Sid was impressed and thrilled: *Kurt is determined to try this out, now.* "Thanks, Jeremy. See ya later." He hiked himself up onto the dock and walked over to Bruce, fast. *Bruce knows who Jeremy is—this is perfect.*

"Am I s'posed to go over there?" Jeremy watched Sid going over to Bruce.

"Yeah, probably be a good idea… you need to be close to him for the Buddy Whistle." He figured Jeremy didn't know what was going on.

Jeremy looked at Kurt. He was impressed that he'd take Sid for a ride! *Sid really deserves it, too.* "I bet Sid will really like it, Kurt. What a neat idea!" *Kurt's power will really impress him.*

Kurt smiled back… *if Jeremy only knew.* "See ya, Jeremy. Thanks." He pulled up onto the dock and headed for his cubbyhole.

Sid was slightly embarrassed. He was half way up, and the snorkel was not exactly a good shield. As he got to the cubbyhole, he saw Kurt putting on his clothes. *excellent!* He stepped up and tried to hide his problem while he reached in for his towel. Kurt was only two feet away.

"We're supposed to be dressed when we take out a boat or canoe," Kurt explained. "We gotta get the lead out, too. There isn't a lot of time left."

"Yow… I didn't think about that." Sid rushed it… *I can dry off later.*

Leonard noticed Sid's problem. *delightful…* he nodded his approval to Kurt. He had to wonder about this sudden arrangement… *most curious. what in the world could have inspired it?* He looked at his watch. *hmm.*

"You need to be careful about the time; the gate will close at 4:45, remember." *they won't have time to do very much.* He nodded a silent good luck as they scurried over to put their badges on the canoe board. *what are the odds, I wonder: will they be in the canoe again in the morning? I'll bet they are… they do make an odd pair.*

Kurt waited at the rack for Sid to catch up. "Help me get this in the water." He took the lakeside end and Sid took the other.

Sid followed Kurt's lead and helped lower it into the water alongside the dock.

"Hold onto the side while I grab a couple of paddles."

Sid bent over and held on. He had never been in a canoe.

Kurt stepped back to the rack; he pulled a couple of floatation vests from underneath and fetched the paddles.

"How do you get in?"

"Let me climb in, and I'll show you... It's a cinch." Kurt handed Sid a vest. "Put this on first." He slipped a vest on and climbed into the stern end. "Hand me the paddles."

Sid handed them one at a time.

Kurt shipped the paddles, one on each side.

"Now, I'll steady it while you climb in." Kurt pointed to a stretcher aft of the bow crossbar. "Put your hands on each side like I did. Always step on one of those stretcher boards, not right on the bottom. When you're in, sit down on the seat and rest your back against that cross bar. You can see how I sit—do the same thing."

Sid studied the problem and reviewed the instructions Kurt had just given. He focused. *boy, this is a challenge...* he counted to three and... he was kneeling in the canoe before he knew it—and the canoe barely rocked an inch!

"Hey, you're a natural!" Kurt was impressed. He half feared they'd come close to tipping over. He handed a paddle to Sid. "This is really your first time?"

Sid looked at him—*oh—he means in a canoe.* "Yes. What am I supposed to do?"

"You paddle on the left side, I'll paddle on the right. We're going down the west shore a short way." Kurt raised his paddle. "You need to turn around and face the other way." When Sid was settled, Kurt lowered his paddle into the water with vigor—he pulled hard.

Whoa! Sid was jolted back—he wasn't expecting such a sudden start. He followed along, clumsily at first—*I didn't know I'd be in the front. how am I supposed to hold the paddle, exactly?* He glanced behind and saw how Kurt was doing it. He tried to mimic that. *we're going ahead full steam, somehow.*

Kurt was adept and compensated for Sid's awkwardness. He had twice the arm power, and his J-stroke kept them on course. "I know an inlet that looks... well, let's say that it's not very crowded, if you know what I mean."

"I know exactly what you mean." This was Sid's very first ride in a canoe. He was sold on it instantly. It took a while to get the hang of it, though. He worried about balancing Kurt's paddle strokes, but it seemed to go all right. Kurt was incredibly strong.

"See that inlet? The second one after the big rock?"

"Yeah."

"We'll swing in right there; it bends a little to the left after it goes in. There's a great place to land."

Soon they were there. Kurt steadied the canoe with his paddle. "I'm going to pull up and touch the shore just a little and steady the canoe. You step out first, carefully. We're gonna get our feet wet, so let's take off our shoes first." Kurt knew the spot well enough to tell it was barefoot safe.

Sid took off his shoes and socks and put his left leg over the side— *eew*. The silt oozed up around his feet and between his toes… *luckily, it isn't too deep.* He lifted his left leg out. *barefoot is the only way.* It was only a couple of steps. He used the grassy bank for a doormat… the sensation of mud squishing between his toes was not very pleasant. *no point in complaining.* He watched Kurt lift the front onto the grass. *what an adventure!* Sid was having a great time… *oh. I just remembered why we came here.* He glanced around… it was very secure and quiet. The swimming area was completely out of sight. The configuration of the inlet masked the canoe completely. "Man, this is something! Is this inside the camp?"

"I don't know, to tell the truth. I was only here once before." Kurt was a little embarrassed. "I was under some pressure, y'know? I didn't want to get caught takin' a whiz in the lake, and I whipped in here. Jeremy stood guard."

"Your secret is safe with me. In fact… a whiz might not be a bad idea." He looked at Kurt.

"Oh. You're right. I didn't think about that," Kurt laughed. "Follow me—there's a clump of grass back here that needs another watering." He led Sid into the small stand of beech saplings.

The urination was brief on both their parts; they had seen each other before, but a new glimpse seemed to be in order, considering.

"Better shake real good!" Sid tried to lighten things up a little.

"Mmm."

They shook themselves thoroughly. It had the salutary effect of preparing them slightly for the next ceremony.

Sid looked around briefly... *where should we do this?* "I know! I'll get our towels from the canoe."

"Yeah... good thinking. It could be worse; at least there's no sharp branches or rocks." Kurt looked around... *this spot is as good as any. no need to wander around or explore... time is short.* He brushed away a few stray twigs. The ground was fairly smooth—no problem being barefoot. He took off his clothes and placed them neatly to the side. *I'm on the way up, all right.* After watching Sid right next to him just now, he had a hunch that this was going to be a good time.

Sid returned with the towels and saw Kurt taking off his shorts. *wow: the time has come—Kurt's planning to do it right here! excellent.* He undressed; his clothing was damp so he spread it out to dry. His heart rate was increasing... he was a little surprised at himself. He wasn't the least bit attracted to Kurt... *I certainly envy his muscles. but I'm getting horny as the dickens anyway.* He reminded himself that this was his "first time," officially. The session with Julian was to remain absolutely secret. *of course, I'll utilize as much from it as I can remember—which is every second! I hope Kurt's as good at this as Julian... I'll play younger kid for all it's worth while I teach him all I can.*

"How do we start?" Sid looked down... *almost ready.* He looked at Kurt's. *wow... he's really ready. it's a lot bigger when he's standing up!* His eyes went wide. He looked at Kurt in wonder.

"Seven and a quarter inches." Kurt was proud of that.

"Almost six." Sid hadn't actually measured in a while.

"Let's see. Those guys were in a contest, you say?"

"Yeah. They had this stopwatch, and they passed it back and forth; whoever was standing watched it, then handed it off when they went down."

"Hmm... we don't have that. We don't have the water." Kurt thought for a moment. "What the heck! We don't want either one of those, anyway... we just want to do it, let's be honest about it, okay?"

Sid blushed. "Yeah."

"Okay. So it's a matter of who goes first then, right?"

"Yeah... obviously." *so far, Kurt is doing just fine... I like Kurt getting most of the credit for this.*

"Well, since you're the one who saw it, I guess that means you get to go first. You show me what to do, in other words, right?"

"Yeah, that makes sense." Sid spread out his towel and got down on his knees in front of Kurt. *I'll do my best to replay exactly what Julian did. oh-oh. the names... ah. I'll just say first guy second guy.*

"Okay. The first guy held the other one by the buns." He reached around and grasped Kurt's buns... *man! muscles!* "Then he squeezed them when he did it. Okay?" He looked up at Kurt to make sure he should go ahead. He saw Kurt nod his approval. He looked at it up close for the first time... *wow. lots of extra skin...* he wanted to look for a minute, but thought better. He took Kurt into his mouth and worked his head up and down slowly, as he kneaded the buns. *hmmm... very interesting... very different from Julian... much bigger... much bigger. it tastes very different. stronger or something... hard to describe... but stronger. I like it just fine, though.* He remembered some of the pressure variations and tongue moves that Julian had employed. He enjoyed this. He went down to the balls like Julian had... *it's sure a mouthful... a lot of hair.* He rather liked that.

Kurt was delighted from the very first... he expected he would be. He had one of these around a year ago, so this wasn't a first time... *there's something about this one that's impressive already. man, this kid knows what he's doing! should I pump or just stand here? I'll play dumb a while longer...* This was going to be a very good finish to the afternoon.

Sid forgot to count... *I must have done half a dozen by now. I'll do five more, then go to the other method. I gotta do these really well, too... hmm...* Kurt's buns were surprisingly nice to touch... *real manly.* He pulled off with a nice tightening of his lips around the head, just as Julian did; he slurped slightly and took a deep breath.

"That's the first way; how was it?"

It took Kurt a second to get back... he had started to just plain enjoy it. "Darn good, I gotta tell ya!" He took a breath too. He looked down at Sid. *to think that this goofy looking kid with glasses could do this!* "Ready, any time," he grinned.

"Okay... This is the second guy," Sid took Kurt's balls into his left hand and rolled them gently in his palm. He put his right hand behind Kurt's left thigh, and pulled forward slightly. He took Kurt cock back into his mouth and pulled the scrotum downward, to tighten the foreskin. Contending with a foreskin was really interesting... he'd always envied guys who had that. He had replayed this technique the last two nights in his mind, and he had it down pat. He worked his head back and forth rapidly, connecting his tongue onto the head with each pull.

"Mmmmm!" Kurt's knees buckled. He could hardly keep standing! *this one needs to be done lying down. man, this one is a winner! I see now what the contest was about!*

Sid knew this would happen, and he kept it up anyway. *I'll let Kurt suggest lying down. do another five...* He really put his tongue to work on this one. He pulled off, and looked up with a big grin.

Kurt reeled. He steadied himself by holding on to Sid's shoulder. When Sid stopped he was about to lose control and become a pumping machine. "Whoo!" He sat down at once, and looked at Sid. "That one must be the winner, Sid." He took a couple more breaths. "Y'know, it makes sense now. They were betting on which **method** would go the fastest!"

"Ahaa! You must be right!" Sid was thrilled that he had done a good test run... Kurt's expression was wonderful. *now... let's see if he believes in fair play.* Sid looked at him expectantly. He didn't want to say "my turn" unless he had to. *I hope that Kurt will suggest the lying down part.*

Kurt's cock felt so good right now... *it's a shame to stop like this. seems better than I remember, actually... oh. Sid's waiting... cripes... now I have to do some. well, this should be pretty easy. it isn't as if I've never done this before.* "Well, you gonna stand up, or don't you want your turn?"

Sid chuckled briefly and stood up. *oh boy... Kurt's gonna do it!*

Kurt grabbed his lifejacket and used it for a knee pad.

that's a good idea... Kurt began method one. *mmmm, yes... not quite as good as Julian was, but nice. mmm... oh. darn it. I was gonna keep count... too late.*

Kurt was surprised... *this isn't bad... hmmm... doing a smaller circumcised one like this has its advantages. I can pay attention to other details, like the tongue and pressure things Sid did; that makes this interesting. how can I tell if what I do feels good or not? or if I'm doing it right? learning how to do this could be a good thing... hmm. this isn't bad at all. oh: how long did he do this one, anyway? I'll pull off after three more... what the heck: another three.* Kurt pulled off and looked up to see what Sid thought.

"Oooh, Kurt! Now I see why those guys looked that way." Actually, it made him wonder why everybody wasn't doing this all the time. "It sure does feel good." He smiled wide. *didn't count... maybe Kurt did more, actually.*

Kurt was pleased. He could see that he had done okay. Now for the second way... "Wait a minute! I just had a thought."

"Oh?"

"Yeh—I think that other style would be better if you were on your back. I could hardly stand up, it was so intense." He looked at Sid. "I don't think it's a big change in the rules, whatever they are."

"I bet you're right," Sid agreed. "Besides, you don't have to do the buns for that one!" He grinned. *Kurt's quick about these things.*

Kurt spread out his towel for Sid to use. Sid grabbed his life jacket for a pillow. He lay down on his back and spread his legs so that Kurt could cozy right in there... *this is the part I've been dreaming about.*

Kurt looked at Sid lying there. *now this makes sense. this I will do very well... left hand on the 'nads, right hand on the—oh. go for the shaft...* That seemed sensible; he put his right thumb and forefinger at the base and got to work. Sid started to buck right away. *what a turn on!*

"Mmmmm!" Sid moaned. *Kurt is every bit as good as Julian on this one! if only he keeps going! this is so intense!* He wanted to hold Kurt's head in his hands suddenly. He thought better of it; *he might stop if I do that. ooohh!*

Kurt got a charge out of doing this; it made him hot! He wanted to take Sid all the way. He had gone longer already than Sid had on him. *I'll just go for a while longer. If Sid wants to stop, he'll say something. feeling this pulsing shaft is such a turn on! I can actually tell what is doing what...* he varied the pace. He began to put himself in Sid's place—almost as if he was feeling this himself. *fantastic.* He wasn't that worried about his own turn right now. *I'm going to take this all the way, in the mouth. I swallowed before and I can do it again. yeah.*

Sid stopped thinking... he enjoyed. *Kurt is every bit as good as Julian now... maybe even better. he's not pulling off, either! that must mean he's going all the way. if he does, I'll do him as well as I can.*

They went for a delicious time longer. Kurt was surprised when Sid tensed up for his big finish. He was pleased—obviously he'd just given a good one. What a surprise... *it was only my second actual, real one. boy it makes me hot! the way Sid reacted... it makes me want to do this.*

"Man, Kurt!" Sid caught his breath. "That was the best one I have ever had!" It was, too. Kurt had replaced Julian... for now, at least. "I better do you pretty quick. I might want to conk out or something." *whoa...* he'd been running his fingers through Kurt's hair. *huh.* Kurt had rested his head right next to his cock afterward, too. *huh!*

Kurt was happy, and very ready. He took the cue and got into position just as Sid had. He had every reason to think that Sid would be good at this. The practice session had proven that.

He was absolutely correct. Sid gave him the best one he had ever had.

They lay down and relaxed afterwards. The rustling leaves overhead calmed, then brought them back to earth... they had been avoiding the awful reality of having to paddle back to the camp.

"Y'know..." Sid thought aloud, matter of factly: "If we practice this enough, we might get good at it."

It took a second. Kurt broke up and guffawed. He looked at Sid. Then he looked up to the sky. "I believe you're right." He was amazed at himself; he fully intended to do just that. He had just discovered a suck buddy. He wasn't about to let him get away, either.

The serious tone of voice Sid heard stunned him completely. He flushed and looked at Kurt. He was looking off into space. Summer camp had just taken a strangely wonderful turn. *huhm!*

9 *Nick enlists Julian*

Nick pretended to be reviewing his notes. His tablet was open to the page about Max's skit. His eyes had blurred... he rehearsed his approach to this once more. His confidence level had eroded since lunch. He flinched suddenly: Julian had just plopped the sketchbook down on the table.

"What d'ya think of this one?" Julian sat down on the opposite bench and slid the new sketch in front of Nick.

hmm. who is this? he looks sort of familiar... Julian is getting good at these. The kid in the drawing had on large round rim glasses... an unruly cowlick, and his hair was sort of rumpled. He had on a scout uniform... *no big surprise there. aha! the background details! this isn't a camp scene!* He looked up at Julian's beaming smile. "Very clever, Julian. It took me a while. This has to be Johnny, the boy in the skit, right?"

Julian nodded his head eagerly. "I tried a couple of the campfire and Max but I couldn't get it right at all. I have to practice flames or something. They were bad. So I thought of this instead. Can you write about it okay, this way?"

"Yeah! This will help, actually." He thought about a possible caption. *this will give me a nice approach, too. perfect for the newsletter. I can skip all that boring stuff about the competition. now all we have to do is win at the closing assembly. no problem there.*

"I'm going to do another one, too—when he rescues the dog."

"Perfect!" Julian made this job fun for a change. Nick pulled out his stack of notes handed in from the patrols. *might as well clear up all this first.*

Fifteen minutes went by very fast... Nick had finished going though his stack of notes. He couldn't delay any longer... he had to have The Big Talk with Julian. He looked at his watch. *yikes... we spent longer on this than I thought... more like twenty minutes; I'm running out of time.* "Y'know, Julian, we have one little problem that I didn't think of until now."

"What?"

"We have way too much stuff for a newsletter. We've got a regular magazine here. I'm gonna talk to Mark. Maybe we could do that! A special camp magazine."

wow. Nick is so smart. if anybody can do a magazine, it's Nick. Julian watched him shuffle through the papers and put stuff away... *this might be just the right time to ask. the other guys will be here for supper pretty soon.*

"Nick? Can I ask you something?"

Nick looked up. "Sure. Anything."

"D'you know Kurt?"

"You mean Zebra Kurt? Yeah, sure. Why?"

"Well... he was over on the platform this morning... y'know, at the lake?" Julian paused. *he was uncertain how to put this.*

Nick could see that Julian was on a touchy subject, or something. With Kurt, he was a little concerned...he wanted to hear this. "Yeah, I know it."

"Nick, I think maybe Kurt is mad, a little." Julian searched for the words. All he had was a hunch. "He didn't say what about, or anything. But since you know Tom so well, maybe you can tell about it."

Nick knew immediately. *after all this time, too.* "What did he say?"

"Well, nothing, exactly. He was telling about his muscles and bodybuilding and karate and stuff. He asked what all we did at Flaming Arrow—as if we did something kind of special, or secret—but it just looked like he was talking about Tom… but he wasn't." Julian didn't know exactly how to put this together. "He was worried that somebody bigger than him was going to jump him or something. It didn't make much sense. I mean, he's really strong! You oughta see his muscles!" He mimed a large bulging bicep.

Nick was relieved. At least Kurt had not been specific. Julian did not need to know about Tom's past inclination to spread open choice little butts. Kurt had been deflowered almost a year and a half ago. *I put out the fire at the time… I thought. well, Tom is cured of that need now… but there's still a repair of some kind needed here; that's obvious.* He looked at Julian. How to start this? Julian just provided an entrée, strangely enough, to what he needed to talk about.

"I may have an idea about this. Thanks, Julian. I'll have a talk with him and see if I can help." He paused. Julian had given him the perfect opening. "That reminds me: I wanted to talk with you about Tom, actually."

Julian was thrilled! *maybe I can tell Nick how happy I am about them.*

Nick looked at that beautiful face across the table. Then he looked again. He saw something else in his eyes… a depth… something he didn't understand. *have I miscalculated?* He had a sudden hunch that Julian was maybe a little more than met the eye. *I better walk carefully here. I'm not sure how to walk, either… get on with it, Nick—he's waiting.*

"You see, Julian," Nick started awkwardly. "Tom and me…" *boy, this is hard!*

"You really like him, don't you Nick?" Julian could tell he had to help just a little. He smiled. He hoped Nick would look at him.

Nick saw that smile. *that's a friend's smile!* He smiled back. He started to feel a lot better. "Yeah. Yeah, Julian, I do." *thank you Julian!*

"And Tom really likes you, too, doesn't he?"

Nick blushed as he looked back at Julian. *there's so much behind that smile!* "Secret's out, I guess." What he didn't know was how Julian had put it together. *we've been so careful in camp—*

"No it's not." Julian ran his forefinger along the edge of the tablet... he wasn't sure how to phrase this. "Nobody told me. I just knew." He paused. He wasn't about to tell that he spent a lot of time dreaming about how to put himself into the same situation—only with Mark. So far, progress was kind of poor. But he wasn't discouraged. *some day, I'll get there*—of that there was no doubt. He looked at Nick warmly. He wanted to tell him how wonderful it was to know someone else who was in love, how they had a special connection because of it. But he couldn't. *until then, I can pretend.*

Nick looked at Julian in wonderment.

"I'm really glad, Nick." Julian recalled the scene he had seen in the tent... Nick holding Tom in his arms... *that's one of the best things I ever saw.*

what in the world could Julian be thinking about! I'm not running this meeting; I've only set it free. I need to be careful, but it looks promising.

Julian was picturing a scene where he and Mark were walking with Nick and Tom—two couples, each holding hands, on the beach... they frolicked some and all joined hands and ran in a circle, splashing in the shallow wash of a wave returning out to sea. The crisscross patterns and teeny bubbles sparkled in the sun. That was one of Julian's favorite fantasies—including Nick and Tom made it even better. It wasn't going to come true as soon as he had hoped, but someday... someday.

"I need to ask a favor, Julian," Nick said, at last.

Julian snapped out of his reverie. "Sure."

"About Tom and me." Inadvertently he glanced over at the Supply tent.

Julian laughed. He was so happy Nick had figured a way to bring it up! He reached across and put his hands on Nick's. "Silly, I won't tell anybody! I think it's super! It's too bad you guys don't have something more comfy, is all."

Nick was astounded. This kid had just swept away an hour's worth of pain and struggle that his brain had not been able to grope through. How did he know?

"Is it really hard? The ground?" Julian frowned. The idea of sleeping on the ground all night was not appealing.

"Boy, is it!" After three nights he could testify to that.

"Sid has an air mattress."

Nick thought about that. Trying to balance the both of them on a narrow air mattress was not a sexy picture at all. They'd always be falling off one side or the other. *I let Tom get away without finding something at HQ again. I need to get back to work on that.*

Julian pictured two cots side by side... nope. "What about gathering up a bunch of leaves or something?"

"Too messy; besides, we have to be able to hide everything at a moment's notice." Nick had looked at every angle already. "Tom has connections at HQ. I'm going to make him come up with a solution."

A bright idea light bulb went off in Julian's head: *featherbeds.* Mark said they had a whole room full. Those would be perfect. He kept a straight face, though... he wanted to make sure it was possible—and he wasn't sure he should talk about the cabin and Mark—that was supposed to be sort of secret. He began to plan.

Nick checked his watch. Amazing. We still have five minutes before the free period is over. What a huge relief! He looked across the table. "Julian... all I can say right now is thanks. I owe you. You have really made my day. You have no idea."

Julian wanted to say otherwise, but he thought better of it. "I like Tom now too," he was pleased to report.

Nick looked at him again. *what did that mean?* He looked for an elaboration.

"Well, at first," Julian paused... "I was kinda scared of him a little. He's so big and strong and everything, and so strict when he runs things. But now he seems like a really good guy. He helped me to dive one day. Man, is he strong! He could lift me right out of the water!"

"When did he do that?" Nick remembered it well, in fact.

"The first day at free swimming. It was real crowded. There was no place to dive from. So Tom just lifts me right up out of the water, just like that! That's when I started to work on my time. I could only hold out for thirty seconds. It was probably really only twenty; we didn't have a watch. Between you and him, man, I'm doing great." Julian had not forgotten about the special squeeze Tom had given him, but he didn't bring it up. His curiosity was cooking though… maybe Nick would tell a little about it. He looked at Nick… his mind seemed to be someplace else right now.

Nick thought about Mark's comment the other night. The conversation just now reminded him that Mark had given him and the others a special responsibility with Julian. *should I say something, or… hmm. just the other day he was all worked up about my comment about his buns. I don't know exactly where or what to say, though.*

"Nick?"

"Yeah?"

"Could I ask…mmm." He was chicken all of a sudden. He blushed and looked down. *It's not right to ask about this; Nick might be angry.*

"Hey! Julian, you listen here!" Nick leaned forward and stared Julian in the face. "You jolly well can ask me anything! I don't know how to say everything I need to all the time, and I apologize for that. But I want you to know how much I appreciate what you have said, and how much I trust you. Okay?" Nick was a little startled by his own intensity. It had been almost a reflex response.

Julian blushed. He knew what Nick meant. Now he felt a little silly. *at least Nick isn't mad at me.* But he was embarrassed to ask about it outright.

"Come on, out with it." He lowered the volume and intensity. "Julian. I mean it. Right now I think you're just about the best friend in the world. You can trust me, too, you know." He wanted to hug him, actually. But jumping over the table would be a little too much, probably. He smiled instead.

Julian chuckled. "Well, it's silly I guess. Maybe kind of personal." He looked up shyly. *Nick's waiting… I have to ask, now. Nick won't get mad or anything.* "Is he as big as I think he is?" He blushed.

Nick was astounded by the question. *I'm so relieved. this is the best question ever!* This told him that Tom had not touched Julian. *now I see what Mark meant… Julian is curious—well, Tom does stand out, after all.* He smiled. "Julian, he is probably even bigger than that!" He looked at Julian gleefully. *I'll brag a little... what fun.*

Julian sat up straight... the happy grin on Nick's face made him grin too. He knew perfectly well how large it was: what he wanted was permission to play with it. That he could never ask, of course.

Nick slid the scrapbook and tablets to the side. "You've seen it limp?"

Julian shook his head. "When he was in the water I didn't look." He thought some more. Nope. "Oh! When they were running down the dock that day—I saw that." He didn't want to admit what he'd seen in the crew tent that one morning.

"Put your arm on the table. Flat."

Julian did so. Nick put his right hand at the tip of Julian's hand. With his left, he drew it to the left toward his elbow, five inches, and held it there.

Julian's jaw dropped. "Soft?!"

Nick nodded yes. Then he moved his hand another four inches, and held it again.

"Whoh! What's it feel like?"

Nick put his thumb and forefinger around Julian's arm, just above his wrist and squeezed slightly and slid it up a ways and stopped. He squeezed as if it was Tom's hard one. He smiled proudly and put Julian's other hand there. "Hold on, right there..."

Julian was thrilled... he could just imagine it. "Nick. You are so lucky. I can't imagine what it would be like to..." o... *I slipped up in a big way.* He clammed up... fantasies were supposed to stay out of sight.

It came to Nick in a flash: he had just come up with a fun idea to work on. How to get Julian's hands on Tom! *brilliant! I'll make it a surprise.* He grinned as his mind began to whirr.

"Sorry." *I better change the subject...* he looked around. He saw Danny's bunk. *that's it:* "Hey, Nick. I just thought of something."

"What's that?"

"Well, I don't want to be nosy, or anything, but—" Julian didn't know how to phrase this. "Do you see much of Danny these days?"

Nick had to think about that one. "Same as usual… breakfast and supper, campfires and lights out. That's about it. Is there a problem, or something?"

"No, I don't think so. He's fun to be with in the morning." He snickered. "He tried his best to cover for you guys, you know." He looked at Nick, amused. "I was too fast for him, though." He saw Nick's smile fade. "No! Listen, it wasn't his fault. I came in too early. He really is your friend." He remembered waking Danny up… boy, would I like to do that one again. "He made me sneak off while he woke you guys up." He laughed. "You have to promise not to tell, okay?" He waited for a promise.

Nick nodded his head, reluctantly. "Then what else?" Nick was puzzled. Clearly Julian saw nearly everything—something to keep in mind. If Danny had a problem, he wanted to know about it. He had to be a part of the team, period.

"I think maybe he's got a new friend or something. I just see him thinking a lot about something. Kind of a… a dreamy thinking, you know? It's a good kind of dreamy, not a worried kind, you know?"

Nick thought about this… he drew a blank… *I'll take notice immediately.*

"I really like Danny. Did you know that he was the one that told Mark to ask me to join the troop?"

Nick shook his head.

"Yeah… Boy, I owe him big for that. This troop is the best thing in my whole life." Julian was aglow with gratitude—at everything, really.

Nick was amazed at this phenomenon. It was the troop that was lucky far more than was Julian. *I had no idea until now how lucky.*

Tom came charging into the camp from the path over to the spring. It was a shortcut from the merit badge areas. "Whew! Am I late? I forgot to take my watch along today!" He assumed Nick had succeeded—*he always does. everything looks fine.*

Nick looked at his watch. "You can go away and come back in three minutes, if you want. Then you'll be exactly on time." He got up from the table and patted Julian on the shoulder as he passed behind on his way to the stove.

Tom raced over and goosed him lightly. His afternoon recreation had made him very playful. Besides, he wanted to be sure the mission had been accomplished. Nick's nod and smile made him want to jump up and down.

"Cool it a little, at least." Nick whispered. What the devil had Tom been up to that made him so juvenile? *hmm.*

Darn. Tom wanted a good smooch right now. Tom glanced over at Julian with a smile. He winked, too—a signal that he knew what Nick and Julian had been talking about.

Julian laughed merrily. *I really like those guys.*

He saw Nick pat Tom on the butt as he walked over to the cooler. He wanted to watch them so bad! *I'll be good.* He turned his tablet around and opened to a fresh page. *it's time to rescue a puppy dog. I can get the basic composition organized before supper.*

First, he tried again to put his fingers around his arm where Nick had held him during the conversation. His eyes wowed: a half inch gap! He looked over at them again... he began to wonder about them. Until this minute, he hadn't thought about what they did together when they were alone. *before this camp I didn't even know about this stuff. I'm just beginning to learn about it—every day something new comes along. what if I hadn't come to camp? man, am I lucky.*

10   *a word to the wise*

Julian was sitting at the table, his back to the door. His head rested on his left hand, propped up by his left elbow. He fiddled absentmindedly with the blue heron feather that Tom had given him... it was interesting; but his eyes soon wandered to that soft focus pastel never-never land where he went during his happy daydreams... he thought about Nick and Tom again. *they're so happy. I'm lucky to know them.* He remembered Nick's arm draped over Tom's as they slept... Tom's straight as wire hair splayed across Nick's chest... the diffused amber light of morning filtering through the canvas wall helped a lot, too. *they looked so soft and wonderful.* He looked at the feather again. *Tom said it was good luck to have one of these...*

Mark finished his evening stroll through the camp a few minutes early. He had planned to stand outside and enjoy the moon a little longer, but he stopped to glance in the doorway. It was odd to see Julian resting instead of sitting up drawing or writing down a last minute note. *his sketch tablet's open... is something wrong?* He went in and closed the door quietly. He stepped across the room.

he's preoccupied by something... he marveled at Julian's ability to go somewhere occasionally with that imagination; he could drop out of the regular world completely. He approached silently. He was able to look at him briefly, as if he were a sculpture—then saw the sun rise magnificently in Julian's face as his eyes focused.

Julian became aware suddenly that Mark was there. He turned and smiled wide. Mark always knew just the right minute to appear. Julian got all goose bumpy and flushed pink at the sight of him.

"You okay?"

Julian sat up and nodded happily. He couldn't tell mark about everything, of course. But it had been a super day, a very super day.

Mark was reassured. He stepped over to the fireplace and pulled the conference chair out a few feet.

Julian giggled. *I love Mark's conferences.* He pulled his chair over and wiggled into place. *A seat pad would be nice, actually.*

"How was your day?"

"Outstanding! Nick helped me a lot at swimming, and I'm almost at half a minute under water!"

"Badges?"

"Okay. I still have a little trouble remembering some of the words in Forestry, though. You know, the weird ones."

"You mean the Latin ones."

Scoutmaster's Cabin

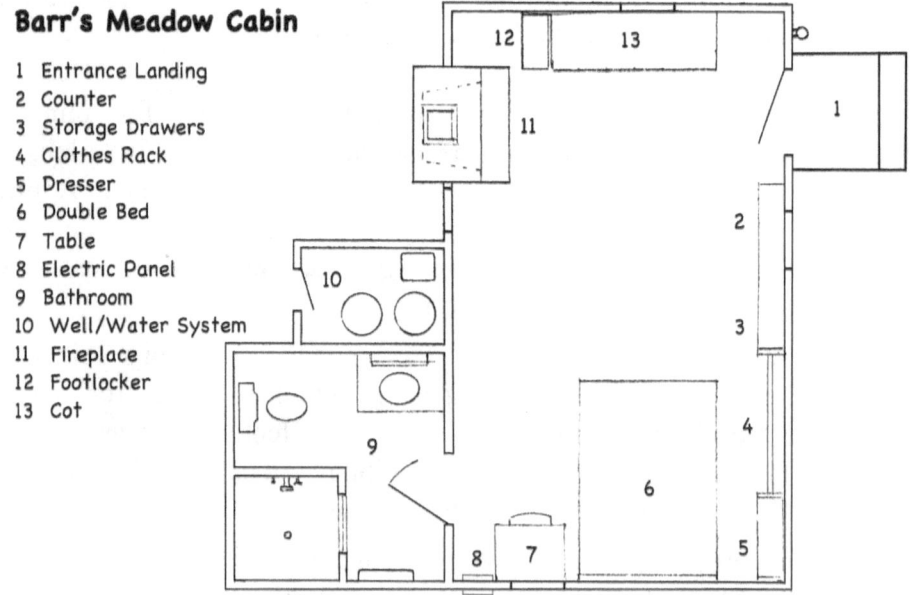

Barr's Meadow Cabin

1 Entrance Landing
2 Counter
3 Storage Drawers
4 Clothes Rack
5 Dresser
6 Double Bed
7 Table
8 Electric Panel
9 Bathroom
10 Well/Water System
11 Fireplace
12 Footlocker
13 Cot

"Yeah. Where is Latin, anyway?"

"It's not a where. Latin is the name of the language the Romans spoke. You should know that!"

"Oh… I forgot." Julian giggled.

you little scamp!   Julian was full of surprises. To think that he could pull an old gag like that. Mark was impressed. *where's that from? I forget… Abbot and Costello?*

"I hit the target today."

"You're not **that** bad, come on!"

"Yeah, I know. But I don't think I'm gonna get that badge. I've never hit the center. I'm just not strong enough. But I can shoot them all now, at least. Correction: Loose them." He was a little bored with **that** word, now, along with fletches and vanes and nocks… *I bet Robin Hood didn't use those words.*

"So what else does Nick talk about?"

"Oh, not much. He helped me at swimming a lot. We work on the scrapbook and newsletter, mostly. Boy, he is really smart, Mark. I really like him." *better not mention anything about Nick and Tom, though. not yet, anyway.*

Mark sensed that Julian had another toughie to deal with. He waited for a minute, but nothing was forthcoming. "Remember, you can ask me whatever…"

"Okay." Julian took a deep breath. He wasn't sure he should ask about this actually. "I see things at camp, sometimes." He looked at Mark directly. He was able to do that now once in a while without going into a swoon. "There was this guy out on the platform a couple of days ago…"

"Who was it?"

"I don't know. He was lying on his back. He had his arm over his eyes. I thought he was asleep at first, and I was worried that he might get burned, you know, like Danny did." Julian glanced at Mark's face… he had to be sure it was okay…

Wednesday night, Mark said you should, remember? Inside guy to the rescue.

okay. "But then I saw he had this big stiffy…" he giggled. "I think he wagged it at me." *I kind of wanted to go over and touch it, but I was chicken.*

Mark was paying attention now. He didn't expect such an open direct question. He kept a straight face. It was refreshing to see such honesty. "And?"

"I looked at it a little longer. It was dark colored. Then it wagged at me again!" Julian raised four fingers. "Four times! I think the guy was awake and peeking at me from under his arm. I didn't know what to do, exactly." He shrugged. "Sid was waiting for me, so I swam back to the dock. I looked back, and he was still there. Do you think he wanted me to go over and touch it?"

"Thank you for telling me about this. You did exactly the right thing. You should never play with anyone you don't know. Not everyone is safe." *I was stupid not to think of this!*

That really pleased Julian. Mark said it was okay to play. *maybe I can tell about Sid.*

"You were with Sid?"

"Yeah! It was so cool. He has this snorkel. I'd never tried to use one before." *I won't tell what I used it for.*

Mark realized that it was time for a serious talk about other dangers. "You need to be really careful about some things. We need to talk about this, Julian. It's possible that you will come across other things at this camp. I had forgotten about that. There are some things that are okay, and some that are not. You need to know about this beforehand." *with all the talk about buns, I need to give Julian a warning.*

Julian recognized the change in tone. He paid full attention.

Mark looked up at the ceiling for a second, searching for a way to deal with this subject. He caught a glimpse of his hat on the shelf above the clothes rack. He got an idea. "You see that hat over there?"

Julian turned around. "Your scoutmaster hat?"

"Yes. I'm going to say a few things with the hat on and a few with the hat off. Do you understand?

Julian tilted his head. This was a different way of talking. *the hat is over there. I'm supposed to pretend it's over here…* "I think so. You mean when the hat is on you are the scoutmaster, and when it's off you are not?"

"Sort of. People have to wear more than one hat. You too. When you wear your scout hat, you do scout things. When you wear your school hat, you do school things. When you wear no hat, you are sort of on your own time.

Julian nodded his head. *Mark is good at telling things.*

Mark inhaled. *so far, so good.* "I have to have my scout hat on all the time when I'm at camp. I don't actually wear it. It's uncomfortable and it looks silly, so I leave it on the shelf most of the time."

Julian giggled. "I think it looks cool. But I know what you mean."

"I'm glad to hear that. So I'll go on. First though, I need you to understand that what I say here is for your ears. I have to trust you, just like I want you to trust me." Mark looked for a nod. "Good. You can share some things, of course, but you have to be careful. If something I tell you comes back to me from somewhere else, what do you suppose I will think?"

Whoa… Julian understood that at once. He started to raise his arm in the scout salute.

"No. No salute. I am talking to you with the hat off. I am your friend as well. That kind of promise is more important than any other kind. It is a promise to yourself most of all. It's the sign that you are no longer a little boy. Once people know you are a man of your word, you are trusted. Nothing is more precious, Julian. When you can respect yourself, you are worthy of being respected by others."

Julian felt something wonderful and new. Mark was talking to him as a person, a real person. Not as a little kid. He felt uplifted and humble. He didn't have the words, but he understood. He smiled at Mark and looked him in the eye.

Mark was reassured. He was also amazed at himself for negotiating these waters as if he knew what he was doing. *onward.*

"When I was a scout here, all sorts of things went on among the boys. If the scoutmasters had ever found out, there would have been hell to pay. We did all kinds of stuff, good and bad. It's natural. The only way to find out some of these things is to explore, listen, experiment, and play around a little. I know that, from my own experience." He hadn't done everything, but he knew about a lot.

Mark is so smart!

"You have probably heard the phrase, "boys will be boys?"

Julian chuckled. "Yeah."

"Well it's true. It would be pretty stupid of me to forget that. I was one myself not that long ago, and I remember a whole lot about it. So I know what kinds of things go on. Okay?"

"Yeah." He chuckled. I wonder if he ever saw two guys sucking each other in the lake. Julian knew better than to ask.

"My point is that some things you have to learn on your own. You can't read everything in a book, you can't always ask someone like your mother or me for an answer. We can give advice sometimes, but you have to discover things yourself. But you know that already. Friends can help too, but it's always up to you. That's one of the famous facts of life. It's true for everybody."

Julian frowned. "So it was it okay to ask about Beefcakes?"

Mark laughed. "Yes, it was more than okay. It was exactly the right thing to do. It showed that you were honest and that you trusted me. I want you always to do that. Now if I can't answer you, I'll try to explain why. I might not know an answer. Or it may be one of those that I can't answer because of the hat. I promise to always try. That's all anyone can really promise honestly, you know."

Julian just thought about Doug and that other kid in the lake. There wasn't any reason to ask about it at all, now that he thought about it. He nodded his head.

Mark had a flash memory alert. Tom and Nick, and the Farting Post. He needed to add a footnote to the matter of open inquiry.

"There's something else you need to understand, Julian. This is kind of important, too."

Julian perked up at once.

I want you to ask whatever you need to, Julian I really mean that. But you need to be careful about some things. You remember a minute ago, when I talked about lots of things going on?"

Julian nodded.

"That was then. But now, as a scoutmaster, I **can't** know about it. Do you understand?"

"I guess not"

"If I find out about some of the things we are talking about, I might have to be like a cop. If I find out, it means they are in **trouble**. Could be **big** trouble. I might have to punish someone, or kick them out, or tell their parents."

Julian didn't see why. "How come? Couldn't you just sort of ignore it or something?"

"No, I couldn't. If it got out that I knew about something, and didn't do anything, then I'd be the one they would punish. They'd fire me, at least." He paused. "That's why, if I know about something, I have to do something."

Mark had seen Tom and Nick going up the north trail on Wednesday. What amazed him was that Casey and Robin were with them. Two other boys from another troop were along as well. He figured they were on their way to have a good time—the free period was just starting. *I was on my way to the ropeyard. otherwise I might have been tempted to spy a little. it reminded me of old times. what a blast I had.*

"Oh... I get it. Man, that's tough."

"Yes, it is. That's why I don't want you telling me too much about what you see. I know you trust me, but by keeping some things to yourself, you are actually helping me, too. As well as the boys." He suspected Julian knew something; *I want him to understand the importance of discretion.*

"Whoa." He thought instantly of Nick and Tom—and Danny, too!

"**Except**: if you ever see anyone getting hurt, or in danger, that's different. There is a big difference between boys being boys, and bullying or abuse."

"Mmm-hm. What about telling Tom or Nick?"

"Now that's a good thought. If you think it's safe enough, talk to either of them first. They could help you decide if I should know."

Julian was so glad he had not said any names. How could Mark be so cool!

Mark considered for a moment. How would Julian know? "Julian, a good rule of thumb is whether guys are the same size, roughly, or the same age. If they are about the same age, they are probably just having fun, or finding out about things. That's all right. It's probably **good**, in fact. But if one of them is a lot smaller, or younger, then there could be a problem. That goes for you too, you know. I expect you to play some too. I want you to. Some things you need to learn for yourself. It's the only way you can, really. All I want is for you to be careful and safe. I don't want anyone to hurt you. I know you won't hurt anyone else."

Julian thought about the profound thing he had just heard. He did not have to have it spelled out for him. "Are the other scoutmasters as smart as you are, Mark?"

"Well, I don't know. Some may be smarter. I know some aren't, I have to admit. They are all good men, Julian; they wouldn't be scoutmasters if they weren't. Maybe some of them are a bit on the old fogey side."

Julian laughed. *I've met a couple of those, all right.* His laugh was interrupted with a small yawn.

"Enough for one night?"

Another yawn, bigger. "Yeah, maybe so." Julian was embarrassed. *this is the best talk in my whole life. why would I yawn, of all things?*

Mark looked at the clock. "What do you know. The lights out order will be given any minute. This turned out just right." Mark looked at Julian fondly. "Thank you, Julian." He had never expected this to go so well.

Julian wanted to hug Mark and more, but he also wanted to let all this sink in. His inside scold was doing a very happy 'I told you so' jig in there. He stood up and stretched out his hand for a handshake. "Thank you right back."

Mark blushed. He'd never had such a wonderful thank you.

Julian beamed. "Time to scrub teeth!" He hopped up with a giggle and headed for the bathroom.

Saturday

Seventh Day

The first week of camp comes to a close; activity and involvement is at the highest level. Few appreciate that camp is half over: only a week remains, many behave as if they have all summer.

Julian feels empowered and secure because of his talk with **Mark**. He undertakes a unique domestic challenge.

Danny realizes that he has graduated from Geoff's educational program, and revisits his plan to secure Julian's affection.

Geoff moves on to the next challenge. He selects Leonard as his special project. Ignoring the staff/scout boundary comes naturally.

Introducing **Freddy**, an entrepreneur of sorts from another troop. He recruits Andy to join his unauthorized enterprise.

The first week of camp ends with progress milestones for everyone in the leadership patrol. **Danny** gets a major promotion. **Mark** and **Julian** have evolved an aesthetic dimension in their relationship. **Nick** and **Tom** break in their new domicile.

No one suspects that anything might come along in the second week that could threaten what they all presume will be a happy end to camp.

11   *a super good morning*

This time, for a change, Julian thought he might have snuck out of bed without waking up Mark. He sure tried his best… but he couldn't leave without stopping to take another mental snapshot. The way Mark was resting—a quarter turn from his side onto his back, his head cushioned on the pillow just so… he might even be smiling slightly. *probably having a nice dream or something. this could be another nice drawing.* He had several studies underway in his mind. More and more he liked to work on them for a while in his head before starting. He tiptoed to the door and stepped outside, where he put on his shoes. It surprised him to be awake like this… he just woke up all of a sudden.

Julian just had to sneak over to the camp early: the talk with Nick yesterday was so wonderful… he needed to look after them, make sure they were okay. Besides, he never failed to find delights over there in the morning. *according to Mark's clock I have a good ten minutes.*

He stopped suddenly… a cardinal! Perched right there on the farting post, chirping—*is it calling to another one?   birds are interesting—the way they tilt their heads when they look at things…* it fluffed itself up. *ooo…* A call came from the birch tree behind the supply tent… *there it goes!* It took off in a flash, and disappeared into the tree. Seeing it up close like that was neat! Julian continued into the camp.

so… what goes on here today? He walked quietly over to the crew tent. Danny was sound asleep. His body was covered today… *darn.* He was sleeping on his left side facing out, at least. *his head is on this end today… if nothing else, I could tickle his nose.* He stepped over to the supply tent.

Tom and Nick were asleep too. They were the reason he wanted to be early—he wanted to see them together again... and to make sure they were okay. This is new: they're lying butt to butt. They're mostly covered up. Darn again. He returned to the mess area. *here I am, all early and everything, and there isn't anything happening. oh well...* It was good to see everyone happily asleep. *I'll go ahead and start the coffee. I can do that without making any noise.*

Pouring from the canteen made him want to pee. He didn't go in the cabin because he didn't want to wake Mark. *darn... we aren't supposed to go in the brush. I'll have to run down to the latrine after all.* He finished filling the coffee pot and lit the burner. He took off at a trot.

He'd only been here that one time... it looked just the same. Two stalls were in use. He only had to pee, so he stepped over to the open trough. *ug... smells pretty awful... they don't rinse it down often enough.* Some old weathered graffiti on the backing board gave it a rough texture ... a few really bad outline drawings... *I know about some of those things now. hmm. I can do a lot better than that!* Some odd names... how long have these been here? *oo! there it says 1947! wow. no wonder it smells awful.* Some were pretty faded. Some had been scrubbed away. *don't recognize any names... lots of nicknames. that makes sense.* Some are so teeny... he bent down close to read... *eew, stinko!*

He stood away and rubbed his nose. Why were these things here in the first place? Julian had seen writing on restroom walls sometimes, too. *I never did understand why some guys do that. maybe Mark knows.*

He shook himself good and zipped up. He glanced at the occupied stalls. All he could see was about a foot and a half or so of their legs. One guy was sitting down; the other was standing up. *oh-oh... something's going on!* The legs were shaking pretty good. *these guys are about to shoot a good one... too bad they're not in the same booth. I better scoot... I don't want them to see me out here in case they finish up quick.*

On the way back he thought again about how lucky he was... the idea of having to go to that stinky booth to do it! How awful. Why couldn't they just do it in their tent? *wait a minute... I just figured that out: if I was still a Wolf, I might have the same problem because of Sid and Jeremy. before yesterday, anyway*... he shook his head and grinned; yesterday on the platform was so funny!

He trotted up the trail happily. He had a new appreciation for having a real bathroom to use... staying in the cabin was wonderful in lots of ways. *I could never draw at the camp table like I can in the cabin—and I get to be with Mark—that's the big bonus.* Getting to know Mark better was way more important that he ever thought. *the handshake last night... wow. I had a dream about that! what was...? man alive, those fade away so easy. I should write them down or something.*

You better be careful what you write down.

Julian's inside guy was paying attention—good thing, too. *writing down some of those dreams might not be so smart.*

Right: sooner or later the wrong person might read your notes.

An image of Sid flipping the pages of his sketchbook popped into his mind. *yow.* He shook the picture out of his head as he came back into the camp—still quiet. He checked the coffee. Not perking yet, but starting to make a little noise. *I never could figure out where that noise comes from; nothing's moving, no gears... maybe molecules make a racket or something when they heat up. hmm. I suppose if my buns were sitting on that burner, I'd make a racket, too. oop! I forgot to put coffee in! do that real quick—what a super foul-up that would be.*

There. Coffee was on the way... he stepped over quietly to take another look at Nick and Tom. *oh, good.* They were wrapped together again. Julian smiled. He loved how they looked. *oh!* Nick opened his eyes!

Nick held his finger to his lips to tell Julian to be quiet. He mouthed a quiet "good morning." He pointed at Tom's head... still asleep.

Julian flushed all over—that made him feel so good. He gave a little wave and stepped out. *oh!* That had made his whole day!

He went to check the coffee. *aha!* It had just started to perk. Perfect timing... he turned it down a little so it wouldn't boil over. *time to check on Danny.*

Danny was on his side still, but turned partly on his back. He looked handsome, as always. *he should get a patent on that hair. I'll sit and watch today... no pestering.* He remembered the two times they messed around. The first one was really the best. He wanted to do the Paul and Doug thing someday... *Danny's always busy these days, it seems. oh well. maybe after camp, who knows?* He studied the lips... *they're puffy in the morning. ooo... eyes are moving... is he about to wake up? is that what I look like when I'm just about to wake up?*

"I hear the coffee." Danny yawned.

"Yeah. I started it early today. You didn't sleep in."

Danny looked at his watch. "Huh! Look at that! Still a couple of minutes, technically." He grinned suggestively and flashed open his sleeping bag to show off his morning erection. "Did this myself, didn't I?"

Julian nodded. *boy. no skivvies again.*

Danny could see the interest he had created. *hmm.* He pulsed it. *yes. great interest. too bad I have to take a whiz...* he signaled Julian with his forefinger to approach. He just had a thought.

ooo, I didn't expect this! He crawled over to the edge of Danny's cot.

"I don't have a sunburn any more, you know." Danny paused. Some of Geoff's bravado was starting to rub off on him. "Maybe we could find a little playtime someday?" *Geoff is busy today—maybe I can play with Julian.*

Julian's eyes went wide with anticipation. He nodded yes and licked his lips.

Danny saw the tongue and it made him horny. *too bad I have to wait.* Suddenly the coffee started to make too much noise. He looked over at it... the spell was broken. *darn.*

Julian stood quicky and looked. *I didn't turn it down far enough!* He raced over to stop it from boiling over. The day was off to a fabulous start! He waited a minute, then filled a mug with coffee. He waved at Danny on the way to take Tom his first ever cup in bed.

Danny said a quiet damn. *I was going to set up taking a little taste later on! well... maybe I won't have to twist his arm too hard. it's time for Julian to advance to the next level. hand jobs are fun, but wait until he tries out what Geoff taught me. yow—latrine time! I have to get dressed quick... oop... where are they?* He'd gotten so used to sleeping nude that he nearly forgot to put on his skivvies.

When Julian entered the supply tent, Tom and Nick had just finished another good morning kiss. They smiled at him as he entered.

"I thought you would like an early cup today," Julian looked at Tom, shyly. "I never knew if you put anything in it or not, so I just brought it in plain." He waited to be instructed—he was itching to take this in there.

"Man, you are too cool!" Tom was delighted by this surprise. "Bring that right here!" He patted the bag right next to his leg. *I'm gonna do all I can for this kid!* Last night Nick told him all about Julian's incredible support... He watched Julian balancing the mug carefully to prevent a spill. *this kid is super!* He nudged Nick with his elbow and got right to it: purposely, he began to slide the cover off his leg... he had a little show planned.

Julian kneeled down carefully and held out the mug. He watched Tom sip... his lips puckered at the edge; the faint mustache looked sexy. *I bet that's something Nick likes a lot.* He looked over at Nick to see if he approved. He saw Nick squeeze Tom's other hand and smile gratefully.

"Thanks for letting me bring it in, like this." It wasn't something Nick had given permission to do. "You don't drink it, do you Nick?"

"Nope. Afraid it might stunt my growth, y'know." He chuckled... *it hasn't seemed to stunt Tom's any.* Nick watched Julian watch Tom. *what an amazing thing to see... Julian is so captivated. he seems to know, to understand what's going on with us... that's ridiculous, of course. it's lucky to have him supportive, for sure. oh-oh. Tom's going to play after all.* He feared keeping a straight face might be difficult.

Tom moved his leg slightly as he sipped... he was adept at getting things into place sneakily. *while Julian talks to Nick, I'll start the little plan we talked about last night. I didn't expect it this soon... this is perfect.* The last time he toyed with Julian was just before that campfire.

his shocked expression was terrific... I tricked him into looking at my tented shorts. this time I have Nick's permission: this time it's for fun... ha! Nick's pulling the bag his way a little. another inch, and I'll be poking out... he pulsed himself a couple of times.

Julian detected the motion in Tom's lap instantly. He had been trying to not look down there, even though he wanted to. *oh.* It pulsed again! He blushed suddenly... he couldn't help it. He glanced at Nick and saw him try to hide a smile. *that Nick! he has this planned! oh. another one. well, I'll play along with this! I'm not as stupid as they think! on the next one, I'll look and pretend to be surprised. there!* He looked down.

Tom was delighted at the suddenly wide open eyes! Now to see the jaw drop... he crossed his ankles. That was just enough to reveal his masterpiece into a fully exposed view. *yes!* He squeezed Nick's hand.

Julian saw it in its full pulsing glory. He had to stare at it for a minute. He wanted to look, naturally... but he knew that he was being shown. *might as well take advantage... wow. someday I want to see it fire!* He looked up at Tom at last. Julian saw his smile... *these guys!* He smiled wide... he had no idea what to say.

"Nick had a nice talk with me last night, Julian. I guess you know how much you mean to us, now." Tom pulsed his shaft again. He meant to include his cock as part of the "us" without actually saying it. He wondered if Julian would reach over and touch it... *he obviously wants to.* Tom wanted him to. *with Nick right here, this is hot!*

Julian wondered... *am I expected to touch it? this is too easy... no. it has to be delivered. then I'll have no doubt. I'm getting a big stiffy, too... what am I going to do about that?* He glanced down to see if it showed.

Tom saw Julian glance down at himself. He nudged Nick in the ribs; *this is fun.* He reached over and gently pressed Julian's bulge. This was very different from his clumsy grab that day in the lake. He stroked it lightly and waited for Julian to look at him. When he did, he took Julian's hand and placed it on his cock. "I want you to understand, Julian. We're all friends here, now. You've proven you're our friend. We have to prove we're yours."

Julian was overwhelmed. He didn't know what to say or do. He looked at Nick... he looked at Tom. Tears came to his eyes. He was so grateful and so happy all of a sudden.

oh! It pulsed again... he looked down at his hand: *it's on Tom's cock now!* That helped unlock him... he grinned wide. *it's so huge. man is it hard.* He looked up at Tom's face. He looked happy and proud. Julian pulled the foreskin down very slightly. *wow.* He looked at Nick. Nick gave him the wide eyes up and down! He wants me to stroke it! Julian squeezed it gently and moved his hand up and down just a little. He treated it like it was fragile... *it's so warm and alive. it's different from Danny and Sid—it's so big; it needs both hands to hold it right. I can smell it, too.*

Tom put his cup down. He grabbed Julian's hands and squeezed them together tight; he pulled to the top, and pulsed it for him. Then he drew down completely to the base, as tightly as it would go, exposing the head. He pulsed again Then he removed his hands. He looked at Julian. "Thanks, Julian. I needed that." He snickered and elbowed Nick.

"Man!" *I've never felt anything like that...*

"Hey: you guys!" Danny called from outside the tent. "You ready for a little breakfast sausage?" He had just hurried up from the latrine... they had to start breakfast.

The three rolled around in hysterics.

Danny rushed in to see what was going on. Julian was rolling around on the bag laughing his head off... the other two were all doubled up too. "Must have been a good one." He was sorry to have missed it.

"I spilled your coffee! I'm sorry, Tom."

"Don't sweat it Julian. It'll dry by tonight."

Nick got up, hard as a rock. "C'mon you guys, we gotta get crackin'." He looked at his watch. "Tell ya later, Danny." He grabbed the top bag and passed it. "Take this over to my cot, will you?"

Tom stood up, still laughing, still hard. Danny's eyes went wide. *Nick's prize... wow. he can have it...once is enough for me. it looks even bigger than I remember.* He headed out with Nick's bag. *what was going on in there, anyway?*

"Cluster hug!" Tom and Nick wrapped an arm around Julian and hugged him hard. They each kissed a cheek, then each other. Tom patted Julian on the butt. "Pancake time, kid."

Julian jumped with glee and rushed out of the tent. His stiffy poked straight out, but he didn't mind. For the first time he realized that those guys accepted him, really accepted him. Now he was a part of the patrol. He didn't know that until just now. What a great feeling.

12   *inspection plus*

Julian tried not to yawn... but inspecting was so boring. *at least there's only one camp left—the Lynx.* Max and Gary were just leaving. That meant it would be flawless. Gary always did a personal inspection before taking off. *I'll go ahead and check everything off the list, even though we haven't even started...* He wanted to hurry this up; he had an idea he wanted to talk to Danny about. *wha...?* Julian did a double take. He was just about to turn to his left when he saw those muscular calves again. *where have I seen those?* They were fresh in his memory. The guy was in his tent bending over, putting things into his footlocker. *I don't know anybody in this patrol yet. but I've seen those calves. yes— the crew socks at the bottom, pulled up tight. I know! this morning, in the latrine.* He chuckled... *it's the standing up one!* The guy stood suddenly and came out of the tent.

"Hey! How ya doin?" Alex Trent stepped forward, grinning wide. "Never see you much, except at the campfires." He remembered Julian, the scrapbook kid; *he's with Danny, and there's his notepad. the kid's on the ball, all right... working on a story already.* Alex gave him a thumbs up and a wink. Alex was on water can duty today... everything else was done.

"Good, thanks." *it's Alex, the guy I met the very first day at the washbasin! super friendly, blond.* Julian figured he must be Danny's age, about... bright blue eyes. Julian smiled as he passed by. *why does he have to beat off in the latrine? yeah... the first day. I remember now—I noticed those calves then, too. I just forgot about it until now.* Julian studied him some more... a fellow blond. *eyebrows and eyelashes are blond too. hmm. that looks okay.* Julian preferred his dark brown ones—*I have my mom's eyebrows.*

"Hey, come on," Danny scolded. He was headed out already... he was ready to play a little. He hadn't said anything—surprise was the best strategy.

Julian hustled after. He looked back over his shoulder and watched Alex trot over to the spring with the water can; *I haven't paid much attention to ankles before. Alex has nice ankles. I can tell that, even though he has shoes and socks on.*

Back at the Flaming Arrow at last, they firmed up the report so they could turn it in. They were required to sign it now. Danny folded it and parked it in the center of the table with an enamel plate turned over on top so a breeze wouldn't carry it off.

"There! Tom can snag it later." Danny looked at Julian and grinned. He'd been scheming all through the morning tour. He had not quite worked out how to get Julian to offer the cabin again. 'Never fear, the tent is always here,' he said to himself.

Julian was glad the busy work was done. *now maybe I can get his attention.* "Danny?"

"Yeah?" *Maybe Julian is thinking the same thing.*

"I been wondering..." he paused. "About Nick and Tom."

"What?"

"Well, it's not right, you know..." He stood up. "Come here a minute." He went into the supply tent.

oboy! Danny was right behind him, about to grab. Julian had led him right into the romping room!

"See?!" Julian stomped on the hard dirt floor. "Those guys shouldn't have to sleep on the ground. We've got to do something." He crossed his arms and frowned. Kneeling down there this morning was awful! Yet those guys looked so cool.

Danny was nonplussed. He thought that Julian wanted to play. He had to shift gears for a second. He looked around the area. To him, it was the rec room. *Julian, Geoff, Nick and Tom... myself.* He looked at Julian.

"Well?" Julian insisted. "Would you want to sleep on the ground every night?" He couldn't believe Danny was so thick.

114

"They don't have to sleep here, you know. They can always go back to their cots for that." *what's the big deal, anyway? Jollies here, sleep there.* He shrugged. It seemed obvious.

Julian frowned. He put his hands on his hips. "Yes, they do!" He stared his most firm stare at Danny. "This is their bedroom now." Why didn't Danny see this? "We're their friends, aren't we?" Julian was losing his patience.

"Well sure, but…"

"Then we have to help out, somehow." Julian had a solution.

"Whatever could we do?" *wouldn't make any sense to move the cots over here.* He still didn't see the problem, actually.

"I've been thinking… you know that new job you have?"

"Yeah…   What's that got to do with it?" *what got Julian on a kick about this?*

"Well, since you and…what's that other guy's name?"

"You mean Geoff?"

"Yeah. You guys are always loading up stuff from the storeroom to take to the camps, right?"

"So?"

"Figure it out! I bet they have all kinds of things stored there. I bet they have a whole stack of mattresses and stuff there. That's where they keep the tents and everything during the winter, right?" Julian didn't want to mention that he already knew about the featherbeds. *Mark wouldn't exactly appreciate it if I told.*

Danny thought for a minute. "Y'know, you could be right. There are a couple of big storerooms there. I've never paid any attention. We just load up the cart from the list every day and take supplies around— mostly it's just food and ice packs."

"How big is the cart?" Julian was convinced he was onto a solution.

"Pretty big. It's like one of those Chinatown things, y'know? Big bicycle tires, and the box is maybe five or six feet long by three or four wide, two feet deep. It can hold a lot; the whole idea is to do it all in one trip, once it's loaded up."

"Can we go down there now and look?"

"Bad idea. Sarge would never let us poke around while he was there. We have to wait 'til he's off someplace else."

Julian thought a minute. "When's that?"

"After lunch. Geoff and I go and fill up the cart after Canoeing. He's usually gone by then on his route. We just do what the paper says. He puts it on the board."

darn... I have to go to Archery just then. "Why don't we just go and ask the Sarge? Maybe he'll let us look." Julian wanted to see to this in person. That way he'd be sure that Danny found the right storeroom.

Danny could see that this was important to Julian. He took him by the hands and sat him down for some straight talk. "Look, Julian. The worst thing we could do is let Sarge know what we wanted, y'know? He's a real mother hen about all that stuff back there." He patted Julian on the leg. "Tell ya what. Geoff and I will poke around in there today, I promise. If we can find something, we'll snag it and put it in the cart with the supplies. Okay?" *probably a long shot, but worth a try.*

Julian looked at him. He saw no reason to distrust Danny, *but what if he doesn't find those featherbeds? I'll have to figure out something.* He wanted this fixed. Nick and Tom should have a good comfy night. He felt so awful this morning when he kneeled on that hard ground... and those guys didn't even complain, or anything. *that's why I have to do something.* He looked Danny in the eye. "Promise? Shakes?"

Danny grinned. "Shakes." They did the Troop handshake, the sacred oath one. He saw Julian's skeptical expression clear... *I don't know why Julian wants this, but what the heck. there's an advantage to having a mattress or two in here, come to think about it...* He was hoping to get Geoff to come again, and that might just do the trick. Now then... he started to walk his fingers up Julian's leg.

Julian felt Danny's playful little move... it gave him a tingle. He watched the finger walk from his knee upward... he looked up at Danny's face. *gosh, he's handsome.* The fingers advanced slowly; Julian was fascinated... he let him explore. *Danny's horny today!* The walking fingers went right up to his pant leg and stopped. He looked up again... *Danny's smiling at me.* He smiled back.

Danny saw the green light. He continued his finger walk over to the fly. He poked gently, and sure enough, something was happening in there! He walked to the top of the zipper and took hold. Suddenly Julian held his hand in place.

"Not here. We have to go to the cabin. This is Nick and Tom's room, now." He looked at Danny squarely. Danny needed to respect this place now.

Danny felt a strange flush. Julian's intense look… he still didn't understand what Julian was hung up about. But the cabin was a better place for what he had in mind, anyway. *I'm going to play teacher today!*

Julian took Danny's hand and pulled it aside. He stood up and led him out of the tent. Julian was not about to mess around in Nick and Tom's room. *besides, the ground is too hard.*

They went straight toward the cabin—but picked up their notepads from the table as they passed by. When they reached the post they broke into a run. They entered the cabin almost together.

Danny let Julian enter first, naturally. He was delighted when Julian went to his cot at once and got the blanket—but surprised when he took it over to Mark's bed. *I wouldn't have had the guts to do that…* Danny helped spread it out; *this will be a lot better than the floor… Julian thought of this by himself!*

last time we did a hand job with sun cream; it's time for Julian to learn about the fine art of sucking… He was eager to share what he had learned this week from the expert from the wild, wild west! *hmm… how much about Geoff should I tell? the advanced stuff will have to wait, obviously. I won't even bring that up.*

Julian could tell that Danny was really hot this morning. He wasn't, himself, especially—but touching Tom this morning turned him on some… and his experiment with Sid was proof that the Doug and Paul thing would be worth trying—*I wonder if he'd be interested in something like that.* Danny was equipped more like Mark—the few glimpses he'd gotten were enough to tell that much. *I better let Danny decide what to do—he's a lot more experienced. I'm still kind of new at this stuff.*

Danny looked at Julian—he took off his T-shirt a little boldly. Julian did the same. *excellent… Julian will follow my lead.* He undressed completely, and so did Julian. "Do we need to lock the door?"

"I never thought about that. Does it have a lock?" Julian turned to look. There was a surface mount deadbolt. *I never noticed that before. boy... what if somebody had come in when Sid and I were playing around?*

Danny ran over and turned the deadbolt. "Better be safe." At least they'd be able to jump clear and look innocent if they had to. Last time, the chance that Mark might show up unexpectedly had worried him... what a disaster that would be. He hopped up onto the bed and sat on his heels. Julian hopped up and sat across from him. Danny looked at Julian's cock: *I forgot how undeveloped it is, compared to Geoff.* He touched it... it began to grow. *I love the way that looks... it isn't so small once it fills up.*

Julian enjoyed what Danny was doing... he especially liked seeing Danny get hard. The foreskin pulling back by itself... *that's so hot! maybe I can find a way to do the Doug one. that's best for speed.* He remembered watching Danny shoot into his face that first day... he looked forward to having that happen in his mouth!

"Julian, I have something really great to show you. You know Geoff?"

Julian shook his head. "Only his name."

"Well, he's an expert at things." Danny flashed his eyes. "I mean, a real expert, too. He's shown me some things... I just know you will like it as much as I do!"

Julian squirmed. "Ooo!" Danny looked better and better...

Danny wrapped his right hand around Julian's fully hard cock. "Have you ever thought about... sucking?" He squeezed Julian gently.

Julian's eyes went wide. "Mm-hmm...yeah..." that's exactly what he was thinking about. *I'll play like I don't know about it for a little while.*

"Great!" Danny could hardly wait... he presumed that this would be a first time for Julian, and he planned to make it fabulous. "Well, you don't have to think about it any longer. I'm gonna show you all about it!" He was jumping with eagerness. "You have to lay down flat for this."

Julian did as he was told. He loved it when Danny spread his legs apart. *maybe he'll start with a massage, like he did that first day in the tent.*

"There's two kinds, basically. There's the straight up and there's the sixty-nine." He licked his lips. He assumed Julian knew none of this. "Okay if I show you?"

"Sure!" That meant no massage... *good. might as well play beginner...* he was planning to give Danny a little surprise of his own, later on. *I'm pretty good at some of this, from what Sid said. but maybe the Geoff way is just as good...* he was eager to find out.

Danny went down just as Geoff had that first time: he wanted Julian to feel that first super second, and what came after.

Julian flinched at the new sensation... the suction was intense. Danny's warm mouth slid down over him with smooth determination and reached the base. *this is different!* Danny's tongue stretched down the shaft and pressed against it as he pulled his head back up. Danny's lips pressed against his crown just before he slid down again. "Mmm!" *fantastic! this Geoff guy is good!*

Danny's temples glowed when Julian hummed like that... he enjoyed this. Doing Julian was very different... the odor was so mild compared to Geoff. *he's circumcised and smaller...* The ability to control what he was doing was multiplied. *I can go right down to the balls with no effort at all. the sixty-nine is going to be so easy! but this is very nice... I'll do this for a while longer...* He ran his tongue down under Julian's balls on the next one, forcing the cock head to hit the back of his throat. Julian throbbed when he did that. He repeated that a few times, varying with a little twisting to one side then the other.

Danny played a little with his hands now... he massaged the balls, pulling them gently, as Geoff had done. There was no point in stretching the skin... Julian couldn't possibly get any tighter. Danny massaged the thighs... moved up to the side of the buns... then back across the belly, just below the navel. He could tell from Julian's reactions that he was doing very nicely. Doing this massage was different from before. Now he knew better what to do, how to use it as an enhancement. He worked over the entire upper and lower torso in rhythm with each sucking plunge. He rubbed and twisted the nipples until they stiffened and were sensitive to the slightest touch. He kneaded Julian's belly below the navel. This beautiful body! He had wanted to caress it like this for so long! Geoff had shown him how to do this properly... *so much of the pleasure is in doing it.*

Julian had lost his objective eye rather early this time. Danny's technique was so completely different and so wonderful that all he wanted to do was let it go on and on. He concentrated on what Danny was doing... this was something he wanted to learn. *ooo... oh-oh! I'm about to shoot. so soon... that's what Danny seems to want.* He didn't want to stop... *this is so wonderful...* He wanted to enjoy every second... he felt his body go rigid and begin its unstoppable sequence... he grabbed the blanket on each side... "Nnnn!"

It was such a turn on to feel Julian tense and pulse. Danny could hear a muted hum now, too. *oh-oh: I didn't mean to go all the way... I want to show the sixty-nine too.* The rigid torso meant that Julian had reached the point of no return. *I'll have to show the sixty-nine later.* He hummed along with Julian, and stayed with him...

Julian finished shooting; he stayed still and caught his breath. It was hard to believe Danny had just done that... *what now?* Danny hadn't pulled off... Julian looked down... *!!!* Danny started up again! *but it's different... he isn't sucking hard. Danny's curly hair! wow.* It was amazing to see his shaft disappearing into Danny's lips.

Danny worked his tongue around gently, avoiding the sensitive tip. He concentrated on the middle part of the shaft, the part that was the least sensitive, pressing it a little harder each time, until it started to feel hard again. *do it just like Geoff taught... this is easier, actually...*

This was a different sensation. Julian felt his balls being rolled gently in Danny's right hand... Danny was only working on the center of the shaft. *ooo... it's started to feel... mmm...* a whole new set of feelings was going on. A deep tingle began inside, somewhere behind his balls... another new sensation in the center of the shaft, on the top side—very subtle. His tip flared.

Danny placed his hands on Julian's pelvis—it was important to hold him steady for the final move. He washed Julian's shaft softly with his tongue... he slowly pulled upward, gradually squeegeeing with his lips more tightly together... he pulled them deliberately across the most sensitive part of the tip. He was ready: Julian bucked hard and shot one last spurt just as Danny pulled off. Danny sat back and smiled happily, proud of what he had just done. Julian's amazed smile drew him: he leaned forward with a kiss. He opened his lips and slipped his tongue into Julian's mouth... he swiped Julian's tongue with a small quantity of cum. Danny sat up and smiled again as he swallowed what remained.

Julian was stunned... all he could do was stare. The entire event was overwhelming. Danny's wide grin... *Danny just swallowed! oh...* Julian wiped his lips slightly with his own tongue. Suddenly he comprehended what Danny had done.

"Tasty, aren't you?" Danny chuckled.

"Wow," Julian whispered.   *I can't really tell...*   he tried to concentrate on the taste. *huh.* He looked at Danny again. "I don't know... I guess so. It's not bad tasting though... is it?" *it's different from Sid's. huh. I don't like it as much, actually. But it's okay. huh. Sid said he liked it. Danny seems to like it too. I'm glad Danny did that, now. I never thought about it before. it's good to know this...* it made him feel better about Sid having swallowed. *maybe other guys are supposed to taste better than yourself, or something.*

"Not only that..." Danny flashed his eyes: "look at what you've got!" He pointed to Julian's extremely hard cock.

Julian looked where Danny had pointed. His stiffy was pulsing all by itself. It was not going down! He looked at Danny.

"That's what the second part does. It keeps you up!" He raised his eyebrows up and down. The look on Julian's face!

Julian did not have the experience or the vocabulary he needed. "Wow!" That's all he could say. *how will I ever be able to do this to Danny?* He appreciated at once what a beginner he was. He looked down at his cock and watched it pulse involuntarily a few times. It felt harder than he ever remembered... *it isn't an especially good feeling... but it isn't bad, either.* He looked up at Danny with a wide grin. He felt a little stupid right now.

"Do you want me to try to do that to you, Danny?" He didn't want to do it wrong, but he sure wanted to try.

"Of course—if you want to." Danny smiled in anticipation. He didn't expect Julian to do it as well as Geoff.

"Good." Julian rolled to his side and got up. This is something he had to learn; one day he'd need to be able to do this for Mark. He watched Danny take his place, and position himself perfectly. *oo! Danny's already dripping! wow... I haven't even touched him yet.* He kneeled down between Danny's legs and sat on his heels for a minute. *I want to just look for a second. this is a picture I want to remember.*

now. He focused on what Danny had done. Decision one: pull down the foreskin, or not? *yes.* To give that very first tight slide, the shaft had to be really taut. He leaned forward and gently pulled Danny's skin down to the base. He smelled Danny's dripping shaft first, then opened his mouth. *mmmm. Danny is delicious!*

13   *penetrating the fortress*

Geoff was unsettled… restless. He had no plans this morning, no quests, nothing lined up. He wanted to find something—that is, someone—new. Besides, he deserved to be rewarded. He had just scored a bundle of points for his troop. He and Nate would be handling the seating at the Sunday service. Listening to old Sarge's grumbles had tipped him off to the opportunity. He had to spend some time buttering up the Camp Director, but it paid off. He rested his hands on his hips… *well: standing on the HQ landing like this is getting me nowhere. loads of shouting at the lake; might as well check it out. water polo, doubtless.*

surely there's somebody who has escaped my notice. I'll be late arriving—finding a Buddy might be problematic. I could always flirt with Leonard. oh! that's right! Geoff stopped in his tracks. He had thought about doing that. What an intriguing idea. He moved forward slowly… better watch from a distance first. He didn't exactly have a plan. *Leonard is a big boy… he requires a big boy plan of action.* It might not pan out, of course, but the challenge was irresistible.

He sat at the top of the grassy slope, out of Leonard's direct line of sight. *so… there he is, sitting behind that table, as always… it's like a fortress. does he ever stand up?*

why do I want to pester Leonard? well, for one thing, he's the right age. Geoff always preferred men Ronnie's age, and Leonard qualified. Those were scarce at a scout camp, sadly—this one, anyway. Geoff guessed that Leonard was probably… twenty-five or six? No more than twenty-eight. *what are his pecs like? there's no way to tell what his physique is like… he always hides behind that table, all dressed in his Official Blue Waterfront t-shirt. it's reasonable to assume he's in good physical shape… he is the big cheese at the lake, after all. doesn't look like he's gone to seed any... he's uniquely handsome, actually. tan is fabulous, above the neck at least.*

hmm. how do I get him out from behind there? I don't see... aha! I have it—Geoff, you are inspired! He knew exactly what he needed: on the first day, there were two counselors seated there. *all I need is a chair! I know just where to get one.* He retraced his steps up the trail; the HQ building had several hundred folding chairs. In a few minutes he was going to join Leonard... *I'm going into that fortress!*

—ɯ—

Leonard was reasonably content today. Bradley had issued the water polo teams their caps at last, so the lifeguards had a more manageable task. Having the new trainees from Lifesaving was a big help too—the game required its own set of guards. The noise was bothersome, but there was no way to eliminate it. At least the cheering was confined to the boat dock. The alternate teams seemed just as excited about the teams in the water as they were about themselves. *the roar is mild compared to basketball or football... I can put up with it.* The frequent foul ball whistles were a nuisance, but they had become familiar enough. *I should count my blessings... all the organizing and operations are Ben's responsibility. Jorgensen is to be congratulated for seeing to that.*

Leonard panned the swimming area with his binoculars. He did that routinely, just to keep busy. Having to stay on station was a mixed blessing at times. The crowd was down slightly from yesterday... that's one phenomenon that continued to puzzle. He did not know with any certainty what factors were responsible for the numbers at the lake on any given day. Nonetheless, his task was to be ready, regardless.

He had toyed with the idea of rotating the duties, but that really wouldn't work; the head of the command chain needed to be here, not locked in at a guard position. He could close the gate at any time and be free to move anywhere he was needed. *I seem to be the only one who can keep track of who is in the water at any given time.* His talent for remembering names was uncommon. It wasn't needed very often, but when or if it was, it was invaluable.

The same ability helped in unofficial ways as well... it enhanced the pleasure he got from keeping track of sundry romances that developed; some lasted more than a single year. That always pleased. Big Tom was his favorite there—*he and Nick are closer than usual this summer.* His second favorite was a new pair from Troop 2. Water polo was eating into it some, though. He swung his glasses over to check: *yes, Adam is there, sitting on the dock's edge.* He panned to the right. *who's out on the platform this morning? hmm... is that...* his view was cut off suddenly. Someone had just walked in front of him—

"Hi." Geoff cheerfully opened the folding chair and deliberately sat directly in Leonard's field of vision.

Leonard was taken aback. *what's he doing?* "Wha..."

"I've decided to study your **outstanding** setup here, Leonard." Geoff nudged Leonard's left thigh with his right, forcing him to scoot over and make room. "I'm looking for ideas that I can use with my troop." Geoff reached for Leonard's clipboard and slid it close to the edge of the table between them. "I'm sure you'd love to share your professional secrets. Naturally, I'll give you full credit when I announce my reforms." Geoff chuckled, as if he was plotting something and Leonard was being let in on it. Leonard's leg felt very nice.

Leonard blushed. No one had ever asked to do this before—that he could recall, anyway. *goodness...* He didn't have a prepared response to cover this contingency. *well... I suppose... um... there isn't any reason to refuse. I'm not sure what I can do, though.* He opened his mouth to say something, but nothing came to mind.

"How long have you run things here, anyway?"

"Well..." Leonard didn't really **run** things. "This is my fourth year as Waterfront Director, but..."

"Four years!" Geoff raised his eyebrows and patted Leonard on the back. "The powers that be must know a talent when they've got one." He looked at Leonard in the eyes. "Congratulations." He held the stare for three full seconds.

Leonard was so surprised that he had no reaction at all. *such extravagant praise! goodness gracious, what exotic eyes!*

Geoff used his disarming innocence smile. He glanced at Leonard's basket on the way to focusing on the clipboard: he approved of Leonard's shorts. They would show any progress—as it happened. He picked up the clipboard and held it in front of him. He affected a genuine interest.

The cover page was a check-off grid for the Buddy whistles. Three pages of handwritten notes... next was a canoe/rowboat sheet. He flipped the pages with a deliberate eye; *something here should suggest a strategy. let's see...* a list of restricted swimmers... a list of swimming instructors and counselors... a duty roster for the whole camp staff, which ran several pages. There were several sheets of notes after that. A water polo roster was tucked in at the very end. He flipped back to the page Leonard had been using. "How do you use this?" Geoff expected Leonard to lean over and show him. He was not disappointed.

Leonard leaned close and pointed to the staff line. "This is who is on duty for the swim period," He glanced back at Geoff's face. "These are the scheduled Buddy Check blocks." He put his finger on the field of squares. "If it is given on time, I fill it in with an X. If it's early, I use an E, and if it's late, an L."

Geoff had slowly, imperceptibly at first, exerted pressure from his right leg against Leonard's left. Gradually, very gradually, he increased the pressure... *how long will I be allowed to keep this up?* "What if a Buddy check is missed?"

"That has never happened!" Leonard sat back abruptly; he didn't mention the fact that on more than one occasion, his less than gentle nudge to the backside of a chair guard had made it possible to enter an L instead of a 0.

"What happens to these sheets?" Geoff gave Leonard the wide open eyes of a curious, malleable tenderfoot scout. *ooo-oo. the leg hasn't moved away.*

"Well, they are kept and tabulated. We use them to evaluate the program, and, in some cases, an individual performance." Leonard's ego was being massaged, and he enjoyed it. He was taken for granted far too much around here. Having a talented and—ahem—attractive, scout take notice was a very nice surprise.

"I see!" Geoff enthused. "This enables you to speak with knowledge and facts, not general impressions." Geoff put his right hand on Leonard's thigh and patted him gently. "Very clever of you!" He made eye contact and gave Leonard a look of admiration. *this leg has just the quality I've been longing for.   strong, substantial thighs... excellent.*

Leonard blushed at once. He had to look away; he sensed that those eyes were… well, dangerous. He recalled the look he had gotten from Geoff the other day, suddenly. He dared not think…   *well, that would be absurd.*

Geoff glanced down to Leonard's crotch. *oh, yes... we are getting started, aren't we?* "Now, don't be modest." Geoff pressed his fingers gently into the skin just below the edge of Leonard's shorts. "Everyone knows that this swimming center is the very model of efficiency and safety." He removed his hand reluctantly, and flipped to the canoe/rowboat sheet. He ran his finger down the page slowly.

Leonard felt himself swelling. He wasn't sure when it had begun. *should I be worried?* This is not something he had run into before… *I hope it will stop... I don't want it to get any bigger, please...* He was rather enjoying this chat… he looked at Geoff. *he's sitting so close;* the flawless texture of his skin… the oriental eyelids were fascinating—and very sexy. *oh dear... I'd better look away.*

"What does this sheet do?" Geoff smiled and blinked his eyes sweetly. He leaned over in front of Leonard this time, and renewed the leg contact.

Leonard felt a little warm. He hated to admit it, but he enjoyed the feeling Geoff's leg gave as it pressed his… *maybe he'll leave it there a while.* "Oh…" he hadn't been paying full attention. "The merit badge instructors like to know if any of their boys are doing any special practices. And it's nice to have this handy without going over to the Buddy Board to check on who's out in a boat or canoe."

Geoff was getting a hit of his own… *what a nice surprise.* He liked the feel and the presence Leonard provided… *big boys and men always feel and smell better, don't they?* He looked at Leonard directly. "How many awards have they given you?"

"Awards?" Leonard was stopped cold by that question.

"You mean to say that you haven't been recognized for all this?" Geoff feigned being shocked. "For an outfit that passes out merit badges and points every chance they get, I think that's a disgrace!" He patted Leonard on the back and held his hand there for a count of five. "Hmm. I just may have to write a letter!"

Leonard was at a loss again. Getting an award had never entered his mind. He looked at Geoff gratefully. He hadn't been praised for a very long time, either... it felt very nice. He felt silly suddenly—*I'm blushing.*

"Don't be so modest... you do excellent work. The least they could do is give you a certificate to hang on your wall."

Leonard pictured a framed certificate in his mind. *would it have glass?* There were a few of those on the wall in Jorgensen's office. *they're quite handsome.* He shifted in his chair unconsciously... he needed to free himself. These shorts weren't as loose as he needed them to be.

Geoff noticed the progress in Leonard's lap... not quite a third of the way up. It was his experience that a slow grow was almost impossible to halt beyond this point... why not allow Leonard the opportunity to show his full potential? Geoff felt reckless suddenly... he regarded the sensation in his groin to be a positive sign. He didn't know if this was going to go anywhere, but he wouldn't run from it. His tease had just been reclassified: it had become a possible... a potential project. He fanned his legs involuntarily. It helped free the space that would be needed along his left leg before long.

>> *BLEET-BLEET-BLEET!* <<

The Buddy Whistle sounded. Leonard and Geoff looked at each other awkwardly. They hadn't reckoned on that.

"Can I just scoot down while you do your checking?"

"Certainly. Stay right there. You're not in the way at all." Leonard stood up resolutely and scanned the inner left area with his binoculars— that guard was reassigned to water polo duty. What a blessing! Standing up enabled him to shake things loose. He felt his cock drift to the right and head down his leg. Thankfully he had loose underwear on today. As long as he was standing, it could drift freely without having to be handled directly—handling almost always meant... *well, I don't want that, of all things!* He presumed his difficulty had gone unnoticed. He didn't anticipate that it would become a serious problem now; he expected things to calm down momentarily. Unconsciously, he was thriving on this little visit. He was flattered, of course. *what's wrong with having a nice cozy chat?* He hoped that Geoff would stay for a while… it felt good to have him here.

Geoff bent forward slightly, as if to free Leonard's field of view. It enabled a more convenient view of developments… he looked over and saw the bulge. *now that would be a nice one…* he calculated that it would be almost a full eight inches when it was ready to be put into its proper place. Leonard's size had just qualified him. He was now desirable: in a word, a project. *ooo…* it just moved from seven to eight o'clock. The power of suggestion asserted itself: now Geoff had to face the delightful challenge of loosening up some space for his own growing member—not easy, hunched over like this. His binding clothes conspired to speed the process… so be it. He leaned to the right slightly. *with any luck, I can help Leonard make an "accidental" brush against me…* an overt hand movement would ruin things.

Leonard's eyes were behaving at least… he scanned the water to verify that all the arm pairs were where they should be. It was a medium to large-sized crowd this morning… it would take a little time to verify them all. Allowing water polo to ignore the Buddy Whistles was distracting. His mind was not exactly where his eyes were… it wanted to lead him astray. His imagination was starting to wrestle for his attention. It was all very vague… a strange sensation in his stomach didn't help. oh! Something brushed against him very lightly. He dared not look. It felt… very nice; perhaps it would happen again… he leaned forward slightly. He snuck a peek down under the binocular lenses. *oh my… I've pressed against Geoff's shoulder by mistake.* It made his situation… well… it was sort of out of his control. Maybe Geoff won't notice what's rubb… um, **touching** his shoulder. Leonard could feel… *oh dear: am I still enlarging? this can't be happening… not being able to touch or adjust is excruciating! surely Geoff doesn't realize… he's facing the other way… umm… how long do I dare keep this pressure? I'll just see… my, but it feels good! when, oh when will that whistle sound?*

Geoff was delighted. He had not expected such solid results so soon. He knew what was pressing against him, but he was smart enough not to let on. He couldn't move his hand to touch and stroke, nor his face to nuzzle—no point in forcing Leonard to eject him. It's obviously standing at eleven o'clock now. His own erection was full, and having to stay seated and bending forward made it pulse and protest vigorously. He didn't know how to take their condition to the next level—namely, acknowledgement and planning. But he knew it was possible. His morning lark may just have become something very nice. He looked up at Leonard just as the whistle blew. He saw the clear outline of Leonard's erection. He wanted it.

Leonard sat down with some awkwardness. Geoff was still hunched over.

Geoff sat up part way with his hands on his knees. He was smart enough to appear oblivious to Leonard's condition. "How tall are you, anyway?"

"Uhh... five eleven." Leonard blushed. He had to swallow; *where should I look... I can't cross my legs: Geoff is sitting too close... oh, of course: arms folded over the lap... that will have to do for now.*

Geoff sat back in his chair and fanned his legs briefly to allow his hard-on to point upward... *it will be hard for Leonard to avoid noticing.* He put his arm on the back of Leonard's chair. "That's a good height. I like that height." He paused. "I'm five feet eight." He rather preferred his men to be taller than he was. He reached over and ran his finger along the neckline of Leonard's T-shirt. "Is this one of those annoying tan lines?" He looked at Leonard sympathetically, his finger sliding slowly on Leonard's skin.

Leonard blushed again... "Umm... I suppose it is." He did swim with the staff in the morning before swim lessons. Getting a tan wasn't part of the program. No one had ever asked him such a thing before. He just had a delayed reaction... the sensation of Geoff's finger touching his neck...

Geoff ran his finger across Leonard's thigh along the hem of his shorts. "This is too, I suppose." He bent down to examine the leg more closely. He got a good glimpse of Leonard's pulsing member. "This isn't as delicious a color as your face." He gave the hem of the short pant leg a mischievous nudge to reveal the tan line. He was tempted to poke a finger in, but decided that would be going too far.

130

Leonard was buzzing. He was conflicted. He was getting rather *horny,* of all things. He wanted this to stop now, but he wanted it to never stop. He was not equipped for this... what a fine, smooth sensation Geoff's fingertip conveyed... *what did he say? delicious?! no one has ever called me that!* He glanced down to his lap: his erection had become so **total**. *oh dear... has Geoff seen it?*

Geoff sat back again. He looked out at the lake and fanned his legs very slowly. He wanted Leonard to see what he had caused. "What a shame... maybe when camp is over, you can even up your color some." He shielded his eyes and looked out to the platform. "A few hours out there would do wonders, you know."

Leonard looked down at the outline in Geoff's lap. He had an urge to reach for it. It pulsed! Leonard's heart raced. He couldn't believe what he was thinking! He pressed his legs together— *oh!* He looked down... a small wet spot had appeared. He was thrilled and horrified.

Geoff turned to look at Leonard. He's checking on himself— *wonderful.* Leonard looked quite perfect just now. *how can I spirit him up the hill to my supply tent?* He swallowed suddenly. He had started to salivate. *oh. that reminds me: lunch isn't far off.* He reached over and took Leonard's arm. He pulled the wristwatch over in front of his face. He looked up at Leonard, and shrugged. The swim period would be ending in about fifteen minutes.

"I've been a pest long enough." Geoff had gone as far as he should for the present. He needed to plan the next step carefully. Indulging himself now would likely spoil everything. "We have to get ready for the crowds." He gazed into Leonard's eyes. He returned Leonard's arm to his lap and pressed it down gently. "Thanks for letting me visit." Geoff stood and remained as close as he could... he indulged himself by triggering a brief pulse. Leonard had focused on it... *excellent.* "Maybe we can chat again soon." He patted Leonard on the shoulder lightly and gave a small ta-ta wave. He walked out of the gate with just a slight swagger... after all, Leonard hadn't had the opportunity to see his backside yet. That's where he was the most welcome. About ten yards up the hill, he turned to wave again... *very nice.* Leonard was watching. *well, well, well. that's the right word: this started well... very well indeed. walking is not helping much right now... I need to run to my camp quickly... might be a shade late for lunch.* Some things just couldn't be helped.

Leonard was not able to comprehend all of this. He knew statements had been made and erections had occurred. He knew that he had about twenty minutes to calm down. He looked into his lap. He wouldn't be able to deal with this here or now. What trick could he come up with to make it go down?

oh... Geoff left the chair behind. Leonard folded it up and tucked it between the table end and the fence. *I'll just keep that here a while. a few days, at least. oh-oh... the water polo whistle! end of the game already?* He assumed a crossed leg position where he could cover himself. *fortunately, I'll be the last to leave. with any luck, I'll be ready.*

14   *lasagna for lunch*

Julian peeked between the layers of pasta in the middle of his plate. It looked like bits of cottage cheese in there. He sniffed... *hmm. it smells good, so—*

"Yeah, it does look kinda funny." Sid sat down. "My mom's is a **whole** bunch better." Mass production rarely achieved quality.

"That's right! I forgot you said this was your favorite." Julian let the pasta flop back flat. argh... it squished everywhere when he tried to cut it with his fork. "Kinda messy." *aren't these layer things supposed to be thinner?*

"Undercooked." Sid knew all about these things. He attacked with his fork held vertically, systematically spearing a line of perforations across, then another down. He looked casually to his left, then right. *nobody. excellent.* He had to brag now. "So... give in to any bad habits lately?" He used a forced off the cuff intonation. He loaded his fork with one of the squares of lasagna he had created and delivered it up to his mouth.

Julian watched Sid address the brick of lasagna. *good idea; I'll make my squares smaller: two lines down. six bites instead of four. now then.* He had been thinking about other things entirely—namely, the padding for Nick and Tom, so he did not pick up on what Sid said at first. But he had known Sid long enough to recognize this particular ploy. He looked at him... he narrowed his eyes. *what the...?* Sid was not offering any hints, either. Julian was stumped. "Bad habits?" He looked at Sid again. Sid was starting to blush! The sip of milk Sid just took made his mind click... the slurp and grin reminded him of what Sid looked like Thursday back in the cabin after they tried the Doug and

Paul thing… only now he has his glasses on. Julian laughed heartily. *I nearly forgot Sid's wisecrack. that's funny.*

"I wish!" Julian wouldn't mention the little "snack" he had this morning, courtesy of Danny. "That was a good one, Sid. Sorry it took me so long." What he had done with Danny was not exactly a habit; it could become a Way of Life! Julian slipped his fork under one of his smaller squares. He looked at it briefly… *hm… tastes good.* He chewed for a while. *once in the mouth, this is okay…* He glanced at Sid, about to comment on the lasagna… *wait a minute: look at that grin!* Julian's eyes went open wide. "What's going on, Sidney?" This was a cat that got the bird grin, if he ever saw one.

Sid nodded yes. He was bursting to tell all about it, but keeping Julian in suspenders was too much fun.

Julian was being forced to make deductions here… but there was clearly only one that could be made. "You didn't!"

"Did too," Sid gloated.

"Did not!" Julian said. This was a fun game too.

"Did, did, did," Sid taunted happily. He worked his thighs back and forth so fast his knees knocked.

"All right then, who with?" Julian challenged him. *Sid never lies…* he was really intrigued.

"Sor-ry… Hafta guess…" Sid hummed happily as he rewarded himself with a bite of lasagna. A small patch of tomato sauce appeared at the corners of his mouth. He was oblivious to the decoration.

Julian was thrilled to see Sid this happy. He wanted to hug whoever was responsible. *okay… go through the obvious ones first.* Something told him he was in for a surprise, though.

"Not Jeremy."

"Nope."

"Stu." *he'd be the last one to mess around.*

Sid laughed hard. "Puh-leeze!"

"Wait! Not Paul!?"

"Nope. Sorry, you're cold."

"Cold? So it's not Doug, either?"

"Huh-uh; still cold." Sid was oozing with pleasure at this. He looked over haughtily. "Your lunch is getting cold." He feigned an interest in the macaroon, the only item left on his tray.

Julian took another bite of lasagna. "Well, I know it's not Tom, or Nick, or Danny. Sid, you have achieved something here, for sure." He regarded him again. *I have to guess, obviously.* He thought bac k... he'd eliminated all the possibles... The yummy time in the cabin.... *duh, nobody else was there.* The circle on the platform! *how stupid of me! of course!* There was... "Justin?"

"No way!" they said in unison, and laughed.

Julian froze as it hit him. He looked up at Sid, who had been watching him work through this. He grinned wide. "No! **Really**?"

Sid nodded his head proudly. He blushed again.

Julian was impressed. He reached over and squeezed Sid's arm. "Can you tell me about it?" He wanted to hear it all.

"I didn't tell him about us, so you can't either, okay? He thought it was my first time." Sid chuckled. "Technically, it was—with **him**."

Julian got the implication at once. He opened his eyes as if to ask if he was right.

Sid nodded his head. He was serious. "Cross your heart and..."

Julian put out his hands for the official troop dealmaker: "Shakes!"

They did the solemn version.

Sid leaned close. "You must never repeat this to anybody in your life! He called me his new suckbuddy." The word sounded so **daring**.

Julian was stunned.

Sid nodded. "I think we're going to do it a lot."

Julian thought for a minute... He looked at his old friend; Julian was so happy for him. But, after all... *this is Sid.* He smiled a just for Sid smirk and shrugged. "Well, you'll have to, won't you?

Sid looked at him, surprised.

"How else are you gonna get any good at it?"

Sid tipped over and bonked his head against Julian. "'Kay," he laughed. "When I figger out how to do it right, I'll give you a call." He giggled contentedly.

"Deal." Julian giggled. He **figgered** it wouldn't take too long. He figgered if it did, he'd give him a reminder.

"Potty time. See ya later," Sid stood. With a wave he walked away, tray in hand. He had to adjust himself a little. With any luck, there wouldn't be a line at the lavatory.

Julian looked after him. The bounce in Sid's gait was really wonderful. Now Kurt had moved over to his list of good guys.

He looked at the lasagna again... he didn't really want it. But he was hungry now. So he resolved to finish his meal before it got stone cold. He took another bite and chewed; he thought briefly about Sid's new situation. Who'd ever guess such a thing could happen. He washed the lasagna down with a swig of milk. *now, then... about that padding: I hope Danny can find those things. I wish I could help... besides, I'd really like to meet this Jeff.* If all went according to plan, there would be a soft bed tonight for his friends. *I'd like to see what the "expert" looks like... if only I could skip Archery.*

"Hey." Kurt sat down across from Julian.

Julian looked up. *wow. speak of the...* "Hi," Julian was surprised. He couldn't thank him directly. *he sure looks like a happier guy today; Sid must have been good for him too.* He noticed that Kurt's lunch was already half eaten. *hmm. remember, Julian, no stupid questions. you have to pretend you don't know anything.*

"I haven't seen you since we had to make that quick exit." Kurt was looking for an excuse to ask where Sid was. He hung around with this kid sometimes. *I'll figure a way to ask eventually.*

"Yeah." Julian laughed. "That was close, all right!" He thought back. *that's right! Kurt had shot that perfect arc up three feet. he's big, too, about Danny's size. Sid's lucky, all right.*

"So, how is it going with the Canoe badge? What do you guys have to do for that, anyway?" No way would Kurt talk about Sid. *look at those arm muscles.*

"Lots of paddling. We learned how to get back in if we tipped over the other day." He looked at Julian, surprised a little by his super innocent appearance. He remembered Julian's vivid description of the underwater blowjobs... and how Sid had translated it so successfully. *if*

Julian had half an idea how good it was, he'd cream his pants. Kurt fanned his legs unconsciously.

"How does Jeremy keep up with you? You must have twice the muscles."

Kurt was flattered. "The kid does okay, don't sell him short." *he's getting better, in fact. it was kinda rough on him at first.*

"Hmm." Julian had finished the lasagna at last. He looked at the macaroon. *ug.* "You want an extra cookie?"

"Sure!" Kurt squeezed it together with his, plonked them into his mouth and chewed mercilessly. "You seen Sid around?" It felt okay to talk with Julian… *no reason he should get any suspicions.*

"Yeah, actually. He just took off for the rest room." Julian finished his milk. "I think he has First Aid next. He'll probably go right there afterwards." He was glad to give Kurt a freebie like that. It might help later on… he wanted to find out more about why he was mad, maybe, at Tom. He wanted Kurt to know that Tom is really a good person… *I used to be afraid of him too, but that was silly.*

"Ah… not a bad idea. I've got an hour and a half in that canoe coming up." Kurt stood. "See ya!" He took off. He wanted to make sure about this afternoon. He hadn't been able to think about much else since lunch began.

Julian watched him leave. *what a cool thing. good old Sid.* Julian wasn't particularly attracted to Kurt, himself. *maybe Beefcakes aren't my thing. Sid is welcome to him.*

15 *the entrepreneur*

Andy just couldn't hold it any longer. He stepped off the path and ducked behind a large red oak. He took it out just in time. Another second and he'd have wet himself. *ahh...* The stream was full and forceful.

"You're under arrest!" said a low voice behind him.

Andy flinched and looked over his shoulder. "Man, you faked me out!"

Freddy laughed and stood next to Andy and unzipped. "I'll give you some help." He aimed his stream at the same spear of grass. "Ahhh."

"I should have gone after lunch, but the john inside HQ had a line a mile long." The lake latrine didn't have a trough—*taking a whiz in a booth is so disgusting. anyway—lots of trees around.* Andy aimed at a specific blade... *maybe I can bend it over.* "So what did you think of the little show, today?"

"Man!" Freddy shook his head.

They had just seen a juvenile alligator swallow a large rat in one bite. The Reptile Study merit badge featured an occasional gruesome demonstration. The second day it was water moccasin vs. field mouse.

"I've decided to hold off on my field trip to the Everglades." Andy was grossed out, in fact. "Man, it didn't even chew! Swallowed it **whole!**" Maybe that was just as well, come to think about it... personally, Andy would be content to watch turtles and salamanders duel it out.

Freddy was impressed by the solid stream Andy was producing... that blade of grass was putting up a good fight. "Better that way. No crunching noises, at least. I don't know what I'd have done if there was a mess. I almost looked away." At least the rat's protestations couldn't be heard once it was inside the alligator.

"Sure didn't bother Mr. Benson any... he must be from Florida or something." Andy was impressed by his cool attitude... It was funny, the way the counselor jumped. He let the rat loose just in time. Andy watched his yellow ribbon slowly run out. He shook the last few drops.

"I'm glad those things don't live around here. I can't move fast enough." Freddy could visualize his foot disappearing in front of his eyes. He finished and zipped up. "I plan to steer clear of our own little swamp, anyway." He looked at Andy closely. He had been looking for this chance for a while. "You plan to go to free swimming?"

"I usually do, yeah." Andy liked the scenery. There was always the remote possibility Tom would show up in a needy state. *ah... I'm such a dreamer. yesterday was such a wonderful surprise.*

"I thought maybe you were. I've seen you there." Freddy had observed him carefully, in fact, for the last two days. He deferred to Andy to go ahead. It was a single file trail along here. They walked along without saying anything for a few feet. "What troop are you from?"

"9."

Freddy wasn't surprised. Andy's manner in the badge class was noticeably different. He always said "sir," and stuff like that. "I'm from 118."

Andy knew that... it was on his arm patch. *the guy just wants to be friendly... give him a break.*

"I'll make Star at the end of camp. How long have you been one?" Freddy wanted to get him talking. His goal was to recruit Andy to be his assistant. Having a guy from Troop 9 would make a big difference.

"A year. I'll get my Life by Christmas, I think. It depends on my project coming through." Andy was pretty sure Mark would okay his tree planting idea. All he was worried about was getting the school's okay.

They approached the fenced area. A jam of fifty or sixty scouts waited to get through the bottleneck at the gate. They joined the crowd.

"Who's your Buddy?"

"I don't have a regular; I usually find someone who's loose." *maybe Andy will offer… that would make it easier to bring up my plan.*

Andy looked around for Tony. He stood on tiptoe and surveyed the heads. "I usually meet Tony, but I don't see him." He looked back up the trail. He didn't remember what Tony was planning this afternoon. No sign of him up there, either. "Why not go in with me? I don't see him. He can always find someone when he shows up. Sometimes he does other things." He chuckled. "We're not steadies, or anything."

Freddie blushed at Andy's candor. *is he serious? hmm. probably, considering what I noticed over the past couple of days… my chances may have just gone way up.* "Wow, thanks. I appreciate that." He didn't see anyone in particular he'd prefer, in fact. He'd stick close to Andy for the time being. His candidate prospects were here, as he had anticipated. *if Andy likes the idea, he could cinch them pretty easy.*

They fetched their Buddy badges from the board. The line was moving along reasonably well. When they flashed them at Leonard he beckoned them to approach.

"Thanks," Leonard knew these two on sight, but hadn't memorized their names yet. *ha. different troops. that's a good sign.* Leonard highly approved of integration. He smiled and sent them on their way. He looked at them casually as they undressed at their cubbyholes. *nothing going on. they didn't even glance at each other.*

"So, where do I look for you?" Andy didn't see Tony anywhere inside either.

"Along the F dock mostly. I'm organizing a little project. I doubt if I'll be swimming that much."

Andy looked at him. *project?* His curiosity was awakened. This might be a way to pass some time; all he and Tony did was hang around and gawk. He'd pretty much scoped out what there was already. He needed something to do, in fact. "What's your project?"

yes! Freddy sensed that Andy had taken the bait. He held up his pocket-sized notebook. "It's in here, but it's…" Freddy lowered his voice: "sort of top secret, if you know what I mean." He flashed his eyebrows suggestively.

Andy wasn't about to let this pass. He looked for an empty space. "Let's go over to the boat side. You won't be heard there." He looked Freddy in the eye.

Freddy hesitated. It was for effect. He wanted Andy to insist.

Andy took him by the elbow and tugged. "C'mon. You can trust me. Besides, I know where they keep the unfed alligators. You're just about the right size for supper."

Freddy laughed. "Okay, I give." He walked over near the Boat Buddy Board and sat down cross-legged. When Andy was settled, he handed over the notepad. "It's all in there." He watched closely.

Andy looked through the first six pages. The rest were blank. *hmm.* He turned the book sideways and looked at the branching diagram that took four pages. The spaces were all blank. He looked at Freddy. *what an obnoxious smirk. I wish I knew how to make an alligator noise.*

"Give up?" Freddy was delighted to have stumped him.

"Give up what? You start with fifteen and end with one. There are only four water polo teams, so this can't be for them."

Freddy was impressed. Andy understood it without any help. "It's an elimination tournament, all right. But there are no teams. It's fifteen individuals competing in a special 'Shooting Gallery.'"

"What's so special about it?"

"Their weapon." Freddy waited for Andy to look at him. When he did, Freddy mimed an exaggerated jack off gesture.

Andy's jaw dropped. *wait a minute!* He looked at the brackets again. It wasn't quite clear, but the concept was brilliant. "Okay. So how does it work, then?"

Freddy was thrilled at Andy's reaction. "On the first round, all fifteen try to hit the target. The poorest three "shots" are eliminated. The second round, three more of the twelve will be cut. Third round, three of the nine are out. Fourth round tosses three of the six. The last round, a single winner."

Andy's mind whirred. *should I try to enter?* He flipped to the first page. There were fifteen names already listed. He looked over the list. He didn't know any of them.

"Interested? I need an assistant, as a matter of fact." Freddy paused. "You'd be perfect."

"Perfect? What would I do?" Andy was interested, that was for sure.

"First of all, help me get the last three to commit, and then help me set up and run the event itself." Andy's interest was encouraging.

"When is this event, anyway?"

"During the free swim period tomorrow, then the next four afternoons. I was gonna start today, but I only have twelve guys signed up. I've been going for fifteen. I need to get the last three today, or I'll have to go with twelve... not as interesting."

Andy liked the sound of this whole thing. *a big time commitment... but there isn't anything better to do, really. who knows, I might see something I want to play with afterwards.* He looked at Freddy. "I have one condition." He didn't like to decide something this quickly, but he saw the need to use this hour effectively.

Freddy hadn't thought about that possibility. *well, there isn't much choice. I need an assistant, and Andy is ideal... and, I don't have anybody else lined up.* "Okay."

"I get to invite a couple of guys to watch." He had Tony and Tom in mind.

"That's okay—as long as they can keep it **absolutely** secret. I've given each contestant the right to invite one person if they want. The thing I'm afraid of is that the word will get out and the wrong person will hear about it."

"Good thinking." *this will be fun. Tony will have a really good time too... has he shown up yet?* He looked around to see... *nope... I can clue him in later.* "Okay. It's a deal. Fill me in."

Freddy was delighted. He and Andy would have everything set to go tomorrow!

16   *Outfitting things properly*

At the trail junction Julian waved goodbye. Cory was headed to the Trading Post for a practice target. Julian wasn't eager for any extra practices in archery. His arm was feeling pretty good, considering… all his arrows had hit the straw today. Six of them were inside the circle. Even Mr. Samuels said he was doing well. *maybe I can get that badge after all.* He was sorry that he wasn't a better partner. *helping Cory swim those six laps tomorrow will help.*

Julian planned to buddy with Bruce again this afternoon, if he could. *today I'll work some more on my endurance. my goal is to swim out to the platform and back three times without resting.* He paused at the top of the grassy slope to scope things out… not too crowded. *that's a good sign.* He didn't see Bruce waiting anywhere. He looked over to the F. *maybe he came in with someone else… nope. well, it's early.* The Archery Range was closer to the lake than any of the Badges. *I'll sit and look at some buns for a while. I haven't done that for a couple of days.*

He stepped a few feet to the left side of the slope and sat down. *Leonard is talking to a couple of scouts. say… what would be the best way to draw him? he's always sitting at that table… sort of boring. huh. how about a portrait? maybe what he's doing doesn't matter. I've never done just a head before—other than my secret drawing of Mark's head, that is. be nice if I had some examples. I'll put it in my idea box with the Mark drawings I'm working on.*

"Julian! Over here!"

Julian turned. Danny was waving from up on the trail… *that Chinese guy is with him. oh. that must be Jeff! wow.* Maybe they found the featherbeds for Nick and Tom! *I remember him—Nick said he had Choice Buns!* Julian jogged upslope.

"Come help us get things all set up!" Danny was jumping with excitement.

"You got something?!" Julian felt a little guilty; he'd been so focused on his badges that he almost forgot.

"Yeah! Come on, we want to get it set up before anybody gets back to camp!"

Julian hopped up and down. "Where is it?" He didn't see the cart. *those things are big;* he wanted to be sure they'd found the featherbeds.

"We took them already—we had to drop them off first on the route. We had to get the cart back, so we came for you as soon as we could." Danny had delivered on his promise, and he could hardly wait to see Julian's reaction.

Geoff watched Julian with interest. *incredible. there has to be something in the water where these guys live. this is the best one yet. still a little on the tender side, but what a knockout he's going to be.* He watched Danny watch Julian. *oho... somebody has plans for somebody else, do they? well.* Geoff could certainly understand that. What a pair they would make!

Geoff hung back slightly and let Danny lead the way. *Danny will fill in this little beauty on the way.* He looked back toward the lake. He'd hung back here on purpose... *good. it doesn't look like Leonard saw me.* Geoff wanted some time to pass before they met again. He hadn't had any time to plan. Leonard was a very special challenge. He turned and trotted up the trail.

Geoff wanted to enjoy the view for a little while. *yes...* Danny's he knew intimately, of course... he had them in rather good condition, if he did say so himself. From what he could see of Julian, more time was needed to ripen his set. *there's plenty of time... if Danny is smart enough to be patient. the front side of the coin is a tad on the early side too. but that face! it will be hard to keep from staring. this one is too pretty... too tender for me to touch. but I can have some fun with Danny. I'll start to cook on that right now!* He nudged his way between them as they left the main concourse and started up the trail to the Troop 9 camp.

Geoff ran his hands down the backsides of the two lovelies and tweaked a fingertip into the valleys just under the cheeks. It was a naughty near goose, meant to startle and tease. It did both, to both.

"Tell me, lovely one, what is your name? Danny has been keeping you a secret!"

Julian was startled. He blushed. He liked how that felt! He knew who Jeff was, so he wasn't offended... but he was surprised. He wasn't sure how to respond, though. He looked up into his face briefly. He felt bashful for some reason. *Jeff is so cute!   I like the eyes and nose, especially...*   He had to work up his courage a little. Jeff seemed nice, but he had never had anybody talk to him like that before. Julian kind of hoped he'd poke down there again. It gave him a nice tingle. *hmm... a new one, sort of.* He just thought about that day he and Nick were on the dock; Jeff ran by with Tom and those other guys—one was the Beefcake. Now that he was close up, he could tell that he might not be a full-blood Chinese—*looks part white. explains why he's named Jeff, probly.*

"I'm Julian," he glanced back. "You're Jeff."

"Yes, I am. Danny must have told. Too bad. I won't be able to surprise you like I would have liked." He chuckled flirtatiously... he watched like a hawk. He had so many ways he could go with this! He put a friendly arm around Julian's shoulder. A big brother, comfort kind of arm.

Danny was amused. He knew Geoff was playing. Just to show he was savvy, and horny, he placed his hand on Geoff's and pressed. He wagged naughtily a few times.

Geoff lifted his left hand and stuck it down inside the back of Danny's shorts as they walked. He ran his middle finger up and down the crack. *who knows... maybe we can party some in a little while.* He pushed the tip of his finger vigorously a few times and pulled up. It had to be tugging things up front, because he was so far down. He felt a buzz himself, now. *in a minute I'll hold it under my nose.* Danny had a particularly nice aroma down there.

"He didn't tell very much." Julian wasn't trying to protect Danny, but he didn't know if he was supposed to tell about the sucking or not. *I'll pretend I don't know about that part yet.* "'Cept that you guys have a lot of fun pulling that big cart up and down all the trails." He liked the way Jeff's arm felt. He sensed that Jeff would be a good friend. *maybe something like Nick... only a lot sexier.*

Danny had to adjust himself. He put his hand between Geoff's legs and ran it up tight. He knew he was nudging the back of Geoff's balls... he was afraid to go inside. *we'll be at the camp in a minute anyway.* He didn't want Julian to see how familiar things were getting.

"It's a lot better than packing all that junk on the hiking trails like we had to do for that badge." *look at those eyelashes.* "So what do you do that's special, Julian?" He meant sexual, but didn't expect to be told anything about that—yet, anyway.

"I'm Assistant Scribe." Julian held up his tablet, and opened to a page at random.

"Wow... Can I look at that?"

"Sure." Julian handed him the tablet.

Geoff had to remove his left hand from Danny's pants, and his arm from Julian's shoulder... those moves were played out anyway. He ran his left middle finger under his nose briefly before using it to mark a page in the tablet. *yum.* He looked briefly at Danny and winked to show how much he appreciated it.

Danny blushed. He had to adjust again. He was as hard as a rock now.

"What do you do with these?" *these are something else!* He looked at Julian more closely. *this is more than a pretty face.*

"They go in the Troop Scrapbook, mostly." He was glad Jeff liked them. "Maybe one or two will get into the newsletter when we get back home."

They went past the Farting Post. "Can I look at these some more later?"

"Sure." Julian took the tablet and raced ahead to put it on the table along with his towel. He wanted to see what Danny had found; he expected to see a big puffy roll. He ran into the supply tent.

Geoff looked at Danny narrowly. "Have you been naughty?"

Danny blushed. "A little. Only a little." He held up his forefinger and thumb to show a short length, meaning Julian's unswollen state. He mouthed the word "virgin," and pointed toward Julian, just disappearing into the tent..

Julian saw the featherbeds—there were two. They had been unrolled already. And some big pillows! "Wow! You guys! This is **perfect!**" Julian grinned wide as they came in.

"I thought so too… lucky for us we had Geoff there, though," he punched Geoff in the arm playfully. He was too chicken to take these all by himself.

Geoff smiled proudly. "The old coot will never miss 'em, I'm telling you." He looked at Julian. "He has a whole storage closet full of these things, in both sizes. I think they use 'em in the winter time for some kind of overnight events."

Julian stood back to take a planner's look. *good thing this tent doesn't have a center pole.* He paced it off in both directions, and then stood in the far corner. He held his elbow in one hand and put his chin on the other.

Geoff and Danny watched; Julian had taken charge.

"Danny, does Mark ever come in here?"

"I don't know. I've never seen him…" Danny had no clue one way or the other.

"Does he ever need to, you think?"

Danny thought about this. "I don't think he ever does. Of course, he could. He's the scoutmaster, after all."

"What's in all these crates, anyway?" Julian tapped one with his foot.

"Don't know that, either."

"Supplies and equipment, mostly," Geoff looked more closely. "My camp is the same. They must all have a standard set of stuff. Most of it never gets used. It's a training and disaster setup, partly. They have special camps that do other kinds of stuff from what we do. They set everything up at the beginning so they won't have to mess with it between groups, or something. I think maybe they rent it out, too." He tapped a crate with strange non-scout labels. "We're not supposed to mess with this stuff."

Julian was satisfied. "Does it have to be set up like this?" He pointed to the aisle in the center. "What if we make the way in go around one side or the other?" This place needed some privacy.

Geoff and Danny stepped back and looked at the crates.

"You'd have to bend over, or crawl, though." Danny pointed to the side walls. "It's only three feet tall over there."

"Yeah," Julian smiled.

Geoff saw it at once. *this kid has brains. I can use this little floor plan myself. tomorrow, we'll fetch a few of these for Hawk Camp.*

"I don't get it."

"I do. Julian, you are a genius. Let's get to work on it."

"Okay. We put the head over here by the east wall. That way the sun won't kill them when it comes up."

Danny watched, fascinated; Geoff and Julian placed the two mattresses atop each other. *oh... yeah.* That made sense.

Julian looked at the oversize pillows. "Wow. Why'd you bring four of these?"

"Why not? There was a mountain of 'em."

"Well, they can decide what to do with them." Julian tossed one against the east end. Geoff and Danny tossed the others there too. "Now... we can scoot these over..." He paused. He was uncertain about this part. "Which side should have the entrance?"

No one was sure. Julian had a thought. He went outside to the table and turned around to look back. "C'mere, you guys."

Geoff and Danny's hands had just begun to wander over to the other—they took their hands back, reluctantly, and joined Julian.

"Which side looks less obvious?" The entrance had to be inconspicuous.

They considered the question.

"The left side, probably."Danny put his hands on his hips. "Unless you're standing at the stove."

"Yeah." Julian walked over to the stove and checked. He could see right down the existing aisle in the center. It had to be moved, no doubt about it. "What if we moved the cabinet over there more, sort of in the center?"

"They'd notice that right away and wonder why."

"Yeah. You're right." Julian looked at the other side. "You know, the cabinet is already almost in front of that end. How can we... wait! Mark never goes to the stove anyway, does he?"

Danny shook his head. "Maybe to get coffee..."

"I have another idea," Geoff stepped over by the west end. "Why not lower the flaps just a little. That way the bottom part would be covered."

"Yeah! Then all they'd have to do is crawl in behind the flap." Wait... which end? Right next to the cabinet would make the entrance at the foot of the bed: Julian grinned wide. "The opening has to be on that end, that's the foot of the bed. The entrance will be covered unless someone is going in or out!" He hopped up and down with delight.

It was agreed to. They returned to the tent and removed the aisle in the center by rearranging the crates. A couple were heavy, but the others moved easily. It didn't take long. They backed up to the table and looked at their handiwork. Geoff took care of the tent flap adjustment while Danny and Julian looked on.

"Just a teeny bit lower.... there. What do you think, Danny?"

Danny studied it. It looked fine to him. He shrugged. "Yeah."

Geoff rejoined them. He put a hand on Julian's shoulder. "Test run. You get to go in first." He gave Julian a little push.

Julian grinned wide at Jeff; he went over to the entrance and crawled in.

Geoff goosed Danny a good one. "You're next. Better move fast, too." He grinned naughtily. He had mischief on his mind.

Danny giggled and wagged his butt as he crawled in. He was ready. The walk in had primed him, long since.

When Danny and Geoff came around the corner, Julian was standing to one side, his planner's pose ruling again. They ignored him and crawled all the way onto the mattresses. They each took a pillow and fluffed it up, with purpose. They were clearly of a mind... they intended to break this lair in properly. They looked at each other hungrily. They had forgotten all about Julian.

Julian ignored them at first. The new arrangement blocked out some of the light from outside, making it more private, cozy—more secret—better for making love. He was extremely pleased. He had been imagining Nick and Tom there, in their new space. What else could he do to make it ready? Should he bring in their bags? *no, probably they should do that. it's as ready as we can make it for now.* Nick and Tom could make adjustments if they needed to. He looked down at the two laying there. Jeff was starting to play with Danny—he had his fingers on the zipper!

"**No!**" Julian stared at them in disbelief.

Danny looked up, startled: "What's wrong?"

"I told you before. This is their room. You have to ask them. You have to ask Nick." *especially Nick.* Julian was adamant.

Geoff was truly impressed. This near child had a command ability that amazed. There was no room for argument. Though he thought it was probably silly, knowing both Nick and Tom as he truly did—he had to respect what was going on here. He looked at Danny. "He's quite right."

Danny was not convinced, but knew better than to say anything. He wanted to keep things merry, anyway. He rolled over onto his hands and knees. He would be the first to leave. He wagged his butt at Geoff, and headed for the exit.

Geoff grinned; *I'll spirit Danny away for a quickie at my place.* He stood and approached Julian. He held him by the shoulders and looked him directly in the face. "You are a true friend, Julian. I'm glad we met. I hope we'll see each other again, soon." He squeezed Julian's shoulders to emphasize what he had said. He meant it. Julian was the second one of this bunch that had earned his respect. Nick had impressed him too. He went to the exit and crawled out.

Julian flushed all over at the compliment. He sort of understood it... he didn't think it was that big a deal. It just seemed to be right. He moved toward the exit, then turned back. He wanted to picture in his mind Nick and Tom as they would look in the morning. He assumed that he would not actually ever see them. Unless they asked, he would never come in. He visualized the times he had seen them. *yes. this will be better.* He got down and crawled out.

Geoff grabbed Danny's left bun the second he stood up outside. "We have just enough time to get to my tent and do a quick one."

Danny brightened. "What about…"

"Don't worry. He has a plan of his own. You'll see." He turned and watched Julian crawl out.

They stood by the table and made a final inspection. It looked like it belonged.

"You better go get them now, Julian."

Julian turned to Jeff. *I was just thinking that!* He grinned wide. "Yeah. Thanks. Thanks, you guys." He felt a little awkward. His thank you was so dumb. He looked at Jeff and hugged him impulsively. He took off for the lake. That's where they planned to be. He whooped aloud as he passed the Farting Post.

Geoff watched him with admiration. "Let's hustle butt, Danny!" *later I'll tell him what a treasure he has to play with.* Geoff had a need now; he had not been able to get to his camp before lunch; all this foreplay today was getting to him.

17   *the love nest*

"So, you need to deal with Kurt fairly soon, I think." Nick had just told Tom about his conversation with Julian.

Tom was struggling to remember the incident. There were so many, it was difficult to separate them in his mind. "I wish I could remember it better... it was way over a year ago, I know that much."

Nick pondered this. "It's sort of important. You don't want to make it any worse." Evidently this was before camp last summer. "What do you do when you try to remember things?" There were tricks that helped trigger memories sometimes.

"If I try too hard, it gets even tougher to remember." Tom wasn't used to thinking that much. He was more of a doer. Thinking about thinking was really outside of his experience. "Sometimes if I'm working out or doing something really physical, things pop into my head, y'know, memories and things like that."

Nick had a thought. "How about chopping a cord of wood, or something? Maybe the camp needs some kind of basic labor performed." *that would be mindless enough.*

"I know! I'll go out to the quarter mile marker and back. That'll clear my head, at least." Tom stood up. He was tired of sitting around, anyway. He looked at Nick to see if it was all right. He saw the thumbs up. He sighed with relief and drew a bead on the buoy. *let's do a good dive, too.* He stepped onto the diving ledge. He cleared his head, as if he were in a meet. He held his arms out straight, and then performed a classic pike, even though he didn't have a board. He made the bend back to straight just in time to enter the water perfectly. The lake surface was barely disturbed.

Nick experienced an instant rush. Tom was capable of such class and beauty. He felt extremely fortunate just now.

—⟋⟋⟍—

Julian ran through the gate, out of breath. "Are they here?"

Leonard was startled out of his torpor. *it's the budding young artist! what a nice development.* "Good afternoon! There are many here, as you can see." *is there an emergency?* He studied Julian's face. *looks more like hurry than trouble.*

"Yeah," Julian paused to catch his breath. "Sorry." He leaned on Leonard's table. "I need to talk to Tom and Nick. You know, from my troop? Troop 9?"

"Why, yes. They are here, in fact. You're in luck!" He turned to the left and shielded his eyes. *hmm... only one person there.* He held up his binoculars. "Nick's on the platform. Tom must be swimming." He scanned out to the lake. "Yes. There he is. It looks like he's doing some distance practice." He turned back to Julian to hear the request he felt sure was about to be made.

"Oh, wow. Thank goodness for that!" Julian was grateful he didn't have to hunt any further. Time was running short! "Umm... I need to get them a message. Can you be my Buddy while I swim out there? I promise not to stay. I'll be right back, Scout's Honor." He held up his right arm and gave the scout sign.

Leonard was charmed. He didn't remember when he'd been given the scout sign last. "I'd be delighted. You'd better hurry; Nick might jump in any minute, too."

Julian wanted to hug him, but he didn't take the time. "Thanks!" He raced to a cubbyhole and undressed. He waved thanks and did a fast walk out the F dock... he wasn't supposed to run.

Leonard was very taken with this one. The quick walk Julian was doing was a delight. *hmm...* he'd failed to exact a promise of secrecy though. *I'm being awfully flexible this season. I need to be careful, or everyone will be expecting special exemptions. I should take a hard line once in a while... the word might spread that I'm an easy touch.*

He lifted his binoculars. Julian swam out and climbed up the ladder. *Nick's greeting is friendly... Julian is sitting on his heels telling Nick some kind of news. whatever it is, Nick is delighted... he just gave Julian a great hug.* Leonard searched for Tom. *aha. just swimming around the buoy, and on his way back. hmm.* What had Nick and Tom sent Julian to do? Leonard began to speculate.

The Buddy Whistle sounded. Leonard raised his arm and pointed to Julian. He was ready to explain should there be a need. There wouldn't be; he was the boss, technically. He helped scan for raised arms. There was a sizeable crowd today, so it took a little time. He flashed thumbs up to the tower chair, and the all-clear whistle sounded.

He raised the binoculars again... Tom had arrived and was being told the news. *ooo! hugs and... **kisses!** well, it is good news! now then... how am I going to find out about this?* He watched all three dive in. *hmm... has a long lost relative arrived? not likely... all three are on the way.* Leonard was fond of mysteries. And having one involving his camp favorites was beyond intriguing.

He put the binoculars on the table discreetly as they approached the end of the Dock. *next time Julian hangs around I'll make a few inquiries. meantime, which one will dress the fastest? well! it's going to be the messenger. look at him get dressed!*

Julian slipped his kerchief back on hurriedly and ran over to Leonard. "Boy. That worked out just right, Leonard!" *how can I hug someone who is sitting behind a table?* Impulsively, he darted around behind Leonard and gave him a nice hug. "Thanks. I saw your arm, too!" Julian giggled. He ran out of the gate and danced in place, waiting for Tom and Nick to catch up.

Leonard blushed in spite of himself. Julian had just earned another favor. He watched Nick closely for a hint as he walked by. *hmm... an enigmatic smile. Tom is...oh, my.* Leonard blushed even more... Tom was unable to obscure the incredible tent in his shorts... *it must be at least half way up! what is going on?*

Tom saw Leonard's face as he hurried toward the gate. He shrugged and raised his eyebrows, as if to say 'can't be helped.' He smirked as he trotted up the slope... it was fun to taunt Leonard once in a while. Tom was of the opinion that Leonard was a virgin. *someone else will have to take care of that.*

157

Leonard adjusted himself discreetly. *my goodness, what an afternoon!* He checked his watch. *that's a relief: forty-five minutes until supper. I'll be fine in plenty of time. as long as I think about something else, that is.* He looked back out at the empty platform. Whatever could be going on in Troop 9? This had been quite a day! He glanced over at the folding chair. Well, his troubles this afternoon were nothing compared to this morning. He must not think about that, or he could get himself into another state. He was grateful Geoff had not dropped in again, actually. He never stayed after canoeing, of course; he had some other duty or responsibility. Leonard still had not planned what to do when he did show up again. *is it possible that he might not show up? that's a silly idea... why wouldn't he? surely no one will disturb that chair... there's no other place to put it.*

Julian rounded the Farting Post still running full out. He slowed at the table and stopped to catch his breath. His heart was racing—and not just from running. He could hardly wait to see them enter their new bedroom.

Nick and Tom walked up, not winded like Julian, but they did have a need to slow down some. They were amused and enchanted by Julian's enthusiasm.

Nick looked at the supply tent. The gap in the center was gone. He looked at Tom to see if he had noticed.

Tom stared at the tent... *where's the entrance?*

"Well, Julian, are you going to show us the way?"

Julian hadn't thought about that. It struck him as all wrong for some reason. He shook his head. He pointed to the opening they had made over by the west corner. He blushed, smiling. "Later, maybe."

Tom was baffled slightly, but amused. He followed Nick over to the corner. Tom lifted the flap—*there's the opening!* He looked at Nick, amazed.

"After you," Nick winked at Julian.

Tom stooped down. It was too low to walk in, and a squat waddle was stupid. He got down on his hands and knees and crawled in.

Nick gave Julian a parting grin and followed Tom.

Julian alternated his weight between feet; it was impossible to sit down or stand still. He heard Nick whoop happily. Julian hugged his sides and laughed. He hopped up and down a couple of times. What a wonderful sound! It was perfect. He realized he had to leave at once. *this is their time.* He grabbed his tablet. It was still on the table from before... he had just decided on his next drawing. He left the towel.

Tom pounced on Nick, and they rolled back and forth. The mattresses... they were more like giant pillows... but boy, were they the answer. They laughed and hugged and kissed. They relaxed for a minute.

"It looks like you're not the only genius in this patrol!" Tom delivered a short peck to Nick's lips.

"I was planning to beat you up about this tonight. Julian has come to your rescue!" He kissed back.

They looked at each other. Unspoken messages were exchanged. *oh, yes.*

"Julian!" Tom looked at Nick. "We have to thank him first, at least."

"True." Nick had to agree. Besides... he wondered how Julian had pulled this off. "Julian! We want you!"

It was silent. They sat up and looked at the entrance. They expected to see Julian's head appear any second. It was still silent.

"Julian?" Tom crawled toward the entrance. "Really, Julian, come on in." He looked back at Nick. Not a sound out there. He crawled out to investigate.

Nick crawled out too. He stood up behind Tom. "Where is he?"

"Beats me." Tom was confused. Why had Julian gone?

Nick realized what was up. "Genius is an understatement." He put his arm around Tom's waist. "We're supposed to get it all set up. He didn't want to be in our way." Again Julian had surprised him. *amazing.*

Tom put an arm around Nick's shoulder. How had they hit it so lucky? He nodded toward the tent. They dashed over to grab their sleeping bags. It was moving day!

Leonard heard Julian's running feet at about the time he appeared coming down the trail. *well... another surprise. surely nothing has gone wrong. he's only been gone twenty minutes.* He watched him approach, tablet in hand. He looked to be as happy as he could be. *the mystery continues!*

"Hi..." Julian had to catch his breath. "I've been running," he said, happily.

Leonard was charmed all over again. This one made him feel so... what, brotherly? Fatherly? It was quite new and wonderful, whatever it was. He noticed the tablet clutched tightly in Julian's left hand.

Julian saw his glance. "Umm..." he hesitated. He hadn't thought this through. "Can I draw a picture of you?" He crossed his fingers for luck—he didn't want to foul up by asking so boldly.

Leonard was taken by surprise. He was unable to say anything. He felt a blush coming. "Well, I..." He couldn't figure a way to refuse. He wasn't sure about this, though.

"Please? It's for our scrapbook." That was a fib. He just liked Leonard's face.

"Oh." Leonard could see the reason. *good.* That made it okay. He could feel flattered privately... that was better, too. "Why not?" He tilted his head. "I've never been drawn by anyone before. Do I just sit, or what?"

Julian thought about that. He'd probably like a pose, actually, but that might be bad for Leonard's duty. *hmm.* "Why not just do what you always do, and pretend I'm not here? I'll just find a spot and make a sketch. I only have time to start one. I'll work on it some later, too." *that will work. I might try more than one angle.*

Leonard was not used to being an observed object. It took some doing to stay calm and not fidget. He didn't have a blasted thing to be doing right now. *this is… well it isn't hard, exactly, but it's… difficult. yes, that's the word: difficult.* He flipped through the sheets on his clipboard. *how should I sit?* He checked his watch. *excellent. I only have to endure this for ten minutes. should I offer Julian the use of that extra chair? hmm.* Julian was hard at work already, sitting cross-legged over at the base of the Buddy Board. *hmm. I'll have to pick his brain later about what's going on in Troop 9.* Out of habit, he reached for the binoculars. He was torn. He wanted to look at Julian. *I'd better check on the swimmers…* there were no more Buddy checks today. *supper hour is near at last.*

Julian had been composing this in his mind for a couple of days. He had planned a head and shoulders view originally, but now just a head and neck seemed a better idea… that way it could be larger. The detail of Leonard's nose, and the way Leonard's hair appeared along his forehead… those were unique. *this is going better than I expected. maybe… yes. this technique is working. oh boy. this proves I'm ready to draw Mark, too. ooo… I can hardly wait.*

—ɯɯ—

After a brief but intense romp on the new bed, Nick prevailed upon Tom to ease up. He wanted to save the big event for after hours. "It's too hot in here during the afternoon—besides, we need to fix supper before too long."

"Good point." Tom sat up. He felt around and pushed down here and there. All the bumps and hard spots were gone. *what a miracle.* "Can my sleeping bag be on the bottom?" Its flannel was nice and soft.

"Sure." Nick saw no point in arguing. They smoothed out the two bags and crawled back out through the new passageway. They needed to get the rest of their stuff.

Tom picked up his footlocker. He figured he'd put these behind the pillows—they'd make a terrific headboard.

"Uh, I wouldn't do that, Tom." The footlockers had to stay put.

"What's the matter?"

"Just look. See the hole that leaves? We take those away and Mark will notice at once." The three footlockers made a central island right in the front of the crew tent. They had to keep everything looking normal. Mark's canvas stool was only a dozen feet away.

Tom looked back. "Mm. You're right." He returned the chest. "What should we do? Take everything in loose?"

Nick considered the matter briefly. "We leave everything here except what we'll need in the morning. Every night we just take in what we have to. That way, if we ever have to put everything back in place quick, we'll be okay." *besides, having to crawl into the supply tent to get things would be a pain anyway.* He opened his footlocker.

Tom nodded. *Nick's always smart about things.* He sat down on his cot and lifted his footlocker lid. *what will I need in the morning? I can leave most of these socks here, for sure…*

"I'll take my tube—it's practically new." Nick picked up his K-Y, a towel and a set of fresh underwear… a Troop 9 T–shirt… this ought to do the trick for now. He took his armload of essentials to the new bedroom.

Tom set out a pair of socks and a T-shirt What else… flashlight. He fished around… *it's in here somewhere. what's this?* He pulled out a small string of beads.

!!!! Instant rush—he looked over his shoulder to see if Nick was there. *he's in the other tent… what luck!* He needed to be by himself for a minute. His heart was beating a mile a minute. *man alive. how did this get here? must have been in my pack and I dumped it out along with everything else.* He sat back and looked at it in wonder. This showing up right now, right here was… *spooky. perfect timing, but spooky.* He stroked it softly, lovingly. His mind was transported suddenly… he thought of his rock again, of all things.

my favorite rock… He'd given it to Charlie one day. He didn't remember why or what had triggered the impulse to give him that most prized possession—he was only five or six years old at the time. But he knew that Charlie had always kept it. It was on top of his dresser… always in plain sight. That meant so much to him. Charlie, his hero big brother kept that! It meant the world, that did. It was a bond—it proved that his brother loved him, his brother thought he was important. That's why he always loved Charlie more than the others… *Charlie is extra special.*

For the first time, Tom realized why he still had this—why he always kept it in his scout backpack. He looked at the necklace closely. It was simple, really, only a thin strip of rawhide, with a few beads along the front half. Luckily it was still in one piece after all this time. The colors Nick had chosen were interesting—they were arranged in a unique way. *maybe I can get Nick to explain if there was a special meaning behind that.* Knowing Nick, there probably was.

Tom remembered back… three years ago. He and Nick were in the third tent—the Panther tent. The troop was in the Owl campsite that year—Nick's first summer camp. While they were waiting for the supper call that afternoon, Nick gave him this. He'd made it that very day in the Tenderfoot craft class.

It was a little awkward, actually. He sort of knew that Nick had a crush on him, though he'd never said or done anything to show it. Tom didn't want him to, either. It would wreck things if he did that. He didn't want the other guys to think of him as having a steady boyfriend. Especially his brothers. So when Nick asked him to accept the necklace he almost refused. boy… that would have been awful if he had. Something made him think a second time—it was the look on Nick's face. He saw himself there, in a way—it made him think of how he felt when he gave Charlie his rock. He could still see it sitting on Charlie's dresser. The necklace was like his rock. He had to accept it.

Charlie's example had rescued him from another big goof up: he'd remembered how important it was that Charlie accepted that rock. For Nick the necklace was just like that rock. It made Tom blush a little to remember that, but it made him realize that Nick's motivation was pure and honest.

"Thanks, Little Angel," he'd said. He used to call Nick that. Tom shook his head… *I used to be too big for my britches.* But, he had been keeping it his scout pack ever since, faithfully.

well, sort of… I forgot about it lately. Not any more.

how red faced Nick turned when I put it on! I did a strut around the tent as though I was showing it off to a crowd. Little Angel laughed gratefully. He didn't get mushy, thank goodness. Nick was smart enough to know not to cross that line. *amazing. Nick is always a little smarter.*

Tom gave a deep sigh. He looked over his shoulder again… *Nick's still in the other tent. good.* He slipped the beads over his head and tucked them safely out of sight. He did this without thinking. These were now a part of his life. *some guys have little gold or silver chains... I have Nick's beads.* He wouldn't trade them for anything, either. He loaded up his "overnight kit."

man, I feel terrific! tonight I'll give Nick a nice surprise. He smiled to himself... maybe two nice surprises.

18   *Danny's surprise*

Julian pretended to savor his slice of bread—it was oven toasted, and it did taste good. Actually, he was congratulating himself for sitting where Nick usually sat, on Mark's right. His theory was proving correct. So far, Mark had not looked his way. It was his hope that Mark wouldn't be able to notice the change over at the supply tent. Not looking in that that direction would help achieve that goal, and Julian had placed himself directly in the way because Mark rarely looked at him directly.

"Mmm, pass the noodles. Seconds are required!" Mark loved Italian dishes. "Which one of you guys made the sauce?"

Nick passed the noodles to Danny, who was sitting next to Mark. "Tom made the meatballs from scratch." They had been able to start fixing supper earlier than usual. "I boiled the noodles." Gently, he nudged Tom's foot under the table. They had made their move-in cuddle brief; the big celebration would take place tonight after lights out.

"One of my mom's recipes. We don't have all the right spices though." *we needed some garlic cloves, for one thing.* Tom couldn't remember the name of that other spice his mom always used… *green flakes of some kind. the packet that came with the noodles was pretty good.*

"Well, I think putting the olives and the onions right in the sauce is a great idea." Mark's one gripe about Pat's cooking was her aversion to onions and spices. *she's a right out of the can cook. never any lumps or surprises… scout cuisine is vastly superior. this dish is outstanding—a few more meatballs would be nice though.*

"Yeah. This is great, Tom." Danny took a small second helping. He wiggled his butt on the bench unconsciously… the quick one in Geoff's tent was very nice. He glanced again at the crew tent. He was afraid Mark would look behind and see the end of Tom's cot. The blanket had slipped slightly, and the pile of socks was just barely visible... *they're supposed to be a pillow substitute. so far, it's holding.* Danny's bag was on Nick's cot; *looks fine.* The rear cot was in the dark so it didn't matter. *if I get a chance, I'll go over and fix the problem.*

Julian watched Tom use his spoon to twirl the spaghetti onto his fork. *that's interesting... another thing I'll take home to show off.* He stole a glance. Mark was trying to do the spoon thing too. Julian had some left, so he tried... *hmm. noodles are springy... they keep unwinding. why does really tasty stuff always have to be messy?* He used the remainder of his bread to clean his plate. He looked across at Nick to see if he was nervous or anything. He and Tom were doing everything right so far. *Mark doesn't suspect a thing.*

Mark was in a great mood tonight. The first week was at an end and everything had gone perfectly. He looked forward to tomorrow... no classes or special duties outside the troop. He sipped water from his cup. *too bad I can't have a glass of red. Italian without wine is almost a sin.*

Nick worked to keep his eyes moving around and free—he was inclined to stare at the new tent entrance; he could see the corner of it just to the right of the supply cabinet. *miraculously, Mark hasn't even looked in that direction.* The missing passageway seemed to be shouting out in protest. The sudden end to its place in the Flaming Arrow way of life was achieved without any warning. *maybe tomorrow we could restack the crates a little, make them irregular or something. they look too much like a solid wall. no—we can do it after the campfire... once Mark is on his day-end tour of the meadow, I can recruit Tom and Danny. won't take any time at all.*

The rehearsal of Max's skit ended with a loud chorus, in unison: "For ever and ever!" It was so sharp that the troop cheered itself as well as the author. Max bowed gracefully and sat with his fellow Lynx members.

Danny stood. "Only two things to report: we finished twenty minutes early at the laundry today. Mr. Madsen was super happy. Five bonus points go to the Badgers and five to the Tigers, and five each to Don Felton and Tony Johnson, who did the work." He glanced at his tablet. "There's a short Order of the Arrow meeting after lunch in the big hall." He gestured to Mark and sat back down.

Mark went to the front to make his comments and announcements. "Thanks, Danny. And thanks again to you, Max. And a special hand to the laundry crew; they brought the troop a ten point bonus!" He led the troop in applauding Don and Tony, who both took a bow. "I have a few things to say, then we'll dismiss; you should have plenty of time in camp tonight to work on whatever you have going. I have some information about tomorrow's special schedule. As you know, there will be no merit badge sessions or classes. The special Sunday morning service begins at 9:00, so we will leave at 8:30, sharp. Now, this is not required. However, if you have nothing special planned, I would appreciate it if you supported the troop by attending. It will be formal in every way. We will march in formation and sit as a troop. We will be doing the question exercise, so take along a pencil and a pocket size tablet. If you need, I'll supply you with something to write on when we get there. Remember, for points, the service will be just as important as the lunch, which will also be formal. You need to look your very best.

"The lunch is an hour later than usual, and will probably be the fanciest meal served all camp. Be sure to use your napkins and follow all the formal table rules. We will be under a microscope there, for sure, every minute. We'll do the clearing up detail afterwards, just like we did at the opening banquet. As far as I know, there is no program as such. But the people who put on the service will be at a special guest table. If you have the chance, nod at them with respect. If you want to say anything to them individually, be sure to do so only after they have finished eating. You know how to address them." Mark planned to surprise the others by seating the troop right in front, the most exposed position. "We'll leave for the lunch at 12:15, **sharp**. Tom will have command during lunch and assemble us for the return hike.

"You should have plenty of time either this afternoon or tonight to write a postcard or letter home. I'll be awarding points for that, too. I will post them Monday morning. Are there questions?"

"What if you don't want to go to the service?" Josh was a new member of the Badger patrol… he was Jewish and didn't want to attend.

"You may stay in your patrol camp, or use the lake. The boats and canoes may be checked out, and free swimming will be available. The lake will be open tomorrow between 9:30 and noon, and between 3:00 and five. Supper will be in patrol camps at the regular time."

Justin raised his arm.

"Yes! A question from the Zebra patrol?" Mark was pleased to see Justin take an active part.

"Do we do the patrol calls, sir, like when we came to camp?"

"Thank you for the question, Justin." He turned to Danny. "Five point awards, one to Justin, one to the Zebra patrol. "No and yes. We will not do it to or from the service. But we will as we go to lunch. We may do it on the way back after lunch—I'll decide that at the time."

Justin felt a huge glow suddenly—he'd never been awarded extra points in front of the whole troop. He glanced in both directions—whew. No one was looking at him. A pat on the back startled him. He turned around. Jim, his patrol leader gave him a thumbs up. *wow.*

Mark looked for another question. There was none. He raised his arms into a V and counted to five. He nodded to the Panther's patrol leader.

Nathan stood and held his right arm out to the side and extended his forefinger. At the five count, the Panthers gave out their screeching roar in unison. The Tigers went next, then the Lynx. Stuart stood and led the Wolf patrol. And so it went until the Zebras did their whinny.

Mark stood. "Well done! I want to meet briefly with the Flaming Arrow in camp after we dismiss. Tom?" Mark gestured to Tom who stepped up to lead the Troop Cheer. It went superbly.

"Troop 9, Dismissed!" Tom shouted. The race to the latrine was on.

Mark had asked Tom to stay behind. He went over for the water bucket. As he poured, he spoke briefly. "I wanted you to know this ahead of the others. Do you remember a couple of years ago, that special duty I gave you?"

"I sure do!" That was one of the big moments in scouting for him. He picked up a branch and helped Mark stir in the water.

"Well, tomorrow morning is Danny's time for the same opportunity." He looked up at Tom. He wanted to confirm that his hunch was correct.

Tom grinned wide. "That's great!" That meant that he didn't have to go to the service! He looked at Mark with gratitude and admiration. "He'll do it perfect, too."

"Good. I want you to train him, one on one, tonight. Make sure he has it down cold." He poured on more water, and Tom stirred again. "I'll meet with the patrol for a minute and announce it. He doesn't know yet. Let it be a surprise, okay?"

"You bet!" *wait until Nick finds out! Mark is always there with a good move...* although this time Mark didn't know about the new bedroom—or how great it was going to be to stay there after breakfast in the morning, instead of going to that service! He watched Mark get down and run his hands through the soggy ashes. "You want me to help?"

"Go ahead and take off. Do your run downhill if you need to. I'll be over at the camp soon." Mark watched Tom leave. *ho-ho! a skip! well... I just made another surprise gift, somehow. things must be going well... good.*

He noticed suddenly that Josh was waiting to talk to him. "I'm sorry Josh, I didn't see you there." He motioned him over. "You must have a second question." Mark could see his face clearly in the moonlight; he looked troubled about something.

"Umm... I was wondering why you gave the Zebras five points, but not the Badgers." He felt awkward asking, but he sensed a bit of an injustice.

"That's a very good question. Do you have any ideas?" Mark was delighted for this one on one. Best way to connect by far.

Josh was surprised. He had presumed it was a mistake. Now he was confused. "I guess not."

"Well, I'm glad you asked about this. Did you notice anything different about the way Justin asked his question?"

Josh scratched his head. He didn't see anything special. All that happened was Justin raised his hand, and... "Oh."

"So what will you do to get five points next time?"

"I'll ask to be recognized first." Josh was embarrassed. At least it was too dark for his blush to be seen.

"Right you are! Well done." He washed his hands with the remaining water and stood up. "And for stopping to find out what happened, you will be awarded five points as an individual. You have learned two good lessons tonight." Mark wiped off his hands on the back of his shorts, and patted Josh on the back. He smiled as he saw Josh do a skip and run to his camp.

Mark was on top of the world tonight. Everything had gone well at the campfire, and the troop was really pumped up. Plus, three scouts were very proud or pleased, and soon there would be a fourth. His hands splashing in cold water caused the usual sympathetic reaction trigger... *I need to stop off at the cabin.*

Tom couldn't wait to break the news... the second he entered camp he made a gesture to get Nick's attention—he was hanging out near the new tunnel. *he must be as eager as I am to crawl in.*

The jubilant expression on Tom's face took Nick by surprise. "What's up?"

"You won't believe this! We have to stay here tomorrow morning!" He looked at Nick enthusiastically.

"What? I don't..."

"Shh! I don't want the others to hear." He pulled Nick over to the far side of the tent. "Mark is going to have Danny lead the troop to the service in my place! I'm practically ordered to stay in camp!"

Nick saw the import at once. He glanced over at Julian. His brain went into high gear. He had to work it out, but... yes... He had it. He looked at Tom. "We'll plan something after lights out."

Julian looked at Danny. Danny looked back and shrugged. He didn't know what was up, either. They flipped open their notebooks silently and tried to overhear... no luck.

"Rally around, men." Mark came into camp. He sat at the end of the table on his folding canvas stool. He waited for them all to be seated.

"This is going to be short." He looked at his watch. "We have twenty five minutes left. That should be plenty." He looked at Danny.

uh-oh... something's up. a direct look like that from Mark—

"I hope your uniform is in good shape for tomorrow..." Mark started. He wanted to see a head nod in the affirmative. "Good. Tomorrow you will lead the troop into the service and see that they are seated properly."

Danny's jaw dropped.

Julian grinned wide. He knew just how Danny must feel.   *that Mark!*

"Tom will brush you up tonight on what you'll need to do." Mark was delighted with Danny's reaction. "You'll need to have the Troop flag ready, stand and all. On the road you will pull up the rear. After we arrive, you will lead the troop to their seats and lead them out at the conclusion of the service. The only commands I will give the troop will be "Forward March" and "Halt." All the others will be yours." He watched Danny's face closely... it was important for him to adjust, to think of himself as a leader.

Danny's heart was racing. He was so thrilled by this! He looked at Tom and saw support. He looked at Mark. "Thank you, sir."

"Excellent. Tom, you will be in charge here while we are at the service." Mark stood. "I'm going to knock off a few minutes early. You guys can take it from here."

"Wow!" Julian patted Danny on the back.

"Congrats, Danny!" Tom said.

"Good work." Nick nodded to Julian to indicate he wanted a word.

"C'mon over here, Danny, and I'll walk you through things." Tom pointed to the space in front of the stove. The moon provided plenty of light.

When Danny had left the table, Nick sat in his place. "How about you, Julian? Do you plan to go to that service?"

Julian paused. He hadn't given it any thought. He wasn't excited about it. He shrugged. "I s'pose."

"How about you stay here instead? We could sure get a lot done on the Newsletter." He had something else in mind.

"Oh! Yeah, that's a good idea. I think Mark will let me do that. I'd lot rather, come to think about it." He looked at Nick. They hadn't been able to talk about the mattresses yet; *now that Mark is gone, maybe Nick will say something.* Julian was curious, to say the least.

"Good deal. I know we can get a lot done. We won't need to do anything on it tonight then." Nick saw that Julian was sort of waiting to hear something. "Besides, with everyone else gone, we can do a proper job of thanking you for providing us with our own little paradise!" He nudged Julian in the side.

Julian blushed.

"We were surprised that you left this afternoon." He looked at Julian, and took his hand and squeezed it briefly. "Thank you for that, too!" Nick marveled at how Julian, the youngest, seemed to be the most mature in so many ways. *Tom and I are so lucky. what if Mark had picked somebody like Dale to be Assistant Scribe?*

Julian didn't know what to say. Nick's words were wonderful. He nodded his head. "G'night, then." He stood and gave a short wave.

He walked rapidly to the cabin. He was elated by the brief thanks… but the knowledge that Nick and Tom wouldn't have to sleep on the ground was going to make him sleep easier. He was grateful too, because he had a special plan for tonight's conference—he was eager to get started.

Nick watched Julian go to the cabin. *perfect: while Tom trains Danny, I can figure out what to do about that solid wall of crates. now that I look at it… a fix will be relatively simple.*

19   *Mark's first pose*

Mark had just finished pre-setting his formal clothes on the hanging rack. *too bad there isn't an iron here; maybe the wrinkles will hang out overnight.*   He heard the door open, then close quietly… *excellent.* Julian had come right away. Mark was looking forward to the nightly conference.

Julian felt bold tonight. He had to compliment Mark on what he had done for Danny just now. "You're so cool."

Mark blushed slightly. He hadn't expected that compliment. He didn't have a response ready. Julian had a way of disarming him unexpectedly. The praise was genuine and uniquely personal. Mark had to appear as if it didn't affect him personally; of course, it had. He affected an off-hand manner. "I don't suppose you have anything special in mind for the next…" he looked at the clock "…eighteen minutes?"

"Yes, I do. How did you know that?" He looked at Mark's face. He tilted his head one way, then the other. *sometimes I wonder if he can read my mind.*

Mark smiled. "I'm a good guesser." Actually, in this case that was quite true. *what is he planning?*

Julian pointed to the folding chair by the fireplace. That was what Mark sat on during the nightly conferences.

Mark kept a straight face. Julian looked comically charming when he assumed command. Although—*he doesn't look quite so puppy-like tonight.* He stepped over and pulled the chair out into the room.

Julian had very mixed feelings about this. Drawing Leonard this afternoon had given him a sense of purpose and strength. *still, this is*

Mark. The idea of showing him the old drawings was still scary. But now he could see that they were the best argument he had. After all, if Mark refused to let him do a portrait, what would that mean? That was something he did not want to even consider. So he was very afraid. But this had been planned out carefully this afternoon—he'd met with his inner boss via the bathroom mirror on purpose. *we decided it was worth the risk.* He opened the tablet to the Leonard sketch.

Mark noted that Julian was not pulling the other chair over... *he's thinking about something. how intriguing.*

Julian walked over to Mark and handed him the tablet. "I drew this this afternoon." He didn't ask for an opinion—he never fished for compliments. But what Mark thought was very important.

Mark looked at the drawing... *it's Leonard!* He looked up, but Julian had stepped over to his footlocker. *what's he...?*

Julian fished the drawings out from the bottom of the footlocker. He had hidden them there after Sid had been leafing through the tablet. He'd put the bun page there too—he left that one behind. These were the secret studies he had done of Mark. He turned around and held them behind his back.

Mark looked down at the tablet quickly—he felt slightly guilty for watching Julian instead of studying the drawing. He looked at the sketch—*mercy. this could have been done by one of those instant portrait artists on the Atlantic City Boardwalk. Erik and I watched that guy for an hour one afternoon... odd how Julian is continually reminding me of Erik.*

Julian waited patiently for Mark to finish looking at the drawing. *no way to tell what he thinks, but he always likes my drawings.*

"Julian, this is remarkable." He looked up. "When did you do this?"

"This afternoon during the Free Swim period. Leonard was very nice about it. I fibbed and told him it was for the scrapbook. I just wanted to draw his face. I didn't have time to do any more than that." *one day maybe he'll let me draw a full figure.*

"The thing is..." Julian took a deep breath. "The thing is, it proved to me that I could do it."

"You're sure right about that!" Mark looked at it closely. He'd be hard pressed to suggest any improvements.

Julian brought his hand from behind his back. The drawings weighed a ton, suddenly.

Mark looked up at Julian's face. *what is that expression?* Julian thrust a handful of paper forward. Mark took them as offered.

"I wasn't going to show you these, ever. But I changed my mind. Before, I always drew you from memory. That's why they're so bad." He looked at Mark gratefully. "Now that I get to look at you so much more than I ever thought I could, I know I can do a whole lot better. I'm learning how to draw better all the time." He watched Mark examine his really crude drawings. They were sort of embarrassing. "You can see why I need to do this the right way."

Mark was amazed and flattered. This is the drawing he had gotten a glimpse of on the bus! He examined it carefully. The studies of his hand and fingers on the next sheet were amazing… there were three. Another sheet was a half figure viewed from the back, from the buns up. Two arm studies with elbows had undergone many revisions. *the two heads are interesting.* One was from below, and had remarkably well drawn nose and eyes. The last one was a profile. *these are very good… but Julian is correct… his skills have advanced.* However, these were not to be called "bad," by any standard.

Julian reached over and pointed to the head from below drawing. "That's when you came to visit the very first time. I remembered from sitting down on the floor." It was still his favorite. He looked at Mark… his eyes were operating in that special mode he had discovered; he called it his camera eye. It enabled him to see forms, lines, shapes without being distracted by other factors, such as name, place, or even sex appeal. He had used it to great advantage when he did the sketch of Leonard. That was one reason he wanted to do one of Mark tonight. He knew he could do a much better one now. Even elbows were under control. *nearly, at least.*

Mark just realized what Julian was asking. *he wants me to sit for a portrait!* Mark felt an odd rush—it felt good, but it felt dangerous. *should I allow this? arguments against it… there must be some…* they didn't pop into his mind. *what would Julian think if I refused?   that would be a huge mistake. I have to agree, don't I?*

Julian was setting up the pose in his mind... *by the table, with the lamp.* He glanced over. *yes. the light will be better over there.*

"Thank you, Julian, for showing me these." He was unaware that they had been removed from the tablet. He ran his fingers along the edge of the pages where they had been torn out. He didn't know what to say, exactly. He saw that Julian's eye was ruled by genuine affection and... well, he had to admit, beauty. He had not ever thought of himself as an art object. These drawings were not what he had expected to see. He was seeing himself in a very new light—Julian was giving him a glimpse of what he saw. It was quite humbling. Julian had done it to him again.

"I took them out of the tablet because other people were starting to look at my sketches." Julian shrugged. "I thought maybe it would look kind of... well, strange, or something, if they ran across them." He needed two drawing tablets.

Mark felt slightly chided. *Julian is far more savvy than I gave him credit.* He looked at Julian again. *oh... I wasn't paying attention— Julian is clearly waiting to draw: I'm now a subject. that's what he has in mind for tonight.* "I'm at your disposal. What would you like me to do?"

Julian grasped Mark's right hand and led him over to the table. He grasped the back of the chair and turned it outward; he gestured for Mark to sit. He turned on the desk lamp and stood back... the light had to be just right for his new portrait of Mark. He sat on the edge of the bed and turned to a fresh page. He looked at Mark's face. *hmm. should he be looking to the side? up or down?* He squinted. The sharp shadows caused by the lamp were unexpected. *this changes things completely. hmm...*

Mark watched Julian closely. He was seeing a very different person. Here was someone who knew what he was doing. Mark marveled that he had not understood that until this minute.

Julian had an idea. "First, sit so you're comfy." He waited for Mark to say he was comfortable. "Now slowly move your head up... okay, now down... stop! Back up just a bit." *ooo! this is a good way to do this!* "Okay, now swing it to the right, real slow... yep. That's perfect." Julian got right to work.

Mark snuck a glance at Julian's tablet... the outline of the head was forming. He looked up to check: *yes! Julian's tongue is right there, poking out of the right corner.* That was so endearing. It gave Julian's beautiful face a nearly comical quality... yet he knew it meant that Julian was absorbed completely. Mark had never imagined he would sit for a portrait. He was flattered... but conscious that he wasn't just indulging a whim. *Julian never seems to have whims.* He had not had that perception until now, either. Sometimes, he was embarrassed by how long it took him to see the obvious.

Julian began the inner composition. *wow... that shadow is my best friend here! man, this is the way. the bright sun this afternoon washed away all the depth in Leonard's face. I'll have to do that all over again. Mark's eyebrows are such a wonder. and the line of the nose*—he quickly formed the nostrils and started on the lips. Having drawn Mark so often in his mind made this more like polishing than starting something new. He seemed to know already where the line would go... the right ear: *the distance from the jawbone is just so...*

Mark watched in wonder. Julian worked with such intensity. *how fleeting the glances are... clearly Julian had this planned. how long can I stay fixed in one position? so far, so good... I must have been here more than five minutes, and I feel just fine.* He smiled slightly. *oh... does smiling cause a problem?*

Julian began the ear. *this is going so well*—doing all that prefiguring made a huge difference. It made it possible to focus on the curly channels in the ear better, because he knew the outline by heart already. *hmm. I'm not sure about showing the teeny whiskers...*

Mark alternated between watching the image form on the page and watching Julian's face. Suddenly he had a flash memory of himself a week ago—*I was sitting on the basement floor waiting for my clothes to finish drying. I was so worried about Julian's crush that I couldn't see anything else.* Now, after living with him for a week, he could see how mistaken he had been. *well, that's going too far... not entirely mistaken. Julian is a very complex person. either he has grown out of that, or he has learned to control it. in any case, it's a minor issue in the scheme of things. one look at that tablet is all it takes to see that.*

Julian had nearly finished. The head was complete; all he needed was a good tail line that showed the shoulder line's direction.

Mark wasn't able to look at the clock, but he could sneak a glance at his wristwatch. Three minutes until they would hear the lights out warning. *what to do: should I allow Julian to extend that, or not?*

Julian stopped suddenly. He held the tablet up between himself and Mark so that he could compare. His eyes darted back and forth rapidly. He dropped the tablet back into his lap and modified the eyelash and the lower lip. He raised the tablet again. *hmm.* His eyes scanned vertically. This time he modified the hairline on top, and the intersection of the chin and neck.

He held the tablet to the right, as far as his arm allowed. He swiveled his head back and forth between the two. "There." He took a final look. "I can do the shading later." He had broken his own spell. He looked at Mark and smiled. "Wanna see?" He handed Mark the tablet.

Mark was not prepared for this. He blushed instantly. His mouth dropped open. How could this be so well done in such a short time? He bent close. There's not one erasure!

Julian's attention had shifted entirely. Outside the two minute warning was being given. *I have to get ready for bed!* He leapt up and ran over to his cot.

Mark was a mix of things—he was not qualified to offer a critique of this, for one thing. For another, he had made that ill considered rule about lights out at ten. *I have to say something, though.* "This is wonderful, Julian." *I'm glad I sat for this, actually.*

"Thanks, Mark." He could tell that Mark really did like it. That meant a lot. He walked over to the pipe rack to hang up his shirt. "Thanks for letting me draw you." It was a huge relief, actually. He looked at Mark, satisfied. He could see the clock. He grinned mischievously. "You better hurry; I hafta turn off the room light in a minute, y'know."

Mark's head snapped to the right: the clock said it was almost ten! He jumped up and ran across the room to undress. *shower will run overtime... no problem.*

Julian giggled happily and raced to the bathroom to brush his teeth. He planned to do this very very carefully, too... with an eye out for a certain reflected view in the mirror. *this time, I'll be ready.* Knowing Mark's nightly routine was handy.

20 *Nick gets his wish*

Oh, the luxury! Nick wiggled back and forth... not a single hard spot! *we can never repay Julian for this.* He put his hands behind his head. With the aisle gone, the light from the moon, almost directly overhead, was diffused. *very romantic, actually. the new tunnel is dark...* He turned on the flashlight and aimed it at the opening... *Tom needs to see where things are when he crawls in. the lantern on the table outside will be turned off any minute.*

A plot for the morning formed in his mind. *while the troop is off at the HQ being... well, there's no need to be a wise guy.* Nevertheless, it was much to his liking that that the rest of the troop would be **otherwise occupied.** *so: Julian agreed to stay behind. how should we spend that hour?* He had been so concerned about preserving Julian's innocence for the past week... *I haven't a clue about what we might do.* Julian's response this morning at just touching Tom was such fun! *no matter what we do, Julian will be thrilled. we should keep it simple, though. strictly front end, of course. hmm. oh—here we go!* The light just went out.

Tom had turned the valve closed on the lantern. He stepped to the entrance and disrobed. He had a special plan tonight... he gathered his clothes into a compact pile and dropped to his knees. He adjusted the bead string slightly—the blue bead had to be in the exact center. He crawled forward... the beam of the flashlight was spread across the floor at the end of the passageway. *excellent. Nick is always on the ball.* He moved in slowly, with purpose—a pretend stealthy approach... obviously he was expected. He stopped at the corner and peeked: his prey was right where he was supposed to be. He deposited the clothes to his left where he could find them in the morning.

Tom started his old Panther growl and slowly crawled toward Nick. He increased the volume gradually. He paused at the foot of the mattress. "Here's the Night Panther. He's hungry again." Tom growled with a lilt. He tried to make it sound sexy. He reached forward and lifted the edge of the cover sleeping bag, exposing Nick's feet. "He smells man meat." He growled again and clawed Nick's right foot with his fingers.

Nick giggled. *what a brilliant idea! as if I needed any arousing!* The sensation of Tom's fingertips was electric. He quoted a line from Max's skit. "Help, help." He said it softly, invitingly. He clicked off the flashlight.

Tom flipped the bag off to the left and velvet clawed his way lightly up Nick's bare legs... he paused at the knees. He elbowed them apart so that he could crawl all the way up. He tried to purr but couldn't. *how do cats do that, anyway?* He compromised with a low hum. He flattened his fingertips and pawed slowly to the crotch. He sniffed at Nick's thigh. "Mmm," he hummed. He licked the thigh briefly. "**Mmmm!**" He licked a path upward, wider and slower, imitating a cat giving its kitten a bath.

Nick's heart raced. This was such a turn on! *how long can I just lie here? I don't want to break the spell.*

Tom licked over to the crotch, and began to bathe the balls. He washed them thoroughly with his tongue. He turned the cat paws into massage fingers that went up past Nick's waist and caressed his abdomen. The soft filtered moonlight made Nick look incredibly sexy. Tom licked the shaft from base to tip, but he did not take it into his mouth. He planned to save that. He licked both sides, curling his tongue as far around as he could, pressing the shaft against his nose. His hands moved down to Nick's left leg; he lifted the knee with one hand and slid the foot back with the other. He repeated this on the right leg and spread them wider apart.

Nick wanted to caress Tom's head, his arms... anything. Instinct told him to hold still—he just comprehended something: *this is new— this is not the Tom who wanted to cuddle all week. oh boy! hold on, Nick!*

Tom lifted Nick's balls with his left hand and licked the back of them tenderly. He washed a path down and across as far as he could reach. He grasped Nick under the knees and held them apart as he licked.

He worked all the way to the anus and beyond, broadly covering the entire area. The sensation of Nick's balls laying on his nose and forehead was wonderful. Tom was amazed at how he was able to produce all this saliva. He was even more amazed at how tasty this was. He returned to the anus and massaged it with the tip of his tongue. He pushed, lightly at first. He moved his right hand over and stroked Nick's cock to force a pucker. His tongue was welcomed into the passageway. He pushed it in progressively, as if it was his finger. He worked it in and out a few times, six, seven, then moved back up over the scrotum and up the shaft. He pulled Nick's foreskin downward and slid his mouth tightly down the shaft. He held his mouth in place and briefly massaged Nick's cock with his tongue.

Nick felt a surge. *I don't want to shoot now!*

Tom tasted the new fluid; I have to back off. He reached his left hand over to the edge of the mattress… Nick always placed the tube of KY there. He sat up and coated his cock and first three fingers. He leaned forward and put his left arm around Nick's neck and sought his lips, his incredible lips. As they kissed, he began with his forefinger. His tongue had prepared the path well.

Nick was in ecstasy. He had his man back! *he's better than ever! no—he's new, different. he's a lover now.*

Tom wasted no time. The second finger went in effortlessly. He was gentle anyway. He was in the mood for love, not passion. Finger number three. He decided against sucking any more; he didn't want Nick to shoot before he did. Tonight, he wanted them to arrive at the same moment. He removed his fingers and pulled down his foreskin. He entered Nick at last. It seemed like the first time, yet it seemed like home. He lifted Nick's legs up onto his back and drove in to the max. He held while he returned to engage Nick's mouth.

Nick could not be passive for another second. His arms surrounded Tom's back, his fingers massaged opposite shoulder blades. He inserted his tongue into Tom's mouth and hummed.

Tom began a slow in and out. Nick pressed his feet down to reinforce Tom's every push into him. They were a throbbing unit. Tom's fingers fondled Nick's hair… massaged his shoulders… it was all one…

The mattress made so much more possible than they had imagined. They were free to explore, experiment, flow where the laws of nature led them. They did everything they could to prolong, extend, delay.

Tom's abs tensed. His cock enlarged and he pulled back to the very tip and froze in place. He focused on Nick's lips and moaned.

Nick knew this was it. He pulsed his lips just the way Tom liked and squeezed his sphincter tightly around Tom's tip and hugged him as forcefully as he could.

"**Mmmm!**" Tom drove in at full force and shot. He felt Nick's cock jet between them—the pulse of Nick's shaft was powerful—its pumping action felt like a flexing muscle. It drove Tom to pump in response—it was like a brief antiphony, a perfect back and forth dialogue. There were six each. Tom stayed all the way in at the end for as long as he could. He pulled out at last, and rolled to the left side, maintaining his embrace.

They had to catch their breath. They were both stunned by what they had just done. Neither one had planned to rewrite their book, but that's what had just happened. Neither knew what to say. They had to be quiet for a minute. A long minute…

Nick snapped awake suddenly. He had just shivered. Goosebumps had popped up on his upper arm—his back and butt were cold. *wow—* he and Tom had relaxed so completely afterwards that they'd fallen asleep without pulling over the top sleeping bag. *it's still bright outside. I forgot to take off my watch… almost midnight. no wonder I'm cold.* He slipped the watch off quickly and put it to the left. He reached across Tom; *maybe I can grab the edge without waking him up—*he stopped midway. His forearm had rubbed across something—*what's this?* Tom was in his snuggle mode again… it took a moment to get a good look.

He felt an instant rush… the trade bead necklace! *I thought he lost this.*

oh, Tom. Nick felt a flood of emotion unlike any he'd known before. A tear ran down his cheek. *boy am I glad you're asleep.* He recovered quickly and pulled the sleeping bag over the rest of the way.

"Mmm... **tchupp-tchupp.**" Tom hummed and smacked his lips as he snuggled tight. Sound asleep, he welcomed the cozy sensation of being covered.

Nick responded to the snuggle in kind, but resisted the urge to give a kiss. He didn't want Tom to awaken. *the beads! I gave him that necklace when I was a Tenderfoot. to think that Tom has kept it all this time.... I made it myself the third day of camp. it seems so long ago. I was so in love with Tom then. it was before we ever had sex together... I doted on Tom's every move. he was a big brother and a hero in those days. it meant the world to me that he accepted the necklace. he even put it on for a while! it's so wonderful to remember!*

Tom wearing that necklace meant twice as much now. Nick kissed the top of Tom's head softly and wiggled his happy butt. *and this bed is heaven!* After a few minutes he calmed down. He was planning to talk about the morning surprise for Julian, but they fell asleep. *we'll have time before breakfast. how perfect things are!*

The necklace... *should I say anything? I'd better figure that out. I'm not used to Tom pulling surprises like this.* How thrilling that was, actually. *where has he been keeping it all this time? Tom's a little deeper than I thought... maybe a lot deeper. you have your man back, all right, and more... better get used to the idea of being surprised from time to time.*

Second Sunday

Sunday, Eighth Day

Sunday is set aside at Camp Walker much like it is at home; a day of rest and reflection. Merit Badge and rank advancement classes are suspended. Relationships formed during the past week are in full swing however, and new ones will form during the final week of camp; conflicting interests arise as well, and unexpected tests of character are varied.

Troop 9 has a banner day showing off. Scoutmaster **Mark** provides **Danny** his debut as a leader by assigning him to lead the troop in place of Tom, the Junior Assistant. **Nick** has asked **Julian** to stay in camp instead of attending the special service. He and Tom have a ceremony planned to thank him for his effort yesterday to secure mattresses for their bed.

Geoff takes up a new quest—his greatest, most daring challenge yet. He becomes obsessed.

Julian's drawing skills continue to advance and attract a wider audience. **Mark's** growing personal happiness is infectious; it feeds his enthusiasm for coaching water polo, and it makes him a magnetic figure in unplanned and unexpected ways.

Circumstances force **Kurt** to confront **Tom**, who has to set things right.

Justin and his private demon are explored. Mark is able to help.

It's opening day at **Freddy's** Shooting Gallery; **Andy** and **Tony,** still swaggering from their success in ambushing Tom, add their talents to the operation—they try to offset the annoying security precautions.

After hours: **Robin** sneaks out of bed for a rendezvous at the lake. He and **Jack** planned this daring exploit during the afternoon free swim period.

21 *Sunday fun 1*

Danny looked at himself one last time, critically... he was using the big mirror on the table down at the Lynx wash station. *looks good.* He straightened his kerchief slide slightly... it wanted to twist to the left for some reason. He rechecked the angle on his cap. Wearing a cap always made him feel dressed up and important. He jogged back up to the Flaming Arrow to report to Mark. *boy, is this going to be something!* He was about to help lead the troop to the Sunday service at the HQ! Tom told him last night that Mark always tested potential Junior Assistants this way... *to think Mark might be thinking of such a thing for me is amazing.* Danny had never led the whole troop. He'd only been a Patrol Leader for a few months when he was promoted to Flaming Arrow, so his experience was a little thin. He was worried about fouling up. Tom told him not to sweat it and showed him everything last night; he felt pretty good about it. *there's Mark, right on time, as always.* He trotted right up and gave a sharp salute.

"At ease," Mark saluted back. He inspected Danny from head to foot, then walked around behind.

Julian waved at Danny urgently when Mark turned his back. He tried to mime zipping up his fly... *oop. Mark might see—*

Danny saw Julian trying to signal something... *what the dickens is he trying to say? too late... Mark's back in front.* He looked forward again.

"Well done, Danny," Mark leaned close and whispered quietly, "except that your flag is at half mast. You should zip up before you leave camp." He stood back and saluted. "Assemble them by patrol, single file, at the camp assembly exit." He dropped his salute.

Danny turned red instantly and looked down at his fly. "Oop." *cripes! I must have been running around this way since before breakfast!* He zipped up. *man, how could I be so...* he set out for the campfire assembly area.

Mark wondered how much of this had been witnessed... no way to tell. *these boys are such a reward. not one snicker... I'll bet they all saw it, too.* They'd learned to never laugh at anyone publicly. Privately, a good razzing was fine. He looked around. oh... Tom and Nick were out of sight already... *probably off to the latrine. they're staying in camp so that Danny can get his first leadership experience.*

He looked at Julian. He was seated at the table, concentrating... the tongue poking out of the corner of his mouth meant he was completely absorbed. He glanced at his watch... *plenty of time.* He approached the table quietly. *let's get a peek at what Julian is drawing.* He moved around to look from behind. *it's a puppy, trying to jump up out of a deep hole. must be for the story about Max's boy hero in the Lynx skit. I don't know anything about drawing, but this is leaps ahead of that bus ride cartoon Julian drew on the way to camp. and last night's incredible sketch!*

Mark had a pang of guilt: *I haven't thought to talk with Julian about his career goals. that's your job, Schaeffer. get with it. obviously this talent is key. once we're home, that will be on the top of the list.* Mark indulged himself briefly—watching Julian draw was fascinating.

Julian was on a roll... *the light is perfect, and there isn't any wind this morning.* The mental block he'd had about Max's story seemed to have dissolved or something. The floppy ears just appeared like magic under his pencil tip. The nose that had eluded him was there now. The tail wasn't right yet. He had never owned a dog... he wasn't sure about some things. How much tail would show from this angle?

Mark shifted to the side to see better.

Julian smelled that wonderful something suddenly, and looked up. "I figured it out, I think," he inhaled deeply. Mark was all dressed up with long pants, shiny shoes and everything. But he always exuded that distinctive aroma that Julian couldn't resist. He handed Mark the tablet... maybe he could suggest an improvement.

Mark studied the drawing more closely. "What color of fur would he have, do you think?" He handed the tablet back.

"Hmm!" Julian pondered. "I didn't think of that." He looked at the drawing narrowly. "That's it!" He beamed at Mark for providing just what he needed. *I'll add brown spots to a white coat... twice as cute that way!* "Thanks, Mark!" He started the revision at once.

Mark looked on, amazed... he wasn't sure just what he had inspired. But it was time to take off. He glanced around the Flaming Arrow camp... he didn't see either Tom or Nick around... he wasn't sure what they were up to. Danny had the formation nearly ready down by the assembly area. He gave in a little, and squeezed Julian's shoulder near the neck. "See you later," he said as he put on his official hat. He stepped over to the crew tent and detached the flag and stand from the corner on his way to join Danny and the Troop.

Mark's magic touch! He mellowed out whenever Mark did that... it made his balls tingle, too. *he hasn't done that in a long time. look at him walk down the trail to head the line... he's so cool with that hat! wow... looks like most of the guys are going. it would be nice to go along, but I want to draw instead. and this way I don't have to put on my uniform until later. Mark doesn't care if I miss the church stuff. Nick will be back to work on the Newsletter before too long... he hasn't seen this puppy yet.*

Inside the supply tent, Tom waited for Nick to give a signal. Everything was ready. Last night they had fed Julian a story about working on the Newsletter. *leave it to Nick to figure out what to do... spending last night on these soft mattresses was thanks to Julian, and he deserves a special thank-you party. the rest of the troop will be out of camp for more than an hour.*

"Joo-lee-an!" Nick called softly. He was on his hands and knees, peeking out of the new entrance at the west corner. He and Tom had snuck out of sight and hurried to get things set up while Mark was busy with Danny. Mark just walked off... *I thought he'd never leave.* He cupped his hands and called again. "Jooo-leeee-aaan!"

Julian had forgotten all about them, he was so wrapped up in his sketch. He turned around. Nick looked funny down there. *oh... he's calling me...* Julian jumped up and hurried over.

"You're invited to a special little party we're having. It's just for you!" He smiled brightly. He and Tom had come up with this little scheme before breakfast.

"Wow! For me?" Julian was thrilled. He realized these guys were grateful, but he didn't expect a party, or anything. He got down on his hands and knees and followed. *what fun!* Nick was going in backwards! He had a mischievous expression... Julian was intrigued. He hadn't been inside the new bedroom since they got it set up.

Tom looked forward to this. Here comes the first treat: Nick's bare butt backing around the corner. *I better close my eyes.*

When Nick's head was even with the corner he stopped. Julian almost bumped into him. "Special party rules, Julian. Okay?"

"Yeah!" He'd never seen Nick so playful. He stopped and looked at Nick's happy face.

"This is a no-clothes-allowed party. You have to take everything off right where you are: shoes, socks, the works. Okay?"

Julian was delighted. "Sure!   He hadn't noticed that Nick was undressed. It was a little awkward, because he couldn't stand up. He sat and took off his shoes and socks first. When he was stripped bare he folded his clothes in a small pile on his shoes. He looked at Nick again.

"Now, we have to back in. No fair seeing where you're going. You'll know when you're there. If you start to go the wrong way, Tom or I will tell you how to turn. Just back in slowly. I'll be right in front of you, so don't go too fast, or you'll bump into me. Okay?" The eager expression on Julian's face was terrific. *is he ever in for a surprise.* He chuckled and started moving.

Julian laughed gleefully and turned around. "Tell me when to start!"

Nick backed onto the mattress and moved up, lifting the cover sleeping bag as he went. He pulled it over his back and waited for Julian. "Okay, come on in now." He held the bag with his right hand so that he could lift it when Julian backed in beside him. "Turn right just a little," he prompted. "No—that's left. The other way—yep, there you go!"

This was unlike any game Julian had ever played... that's one reason it was such fun. Backing up on hands and knees... silly, but fun. His feet hit the edge of the mattress. "Am I going the right way?"

"Yep. Just keep coming, up onto the mattress." Nick watched Julian's cute little butt coming at him.   wow.   He had a sudden appreciation of Tom's preference. Under other circumstances, he might do something a little rude, himself. He compromised by pulling the edge of the sleeping bag up from below, wiping Julian's butt as he slid it over his back.

"Ooo!" Julian cooed. The bag slid up his legs and onto his back. It grew dark as he backed under the cover. Soon he was right next to Nick. Even though it was kind of dark, he could still see Nick was smiling, and up to something.   *boy*—the mattress under his knees... *what a difference!*

"Welcome to our little place, Julian. Now we turn around to go the rest of the way. At the other end, we stop and lay down on our backs." Nick nodded to indicate that Julian should turn to his right.

As Julian turned, he saw toes—Tom's bare feet! He followed the line of sight all the way as he turned... *ooo...* his head was moving directly over Tom's bare cock as he turned. *wowee. it's limp, sort of; I can't see it very well...* Boy, did he want to play with it! He could **smell** it, though. He kept turning and crawled forward. *it's warm under here... smells sexy...* his head came out into the light. To his left Tom was smiling at him. He was propped up on one of those big pillows.

"Hi."

"Hi." Julian flopped down onto his back as Nick had told him to. He looked over at Nick... he was propped up on another pillow. *I'm right in the middle... a pillow is here just for me!* He didn't know what to say, exactly.

"We only have a short time, but we wanted to do a little something to say thanks, Julian. Danny told us all about how these mattresses were your idea. You seem to be the only person who understands what's going on."

Nick's discovery on Friday that Julian was fascinated by Tom's size inspired their plan for this special party. The quick peek yesterday was spoiled when Danny's breakfast call interrupted. The idea now is to give Julian a bit more fun—uninterrupted this time.

Julian blushed. *why all the strange stuff, though? oh! here it goes:* Tom on one side, Nick on the other, had started to massage his chest lightly. *gosh...*

—◊—

22   *Geoff on duty 1*

Geoff stood at the HQ entrance, more or less at ease, his left hand full of program sheets. He was grateful that the entrance was on the west side, because the shadow of the building protected him from the discomfort of standing in the morning sun. He felt thoroughly righteous this morning. He had been allowed to volunteer for this duty. All he had to do was greet troops at the door and distribute the program as they entered. Nate was tending to the seating inside. His troop was going to get a bonus in the points department because of this. It would help a lot; Troop 419 **had** to be on the low, **low** end. Distributing supplies with Danny had enabled him to get better known around here, and his initiative enabled him to take advantage of opportunities of many kinds.

One of them was being appointed officially to watch this morning's parade of overdressed lovelies! Cruising seemed a little bold, given the occasion... *but I'm practiced at being cool. I won't do anything indiscreet; I'll stand up straight and proper.* He'd seen a few very nice baskets, in fact... several of these specimens were new. *whooo. speaking of baskets! there's another short guy... it's amazing how many small guys are so well hung.* The early morning angle of the sun certainly helped highlight areas of special interest.

Geoff calculated that about half the troops were inside. *at last... here comes Troop 9 down their trail... this will be fun.* He had a special, **intimate**, knowledge of this outfit. *it will be nice to see what other yummies remain to be discovered in this magical troop. oh, yes... now this made the duty a privilege: their hot scoutmaster is leading them in a line! wearing a silly state trooper hat just like the other scoutmasters.* He'd wanted to get a closer look; thirty feet away on the water polo dock the other day was such a tease.

wait a minute! Geoff did a double take: *they're in perfect step! when did they have time to practice that?* It had to be something they did back home. They looked like a military school. As the line approached he felt a caution alert sounding... *how am I going to avoid checking this Apollo out as he walks right up? there's no way. seeing him up close is going to be very nice.* His peripheral skill was considerable. *I'll wait until the last minute to glance directly...* that would be his concession to propriety.

Dress uniforms were so annoying; they hid things altogether too well. But Geoff had seen this one on the boat dock: he had an idea about what was underneath all that bothersome cloth. And the process of walking was helpful in suggesting what was in there... **especially** *if, like today, he's wearing the right kind of underwear*—shifting and tumbling manhood was a satisfying thing to watch too... this set was **entirely** satisfying... it stimulated the imagination. *where would we be, if we had no imagination?* This man walked like Ronnie—proud and erect. thighs. *look at those thighs!* He had to look above the waist at once. He was beginning to tent.

As he approached the HQ entrance, Mark couldn't help notice: the scout on duty had a growing problem. He would pretend otherwise and ignore the obvious. The boy was properly outfitted... *he wears a JA Patch.* He looked vaguely familiar... part Oriental; *I've seen him somewhere.* As he came within ten feet, Mark held his right arm out to the side, then up as he stopped. The troop stopped, but continued to march in place. He did a smart about face, and gave the command to halt. The line stood at attention. Mark turned around and gave the scout on duty a salute.

"Good Morning. Is there a handout to distribute?"

"Uh... Yes, there is. Er... sorry." Geoff fumbled the salute badly. He had been taken completely off guard. He held up the small bundle of sheets that were in his other hand. It was a simple half page program, mimeographed on one side.

"Ah. Would you distribute them out here, rather than inside? My Senior Patrol Leader will assist, if you'd like." He looked at Geoff as though he were fully competent and in control of himself. *the boy will settle down and do fine, given a chance.*

"Oh! Yes, sure." Geoff was blown away. This was a voice and a face that would **seriously** haunt. He gazed at the scoutmaster with more than a little awe. His tent would not recede... quite the contrary.

Mark did a precision about face, stepped to the side and walked forward a few feet. He nodded to the end of the line where Danny stood. Danny did a smart right face, stepped forward two paces, and then stopped. He did a sharp left face and marched right up to Mark and presented the flag. Mark accepted the pole, snapped open the stand at the base and placed it to his left.

"Have the troop stand at ease in place. Then you will help this young man distribute the program. Return here to wait for me." He saluted, and watched Danny execute the order.

Danny did a smart about face. "Troop 9!" he said loudly. "Stand at Ease."

They did so with precision. Mark was satisfied. He turned and spoke to the scout. "This is Danny Laskey, our Senior Patrol Leader. If you'll give him a handful, he can start at the end of the line while you start here. I'm stepping inside for a minute."

Geoff looked at Danny in disbelief: had he really just commanded the entire troop? And look at what they did!

It was hard for Mark not to allow his amusement to show. Obviously Troop 419 was not accustomed to spit and polish. The boy seemed unable to reply. "I'll be back presently."

Geoff was still slow to react. He barely knew to close his awestruck mouth. He was clueless about all this military stuff. "Oh. Yeah... uh, yes, sir!" *I hate it when I blush!* He stepped over to give Danny a handful. He didn't see Mark turn to go in, but he thought to look back and watch him walk into the building. *man, he's hot!* He looked at Danny and did a small eye wow.

Danny tried to keep a straight face, but smiled a little. He took the programs and went to the end of the line and proceeded to pass them out. Right now he was very proud. He could tell that Geoff was impressed... *I must be doing things right. it's lucky for us that he was assigned to greet today. a surprise, actually... he never mentioned it.*

Mark went in to see the layout... he wanted their entrance to be flawless. His boys could get a nice leg up, or at least hold their place because of this opportunity and the formal noon meal. He didn't need to go into the hall—from the end of the hallway he could see what to do instantly: the side fill. That will surprise them! He went back outside and stood at attention. He watched the end of the program distribution. Danny came up to salute. Mark was delighted that the JA on duty followed Danny's example. *curious... Orientals are rare in this part of the country.*

"All in order, sir." Danny saluted.

Mark returned his salute. "Thank you, Danny. I will address the troop." Mark nodded the cue for him to lead the way. Danny performed a sharp about face and went to the mid point of the line and stopped. He performed a sharp left face. Mark quietly instructed Danny to order a right face. He turned to face the long row.

"Troop 9," Danny commanded, "Remaining at Ease, Right Face."

They turned as ordered, with precision. Geoff was fascinated. He had never seen anything like this. Danny amazed him. His eyes drifted back to the scoutmaster: *must be about six foot two. very nice; those long pants are extremely unfortunate.*

"Gentlemen, we will perform the side fill maneuver. Danny will lead. He will stop at the end of each row and signal the number that is to fill that row out to the edge of the aisle. Do not march in step after you enter the building. Stay far enough apart so that you won't have to back up when the row in front of you has filled. An arm's length should be about right. After the service, remain in place and wait for Danny to direct the exit. It will be in the same order as your entrance. We will reassemble out here by patrol for formal dismiss. Are there any questions?"

Tony raised his hand.

"Tony?"

"How many questions?"

"Thank you for the reminder." Mark turned to Danny: "five points to Tiger." To the troop he said, "the basic three will be enough per person; one tough nut per patrol. Write them on the back of your program or in your pocket notebook. Turn them in at the campfire tonight. Any other questions?" Seeing none, he scanned the troop for any obvious dress issues. They looked fine. Quietly he instructed Danny to proceed.

"Troop 9, Attention! Left Face."

They did so, sharply.

"Dress Front, Dress!" Danny was thrilled to see them follow his orders. The scouts extended their arms forward, just touching the back of the scout in front of them, and returned to attention. He turned and saluted Mark.

Mark returned the salute. He spoke quietly: "Go to the far side and start the fill at the fourth row from the front. No voice commands inside. Caps off as you enter, on as you exit." Danny's performance was exemplary; Tom had trained him well.

Danny stepped to the front and raised his arm. He saw Geoff's amazed expression. Boy, was he proud. He lowered his arm, and led them inside. He glanced at Geoff, but stayed in character. Mark had warned him to stay cool, because they were being judged on everything. That meant somebody was probably watching. He removed his cap as he stepped through the doorway.

Mark moved the troop flag over to the side of the entrance, where it would remain until they departed. Why were no other flags there? Surely they didn't take them inside... that would not be appropriate for a service. He waited for the end of the line to pass, and stepped into place. He nodded to the JA as he went by him into the building. The expression on his face was worth the walk from camp. Mark had no basis for guessing his precise ethnicity... mixed, undoubtedly.

Geoff enjoyed the parade to the extent possible... but he was waiting to study the scoutmaster's face as he went by. He looked too much like Ronnie for comfort... the blue eyes especially. He tried to visualize a bikini and long flowing hair. *no no... those would not fit this man, at all.*

But he looked just too delicious anyway. Geoff had to remain true to himself, didn't he? *what is his name...* Nick had called him by his first name... *hmm. well, whatever it is, he goes to the front of the quest list, as of this minute.* Geoff watched his backside go by. Those trousers did not do him justice. Those were an enemy. They must be eliminated. The memory of him in that huddle with Tom and the water polo team teased him mercilessly... it was so short a time, and so far away. He began to undress this masterpiece in his mind... that would have to do for now.

drat.   here comes another outfit.   He wanted to go in and get started with this new challenge. He smiled vapidly and passed little sheets of paper out once again. His tent was lowering, finally. It had gotten an occasional glance. Well, he didn't grudge providing the show at all. There was no way to hide it, anyway. He felt magnanimous this morning. And impatient.

—◊—

Above in the conference room, the small group of scoutmasters stepped away from the window. It had been opened to circulate the air, which made hearing the activity below very easy.

"What was that question business?" Soames scratched his head.

"I'll see if Sarge can find out. The patrol leader is one of his delivery boys." Jorgensen was not surprised at the performance. He'd wager there was a lot more coming today... obviously, Schaefer had ceremonial ops figured out. He felt a little guilty about using this spying technique. But it seemed to be the only way he could find to prove to these men that Schaefer was the real deal. He did not rely on gimmicks. He earned it all. Look at his turnout, for one thing.

Henderson was pensive. "I'm going to watch their deportment during the service. Taylor is supposed to monitor their entrance and seating. I'm betting Schaefer takes us all to the cleaners again." He left the room. Soames tagged along.

—◊—

Mark entered the large room at the end of the Troop Nine line; Danny had begun to fill the empty south end of the rows. Presenters valued compactness in the congregation. It enhanced audience involvement and seemed to buoy the speaker as well. Moreover, latecomers had to sit in the rear or stand, and were less disruptive.

The ragged, irregular scattering of the audience this morning was unexpected... presuming the Troops would sit as units was incorrect. He was glad for his plan now: there was no way they could have sat in a solid block—the scouts already present were scattered randomly enough to make that impossible. Danny gestured to the last four scouts... there was room in this row for both of them as well. He gestured to Danny to go in first. Mark preferred the aisle seat, given his long legs.

these folding chairs won't be much fun...   it's only for an hour. He'd suffered worse; he read through the program... standard fare; the reverse side was blank—ideal for the boys to jot down their notes.

Geoff was frustrated. Having to wait outside until the last minute meant that the best seat he could find was a spot three rows from the back... **terrible** for viewing. All he could see was the back of... *hmm.* For the life of him, he could not recall that man's **name**! *Apollo. that's what I'll call him for now... it suits perfectly. at least the hat is off. so: what to do... first, I'll give priority to devising a scheme. there are five plus days left. I'll find a way... after all, I've taken most of the leadership patrol now, plus what... two more, sort of. by the way: where are Tom and Nick?* Their absence was surprising. *ah... of course! they're playing in their new bedroom suite while Apollo is away from camp.* Nick was smart enough to engineer something like that. *Apollo... Apollo: what is your name... let's see if an E.S.P. signal has any effect.*

Mark listened to the proceedings with one ear. The homilies were tedious... but apt, he had to admit. It was better to have these things spouted by the pros. The boys needed this kind of guidance too. He wasn't convinced that adding it to camp was such a great idea, though. *they didn't need this kind of a service when I was a scout.   but it's part of the program now, so I'll play along.* He was curious about what he would read in the questions that would be turned in tonight. It never hurt to know what the boys heard and thought. *hmm.   the presenters might find them interesting, too.   I'd better ask Jorgensen about that... no need to rock any boats.*

Mark looked across the sea of heads in front of him... they're on task. He never doubted them for a minute. *hmm...* he felt strangely uneasy... an odd feeling had been bothering him for a while. He could swear someone was staring at him... he could sense it. There was no way to tell without turning around to look. *well, it's pointless to worry about it.* He turned his attention to water polo. This was a handy opportunity to deal with that. *we have to work a little harder to score goals than I expected; maybe I should examine where I placed some of the players.* He took out his pocket tablet; *this is my "tough nut" assignment.*

Scoutmaster Henderson moved along the west side of the room in calculated increments. He wanted to see what was going on without being noticed. It wasn't hard to tell the Troop Nine scouts from the others. The uniforms were the same as everyone else's, but that was all. Schaefer's boys were all rapt and paying full attention. He'd seen one or two actually jot down something that was said from the lectern. Scouts from the other troops were behaving, being polite—but he doubted if many were actually listening. There was no way to tell. Schaefer himself seemed to be taking notes. That didn't fit... *what's he up to?* So far, everything said by the speaker was standard fare for this sort of event.

23   *Sunday fun 2*

Tom tossed the top sleeping bag down on his side, and Nick did the same. It hung up on their feet, and they kicked it off. "That's better." *too hot with that on—we should have brought over the blanket.* Tom looked at Julian. "I wonder if you would do me the great honor of getting me hard, Julian?" He flashed his eyes.

Julian was stunned. *did I hear right?* He looked at Tom, uncertain. He looked over at Nick.

Nick nodded yes and nudged him to sit up. "Him first, me second," he grinned.

Julian sat up and turned around between them. wow. He looked at Tom's, then Nick's. *what a surprise! I never thought about something like this! hmm... they might get hard on their own if I don't hurry.* He looked at Nick apologetically—for having to do Tom first. Then he reached over and touched... it. He looked up at Tom again; Tom gave an impatient nod to go ahead. Julian lifted it up and held it in both his hands. It began to swell. His eyes bulged as he watched. *whoa...* holding it while it grew hard was really something! He remembered what it felt like yesterday before breakfast... *boy, it's sure better on the knees with these mattresses here.*

The rest of the world receded. Julian was now doing this. He wanted to see, feel, and remember it all. He began harden himself... that felt very nice, too.

Tom's cock enlarged rapidly. He pulsed it once, hoping that Julian would squeeze harder. yes... he pulsed and held—how smooth and strange Julian's hands felt; watching the expression on Julian's face enhanced the experience. *this is more exciting than I expected...* full up; he nudged his hips upward. ohyes... Julian understood.

Julian was captivated. Doing this was hot and exciting, but it was **fascinating**. *this thing is so much bigger than Danny's!* He bent down to get a whiff. *mmm! strong.* He grinned at Tom; he was getting a little horny, actually.

Tom had a sudden inspiration. He nudged Nick in the ribs with his left hand and sat up slightly. "I want you to take me all the way. Will you do that?" He looked him directly in the face.

Julian flushed. He could tell that Tom meant it! He would get his wish to see this masterpiece fire! He swallowed rapidly. He could feel his heartbeat start to increase. *boyohboy.* Tom didn't have to ask twice! He got right to work. He thought about what he had done with Danny yesterday. *that's exactly what I'll try to do here. o-kay... what should I do first?* He tested all the limits—how far down he could pull, how far up.

it's too awkward like this. He climbed over Tom's left leg so that he could address this task properly. *there... much better.* He pulled the foreskin down with his right hand, and handled the balls with his left as he sucked on the head really tight. *strong taste! man. it's gotta be twice the size of Danny's.* An inch or two was all he could get in his mouth! He wrapped his tongue around the crown. *ooo, did that make Tom swell!* He rubbed his nose across the tip so the aroma would stay there while he worked.

Nick's jaw dropped. This was not part of the plan!

"Ohmmmm!" Tom moaned. He looked at Nick and flashed his eyes. *do you see what this kid is doing?!* He wanted Nick to do this very thing! He gestured his sentiment to Nick with an emphatic nod. *whoo! this is not what I expected.* Julian had a technique that was different, unlike anything Nick had tried.

Julian knew three techniques. The newest was best, but there was no way he could do that one here. That's the one Danny had shown him. Tom was just plain too big. The Doug one wasn't that good either, for the same reason... and because Tom was lying down on his buns. The Paul rapid up and down on the tip while holding him tight was possible. But that one went too fast. He wanted to savor this once in a lifetime event. So he used his tongue to lubricate, and did the spiral thing... That was a good way to give his mouth a rest. Tom was so darn huge, he couldn't suck for very long at a time, even if he didn't go down very far.

besides, it's more interesting to look at it.   what does Nick do with this thing!?

Nick was dumbfounded. He never imagined that Julian would even think about using his mouth... Julian was full of surprises... *fascinating, and super hot!* He had never actually seen Tom's cock like this... he appreciated it in an entirely new way. It made him incredibly horny... it was all he could do to not touch himself. He was completely surprised by Julian's evident ease at doing this. When Tom changed the plan he was afraid that Julian would be spooked. He'd expected him to be awkward, at least— flustered, certainly. *not a bit!*

Nick watched with affection. Tom's idea to turn Julian loose was just the thing! He scooted close and massaged Tom's chest with his left hand... he nuzzled briefly, then stretched up for a kiss. It turned in to a very long one. Tom reached around his head and pulled him into a tight lip lock that went to tongues, slobbering tongues. After last night, he never expected to get this turned on.

Tom broke off at last so he could watch Julian for a while. *man alive, this kid is good!* He worked his hips back and forth. Too bad Julian doesn't know enough to put a finger in while he does this... His butt had started to buzz too... he wanted Nick inside him, actually. *man, Julian is doing some new things here.   way more than I thought was going to happen.* He was coming around second base...

Julian sat back to look as he stroked. He was practicing the tight squeeze. Tom really liked that. *oh-ho!* A drop appeared, a clear drop. He bent close to look. He squeezed and pulled up ... another one oozed out.   He put his head down and licked it up slowly onto his tongue. *mmmm.* No question about it: he loved that taste! He looked up... *they're watching.   boy do they look turned on.* He squeezed out some more and sucked. He poked his tongue into the hole and moved it gently.

"Mmmn!" Tom jerked involuntarily. *that's new!   a few of those will take me over the top!*

Julian backed off that one. He wanted to control the event a little. Besides, he wanted to watch it shoot. He planned to get the last push into his mouth, just to be courteous. He sensed that Tom was getting sort of close. Julian figured he must be doing a good job, because of Tom's reactions—it helped some to know if somebody liked what he was doing. Tom's body flexed... he began taking short breaths. Julian started a home stretch combination—he spiraled down from halfway to the balls and licked the shaft to get it real wet. He could see the pre-cum ooze. He worked that into the crook between his thumb and forefinger. It merged with his saliva, and helped get Tom real slippery.

Tom was close... he wanted to be kissing Nick when he went. He made a small kissy-kiss sound to get Nick's attention.

Nick heard Tom's call. He saw the fever in his face and knew the moment was near. He wanted to watch, but he was being summoned. He kissed and held.

Julian felt the sudden stiffening—*it's on the way!* He sat back and watched his hands move in the path that would feel the best. He watched Tom thrust forward and freeze for a second. The hole opened as the crown flared and a white drop seeped out just a little. Then Tom pulled back hard and thrust forward a second time, and the jet flashed by out of Julian's view. He held on tight, wanting each thrust to have the same contact. Watching the crown swell and eject was so amazing. After the fourth one he put his head down and took the last two in his mouth. He tucked his tongue in again and got that extreme shudder. He remembered suddenly how Danny had finished. *I'll try that. mmm.*

Tom was spent at last; he sat back. He wasn't sure if it was Julian's lips or Nick's that were the most exquisite. *Nick's, probably. but Julian has magic hands, for sure!* He looked down... *Julian is still on me! what's this?* He looked at Nick.

Nick looked down. *oh! he knows about this? that doesn't make sense. Geoff couldn't have touched Julian, surely! did they have a little session in here yesterday? that didn't figure.* Julian was full of surprises this morning. look at that! Julian was doing exactly what Geoff had done on Friday. *will it work on Tom? I haven't had a chance to try it out yet...* watching, being an observer was a nice surprise.

Julian couldn't get his mouth down far enough to do what Danny did yesterday, so he worked with his fingers instead... maybe that would work. He wanted Tom to stay hard all the time he was working on Nick. He felt Tom harden again... he began the last squeeze... he could only hold Tom's hip with one hand—that would have to do. He did the squeegee. The last drop came! It worked.

Tom bucked hard on that extra thrust. He looked at Julian in disbelief. He looked at his pulsing cock—it was harder than ever. "Julian!"

Julian sat up and grinned. "Good one," he said, matter of factly. "Danny showed me how to do that yesterday after inspections."

"Good one?!" Tom reached over and tousled Julian's hair. "Way better than good." *one of the top ten I ever had, at least.*

Julian giggled; he was glad Tom was pleased. He glanced over at Nick. "It looks like you're already hard, Nick." Maybe Nick wanted to be sucked too... *it's smaller... even smaller than Danny, a little. I could do a great job on Nick!* He looked up to see.

"What do you expect? Who could watch a show like that and stay limp?" Nick looked at Julian... *this boy is a revelation. he clearly wants to do me too!* He nodded yes, instantly. *so... Danny has been playing teacher. that explains it!* Obviously, Danny had been trained by Geoff—probably on their delivery route. *very enterprising... sure has been cool about it.*

Julian saw the nod. *oh boy!* He climbed over and faced Nick's raging cock. "Oop. Looks like you're kinda close already, Nick." Julian pulled down gently on Nick's foreskin and took a swab of his pre-cum on his forefinger and held it up. He glanced at Nick as he licked off his finger. *good taste... not as salty.* He pulled down the foreskin. This was going to get the full Geoff style... *the trouble is, he'll shoot so quick. oh well.* He got to work. *mmmm. this is a lot better...* all the way to the balls better.

Nick watched in disbelief... it's as if Julian was a professional at this! He looked at Tom... he was rapt... and he still had a full erection! *maybe we'll have time for a second inning!* "Ohm!" He looked back to Julian at work. *I won't be able to hold off for long.* He reached over to Tom and made the kissy-kiss signal. *I want to share this one too.*

Julian was having fun... Nick was much smaller so he could do everything. His own cock was bothering some now... *I'll have to shoot pretty soon myself. what if I put Nick's balls into my mouth? mm... the hairs... very different from Danny's... too many... Danny's are better.* He pulled off and did the hand massages instead. *oh-oh.* Nick was growing tense and starting to thrust. Julian wanted to watch him fire too—he sat back. *I'll take the last one or two like I did for Tom.* He did the spiral and pulled down with his left hand. *there!* The pulse became a swell, and Nick fired fast. *wow, he shot right away! his tip is pointy.* It swelled nicely as it shot. On the fourth Julian returned it to his mouth for the finish. He did to Nick exactly what Danny had done to him.

After the squeegee, he pulled off and sat back. He had done well. Nick's moans were fun to hear... they were muffled because Tom was kissing him. Julian was proud of his achievement... but he was now in need. *should I beat off?* He looked down. *oh! a drop!* He put some on his fingertip and tasted it. *hmm...* he did that again. *mm! sweeter tasting, for some reason.* He watched them proudly... *they look so perfect.* They finished their kiss and looked at him. He didn't know how to ask.

Nick was ready to take a break and relax for a moment. *what an event!* He was about to express his gratitude—oh... *Julian is confused about something—of course!* Nick noticed his dripping cock. He elbowed Tom and sat up. "Julian, may I?" He reached out and touched Julian's thigh.

Julian grinned wide, relieved and grateful. He turned around and wiggled back into place on the middle pillow.

Nick got right to work. "Mmmm," he hummed. this won't take very long. He winked at Tom. *I'm going to utilize professor Geoff's method... Julian deserves no less.*

Tom watched Nick... engrossing. How strange and wonderful. He touched Julian's shoulder. "I owe you one, kid. Don't you forget it, either!"

Julian paid attention to Nick's ministrations. *yum.* He was as good at this as Danny! He reached over and held Tom's cock—it was still hard. That turned him on. He shot very suddenly, and Nick took it all. wow.

They lay quietly for quite a while. Nobody knew how to end this. They had to.

Julian looked down. "Everybody's still hard!"

Nick moaned. "I know! Let's go down to the lake. Maybe the walk will do it. We can swim for a while. There's a big fancy Sunday dinner."

Tom had a major duty coming up. "We have to sit as a troop." They had to come back and dress up; Mark counted on them to put on their best show at the banquet. "We'd better hop to it or it'll be too late!"

They got up, reluctantly.

Julian went to the tunnel to get his clothes. He decided to dress out by the table. His focus had returned to his plan for the day—*I just remembered! I'm supposed to Buddy with Cory. I'll skip up to the Zebra camp first and see if he's there... he might have gone to the service.* He looked down at himself... good. Almost shrunk back down. As he pulled on his skivvies, he got a signal from Mother Nature: *hafta take a leak.* He hollered back. "I'll see you guys down there, okay? I hafta go to the cabin." He finished dressing and grabbed his tablet.

Inside the tent, Nick paused. Julian's announcement made him think... he looked at his watch. *why hurry?* He put his hand on Tom's shoulder.

Tom turned to face Nick. "Second helping?"

Nick fondled the necklace gently. He looked Tom in the eyes... he couldn't find the words he needed just now. He hadn't said anything about the beads yet.

Tom returned his look. They held each other's gaze for a short while. They didn't need words, actually.

They undressed again.

"You have to do me tonight." Tom pulled the tube out from under the mattress.

"Um-humm," Nick spread his arms wide and fell onto his back.

24   *Geoff on duty 2*

Geoff's head fogged again… staying awake was difficult. The guy up front was **such** a bore! At least the gospel quartet had shut up for good, according to the program. *it will be over soon.* He had stared at the back of Mark's head so hard he nearly got a headache. His attempt to E.S.P. him into turning around got nowhere… no reason to think it would work; just a long shot. He had not figured out a thing to do, either, except to stake out the water polo match tomorrow. *no, wait… can't do that: Leonard will be there. hmm…* His plan to seduce Leonard had to be put on hold for the time being… *I can't be at the lake without paying attention to Leonard.* The fun chat at his table yesterday went too far. *I'd better stay out of sight temporarily… no need to offend or alarm him. working two projects at the same time is not a good idea. these things require focus.*

He needed to pick a brain or two… he had to be careful about that, too. There was no doubt about the loyalty of Apollo's troop members. They mustn't suspect anything… *oop.* Service over. Luckily, the usher duty was incoming only. *now I can watch.* What for, he didn't know yet.

Mark stood and stepped into the aisle; he let Danny pass by. He watched Danny's performance closely; this was his debut assignment in leadership. So far, he had performed flawlessly. Directing the troop's exit was next.

Danny knew he was being observed; somehow that made him feel more secure. He reached the fourth row and did an about face. His stance wasn't rigid and forced, but formal, just the way Tom had shown him last night. He nodded to Nathan, the Patrol Leader of the Panthers. He would lead the line of scouts up the aisle.

Mark stepped into place a few rows back to await the line Danny was sending. He stood at ease, facing front. After Danny emptied six or seven rows, he would about face and complete the exit process.

Geoff was about to cream in his pants: the overdressed Apollo was standing in the aisle, right next to him for some reason—Geoff could smell him, he was so close. *man alive; I haven't gotten this hard so fast since...* he couldn't remember. *inhale often, Geoff.* He turned his head slightly... *maybe I can see something. nice profile... it suggested the serious package hidden inside, all right. exhale now, stupid, or you'll faint. now inhale another lung full. those infernal trousers! I can't see a thing! only a probable cause. do I dare look up? no. that would be stupid... could put him on alert. that must be avoided at any cost. keep your cool, Geoff. get ready to turn your head after he turns to leave— that's the best you can hope for. look at the scout basket that's standing in the aisle facing him, stupid! hmm... any other day, that one might be interesting; a patrol leader I haven't seen before... Life rank, too.*

ah! there he goes... they're moving out. He watched Mark's backside recede until it was blocked by the row of scouts he had in tow. Geoff wanted to rip off those trousers so bad. *whew. now I can try to calm down...* he needed to be ready to follow them out. *oh! Danny's the last one... excellent. maybe I can catch him for a word.*

At the back of the house Mark turned and led the boys straight out. He put his hat on as he stepped across the entry. They were orderly, but not in a formal line. They had to allow other scouts room to leave; it didn't look like any others were exiting in formation. *Strange... perhaps the others are waiting for my troop to be clear. that must be it; I'll leave plenty of space.* He moved directly out at a measured steady pace. He stood well clear of the building, and indicated to the Panther Patrol leader where to stand as he approached. The Troop formed into patrols automatically, in two ranks, in line with the troop flag, which had remained in place. They ignored the scouts from other troops who were leaving randomly. Several were heading directly for the lake.

Danny was at the end of the line, and as the last patrol formed, he reported to Mark with a salute. Mark returned it. "Call them to attention, please."

Danny faced the troop just as Tom always did. *boy, does this feel great.* "Troop 9: Attention!"

They snapped smartly to attention. The troop knew they were being observed, and responded perfectly.

Mark looked at his watch, and then addressed the Troop. "At Ease. You have about 70 minutes before the formal dinner. Patrol leaders need to report five minutes early, as usual. Formation will be by the assembly area at twelve sharp. You are on your own until then. Are there any questions?"

"Can we hand in the questions now?" Tony needed another five points.

"Nice try." Mark waited for the chuckles to die down. Tony frequently used this ploy to bag some easy points. "Campfire. Your Patrol has to vote on one of them. Just fold it up and tuck it in your pocket. But the campfire tonight is not formal dress; so don't forget it when you change shirts. Any others?" He scanned the troop. He gave a wink to a scout in the back row and raised his arm. He counted to ten; he wanted Tad to get a good head start. "How many of you are going to beat Tad to the latrine?" He dropped his hand fast and the whole troop leapt into a sprint for the Meadow. He watched them take off. *what a joy, these boys. look at them go. the quarter mile run is perfect.*

Mark wasn't sure what to do with the next hour. He had no duties scheduled. He stepped back to the doorway to pick up the flag; *hmm…* no other troop had come with a flag. In fact, as far as he could tell, none of them seemed to be organized for this event at all. *I'll bet it will be different at lunch.* He wandered slowly toward the trail to Barr's Meadow. *maybe I'll just relax for a while. I haven't done that yet this week.* He put the flagpole over his shoulder casually and headed for camp. The boys did well; *I must congratulate Danny at the next Flaming Arrow meeting.*

Geoff stood just inside the door, ready to duck out of sight in an instant. He did not want to be noticed. He couldn't remember when he had felt so drawn and fascinated—and **turned on**. *how can I do this? should I follow him? the man is alone, after all…*

—ₘ—

"Have you ever seen a dismissal like that?" Jorgensen was delighted.

The watchers were back in the upstairs room. Jorgensen planned to hear what they had to say; then he'd put his foot down. *Soames is the difficult one of the bunch.*

"Guys, I can't find a chink in his armor." Soames was frustrated.

"His seating strategy was a piece of genius," Taylor folded his arms.

They looked for an elaboration.

"They were the only Troop that actually sat as a block... he had them fill in the ends of all the rows from the east aisle. That's why, if you noticed, it looked like a solid attendance. There were no empty seats on that side. If they had been wearing a different color, you'd have seen it clearly. He had unit integrity the entire time."

No others could make that claim. They had relied on attendance only as a basis for earning points this morning. Schaefer had matched or exceeded them there, and all the ceremony was a bonus.

"Is he political, at all?" Henderson was amazed by how on task those boys had been—almost as if they were in training for something.

No one knew exactly what he meant by the question.

"I watched that bunch from the floor. That entire troop paid full attention to everything. Some of them actually took notes. Not one head nodded off." Henderson shook his head. "Fellas... I mean, if I had been trying to listen to that, I'd need to have my JA sitting next to me under orders to poke me in the ribs every five minutes."

They all laughed. The morning **was** wholesomely boring.

Henderson shook his head again. "How does he get them to do that?"

Jorgensen stood up; the time had come to move on. "Gentlemen, I think we can agree that Schaefer is not pulling any cheap tricks. I expect you all to remain fair and objective. What I plan to do is ask Mark to set up a workshop in the winter and share his secrets."

"Yeah." Soames had to agree. It looked like a fourth win in a row for Troop 9. "Anybody figure out what that question business is?"

"Maybe we can get it out of him at the dinner table this afternoon." Henderson would make sure he was seated next to him at the head table. He, for one, was going to arrive early, with banners flying. Mark wasn't going to win by default. He remembered that opening day meal. Troop 9 had caught them all napping, just like this morning.

"Okay boys, back to your Troops." Jorgensen had to hunt down the guest speaker and his crew. His was the unhappy task of baby-sitting them until the dinner. Just what he would do for the next hour was anybody's guess.

25 *Sunday morning swim*

Julian was on his third lap to the platform… that was real progress. The practice session yesterday with Nick made a big difference. He was a little tired now… *better rest on the top for a minute.* Up the ladder he went. A couple of guys from another troop lay on the far side... he didn't know them. He just smiled and sat on the edge facing the shore. *after a minute I'll swim back. where are Tom and Nick? they should have been here a long time ago. oh, wait ... I wonder if they... can they go twice in a row? hoo!*

He reflected a little on the surprise party. That made four different ones now he had worked on. He shook his head. A week ago, he had no idea about anything. He never even imagined any of this stuff. *I sure lucked out, being put in the Flaming Arrow. 'course, like Mark said, none of this is scouts. as long as it doesn't get in the way, it only makes sense to find out what I can. I'm not about to learn about this at home!*

He kicked his feet back and forth absent-mindedly. He was suddenly aware that this was a very important step toward making his dream come true. *what if I had done what I was planning? wow.*

You are one lucky kid, Julian. *At least you didn't make that mistake.* His inside voice had kicked in—usual when he was focused on this subject.

what would Mark have thought?

That you're a real stupid kid, of course; and he'd be right. Julian nodded…

yeah... I still am, aren't I? boy, that shot of Tom's... I forgot to check where it landed. It went by in such a jet! *must have gone past the end of the mattress, at least. hmm. they prob'ly cleaned it up by now.*

Julian froze: *oh-oh!* He just realized something. *ooo... I really fouled up. I just didn't think. I told them about Danny! ohmygosh—I have to warn him. how could I be so stupid! ... it's just that Danny seemed to be in on so much with those guys. now I remember—he said it was Jeff who taught him that, not these guys. what if he didn't want me to tell?*

Even though he was pretty well rested, Julian wasn't in the mood to swim any more. He was very worried about his misstep. Preoccupied, he kicked his feet... *platform is too high off the water.* He wanted to splash with his feet like he could off the edge of the Boardwalk. *darn...*

> > *bleet-bleet-bleet* < <

The Buddy Whistle wasn't as loud out here, but it still drowned out any other sound. Julian looked over to the F dock. There... he waved at Cory and pointed. Cory waved back. It was lucky Cory planned to swim today—the small numbers today made it more appealing. Cory needed to get over his dislike of the water—*he's close to qualifying. in a while I'll go over and see if I can help some.*

The second whistle blew. *that was quick! it's easy to do the buddy checks today.*

Julian's thoughts returned to the party. *Nick's is all right... kinda pointy.* He felt a little guilty, though... all I did was finish him off. Nick didn't appeal to him, really. *maybe that's why I feel a little guilty. well, maybe someday I'll try to do it right.* It wasn't Nick's fault he had to go second.

Splashes nearby interrupted his reverie. He looked to the left and saw two familiar faces swimming up to the platform. Tom was inches ahead of Nick. Julian grinned.

"By a hair," Tom boasted, pushing out of the water like a rocket. He grabbed the ladder bars and vaulted himself past the steps. The platform vibrated from the impact. He stood with his hands on his knees to catch his breath.

Julian remembered those arms. They were able to pitch him way up into the air.

Nick climbed up the rungs. He didn't have the biceps to do what Tom did; he stood next to Tom in the same pose. "Did you hang back?" *I did too well...*

"No! You're getting better at this all the time. Your swim coaching has paid off!" He bumped him and nodded at Julian.

Nick laughed and moved around to the other side of Julian and sat down. He nudged with his elbow. "Long time no see!"

Julian broke up.

Tom sat down on the near side and nudged with his elbow. "How many laps can you do now, champ?"

Julian was about as pleased right now as he thought possible. "I did two nonstop out here and back, but I stopped halfway on my third."

Tom was impressed. "Wow. You have come a long way!"

Julian just remembered. He looked around—*those other guys are still here.* He spoke low. "You guys, I did a bad thing this morning."

Nick and Tom looked at him in surprise. They both had a very different opinion.

"I told on Danny, and I shouldn't have," Julian worried. "I didn't mean to, either. It just popped out. I didn't even think about it until just a little bit ago. I haven't seen him yet, 'cause they're not done with the service. I will as soon as I can. Will you guys be nice to him?"

Nick was impressed. "You can count on us, Julian," he looked at Tom to agree.

"Yep." Tom said.

"You guys are such good friends and everything, I just figured you know all this stuff. I'm so new at it all. I'd hate it if I did anything wrong."

Tom looked in wonder. He had not even thought to worry about Julian's discretion. Now he saw why. He hugged Julian hard.

Nick hugged as well. "You are a true friend, Julian, and Danny knows that. Don't worry, please. We didn't know, but we weren't exactly surprised. We've known Danny for a while now." This explained a lot—*he's been taking Mark's request to heart... been running a special education program for Julian. very enterprising...*

Clearly, he had taught Julian well. "On our honor, we won't say a thing—even if he does. Okay? You don't have to talk to him. Maybe he wants to tell us himself some time. Why don't you let him?"

Julian felt a lot better. "Thanks. You guys make me feel so lucky." He blushed. "I won't tell anybody about our party, ever!" He pressed his legs against theirs.

Splashes. The two guys from behind had dived off. Tom looked up.

"Know them?"

"I've seen 'em around. I think they're from Troop 2. The brown haired one is one of the water polo guys—on the A team. Pelicans. The other guy just hangs around." He gave an eyebrow lift to Nick, signaling that they were probably a couple.

Julian noticed the signal Tom gave to Nick. He looked out at the two swimming away. He looked at Tom again. *oh—he's wearing a rawhide and bead necklace. that's new. why is he wearing that, anyway? huh—I made one of those when I was a Tenderfoot. I gave it to Mom.* He noticed something else, too: Tom and Nick's hands were touching each other behind his back. He smiled to himself. *I know more than these guys think...* that felt good, actually, knowing that. He watched the two guys swim toward the dock. *too bad I didn't pay better attention when they were here. I might not recognize them again.*

Suddenly there was more splashing at the ladder. Up climbed Sid, followed by Kurt.

"Hi ho," Sid chimed. He was in very high spirits. He had forced Kurt to come along. Sid was bursting to do a secret brag with Julian, having just had an especially excellent "canoe trip."

Julian and the others swiveled around to greet the newcomers.

If anyone were to glance downward from the waistline, they couldn't help but notice that two rather red and puffy cocks were not yet completely becalmed from immediately recent ecstasies. Of course, all three on the platform did just that. Had they not undergone a recent event of their own, they might have felt a certain envy. As it was, they felt a sudden unexpected kinship. It would go unspoken about, but the private thoughts would be impossible to suppress. The lucky new arrivals seemed oblivious to how they appeared. It must have been a super time.

Kurt was very uncomfortable being here—Sid had insisted. Admittedly, his anger toward Tom had dulled considerably. He didn't want to admit that it was his newfound pastime that had done that, but it was probably true. Still, he was resentful. *it's probably safe in a group like this... be all right to hang around for a little while... safety in numbers and all that.*

Sid wanted to tell Julian all about it, but he couldn't with these other guys and Kurt here. All he could do was look into his eyes and somehow tell Julian the world was a wonderful place. He'd talk as soon as he could—he just had to show off, basically.

Nick knew Kurt's history, and watched him closely. He'd been given a heads up by Julian a few days ago, but had not found a chance to talk with him yet. He had talked with Tom, though. Maybe Tom could handle it by himself... it looked like a possibility right now, at least. Clearly he and Sid had not been out bird watching.

Julian looked at the circle of friends around him. He didn't know Kurt well at all, but he was making Sid happy, so he counted as a friend. This was another one of those it's-great-to-be-a-scout days.

"Did you guys ever meet Sid? He's my friend from over at Wolf. Sid, this is Tom and Nick." Julian blushed. "'Course, you already know who they are." He felt silly, but the silence needed to get busted up somehow.

"Hi Sid," Nick nodded. "Wolf's loss is our gain, I have to tell you."

Tom looked at Kurt closely. He could almost see the chip on his shoulder. Nick had given him the way to deal with this yesterday. He was surprised he'd be able to do this so soon. But it made sense to deal with it at camp. *I might not see Kurt for the rest of the summer. I'll try to catch his eye.* Kurt seemed to be avoiding a direct look.

"Hi." Sid was glad all of a sudden to actually be with the bigwigs. *leave it to Julian to pull this off. maybe they're good guys.* "Do you know Kurt? He's been teaching me how to work a canoe in his spare time." He nudged Kurt with an elbow.

"Hi." *there. I've been sociable. when can we leave?*

"If they ever have a race with those things, here's the winner!" Sid nudged him again. *Kurt is too bashful for his own good.*

Kurt blushed. *dang it. the little guy is about to make me feel good...* He wanted to stay grumpy for a little while longer. He smiled a little at how stupid he was being.

Tom saw the uncertainty in Kurt's face. *he still refuses to let me catch his eye.* He decided to act if there was an opening. He looked at Nick. *yes!* Nick saw it too. Nick would split Sid off... all Tom had to do was jump in at the right minute.

"You must tell us all about it, Sid. Say—could I see those strap things? I know someone who really needs something like that." He scooted over close to look.

Tom nudged Kurt's leg. When he looked up Tom nodded his head to the left. He was asking for a conference.

Kurt had not expected Tom to make a move—his eyes flared... he was ready to challenge. Instead, he was taken off guard completely by an expression he never expected to see on Tom's face. He was expecting a leer, a horny let's go fuck in the brush look. This was a sympathetic, almost brotherly look. He watched Tom scoot over to the lakeside edge. hmm... *Sid's busy with the other guys...* He scooted over, as invited... but kept his distance.

"Hey," Tom said.

"So, what's up?" Kurt was wary, but ready to listen.

"I've been meaning to talk with you for a long time." Tom felt awkward. Nick's talk to him about this was of limited help right now. "See, when I... well, back then I was stupid and inconsiderate and horny as the dickens. I was selfish. I know now what a bully I was, sort of." He looked at Kurt to see if he was getting through. He didn't know how to do this... but Nick had shown him how important it was to listen to the other guy. *that's what I never used to do.* Part of his problem now was not remembering the details of what he had done. *I have to be sort of general about it.*

Kurt blushed. Tom had disarmed him completely. He was still not satisfied, but he wasn't mad any longer. That surprised him. He forced himself to look at Tom. It was hard to do that. It was hard to do with anybody, really. But curiosity was helping—he didn't know what to say, though.

Tom was grateful that Kurt had looked at him. Now he could go on. "See, I didn't understand about things then. I thought if I liked it, everybody else would too. And I think sometimes they did." He leaned over and nudged Kurt. "I sorta know that, because they always came and got me for another one, if you know what I mean."

Kurt's eyes widened at that piece of news. He looked over at Tom's limp but very big one. He had to admit that he had liked some of it. "Well, I suppose I never thought about that." It did figure, actually. He looked at Tom. His courage had arrived. "What pissed me off was being forced into it, to tell the truth. How come you didn't ask, anyway?" *there. I said it, and I'm glad.*

"Because I was a self-centered bully and an asshole. I admit it. My attitude used to be that if somebody didn't like it, it was his problem, not mine. You see Nick, over there?" He watched Kurt look over at Nick. "I have to be honest: he gets the credit for shaping me up. He's the miracle man, let me tell you."

Kurt looked at Nick. *he's the guy who reads the minutes and things like that. doesn't look like a miracle worker...* He looked back at Tom. He had never seen such a transformed person in his life. He looked at Nick again. Miracle must be the right word. Nick looked like an ordinary kind of guy.

"Now, we can't talk for long, so here's the deal. I'm asking this time, okay?"

Kurt was astounded.

"But I'm asking you to do **me**. You have a right to that. If you want to." Tom looked him in the eye. He was completely sincere.

Kurt was double astounded. His jaw dropped wide open. He'd never done it! He'd only thought about it. He looked back at Tom. "But…"

Tom caught on at once. "You've never..."

Kurt shook his head no. He blushed… he'd never had a chance.

"You want a free lesson?" He watched Kurt's face. He could tell that he was afraid. "You'll still do me, but I'll show you how." He grinned wide.

Kurt's mind whirred. He looked over at Nick. *is this part of his miracle?* He looked at Tom again... his eyes were wide and expecting and flashing happily at him. It was infectious. He nodded his head slightly. yow. *what have I just done?!*

"Excellent! Are you available at free swimming tomorrow afternoon?"

Kurt was frozen in disbelief. *this is all going so fast.* He wasn't even sure if he should have agreed yet... *should I back out? I can't. am I safe?* He didn't know. Who could he ask? No one! *yipes.*

Tom could see his panic. *have I fouled this up?* He had to call the boss in on this, now. "Sit tight a minute," he stood up. He knew Nick had been keeping an eye out. He stepped over, and Nick stood up. Tom nodded to him to take over with Kurt.

Nick had been paying close attention; he crossed over behind Julian and stood by Kurt. He put his hand on his shoulder and sat down. "Hi," he waited for eye contact. Kurt looked at him, clearly confused. "I have an idea about what Tom was saying to you." Nick smiled gently. He wanted Kurt to feel reassured. "I'd understand if you need more time with this. Tom still tends to be in a hurry."

Kurt exhaled in relief. Those were the perfect words to hear right now. He looked at Nick. "Could we talk somewhere?" He didn't know exactly what he wanted to say, only that he needed time and support. He sensed that Nick could provide both. He'd never paid any attention to him before—but Nick seemed to be the one he needed. He wanted to back up on this whole thing—way back. Maybe Nick could help out.

"You bet. You want to now? Can you leave Sid with these guys, or..."

Kurt made an executive decision. He had started to defer to Sid, which was silly. Kurt was the oldest; he should be in charge. "Yeah. He can take care of himself."

Suddenly Danny came splashing up the ladder. "Do we own this platform now, or something?" He shook the water out of his curly locks, happily sprinkling Julian and Sid. *that's for skipping out of the Sunday service.*

Tom greeted him warmly, "All went well, naturally?"

"Yeah! Man, Tom, it was so cool!" He was bursting to describe the whole thing. His first leadership assignment! He was on top of the world! Julian and Sid were eager to hear all about it.

Nick nudged Kurt. "Good chance right now."

"Yeah. You lead the way, okay?"

Nick pointed to the ladder. Kurt went to it and backed down into the water. He didn't want to make a splashy exit. Nick kneeled between Sid and Danny. "We'll be back later. There's something I have to show Kurt." He patted Sid on the shoulder.

Sid nodded at Nick; he was kind of glad. *maybe I can get a word to Julian on the side before they come back.*

"…We hafta get dressed up for the lunch today, remember," Danny was saying. "But since we have about an hour I had to come and brag. Besides, nobody was around! I couldn't just sit there…"

Julian noticed Nick follow Kurt into the lake… *wow—they're going to talk about Tom.* He watched them swim over to the dock. *I'm glad I talked to Nick about that. Nick is good at figuring things out. he'll show Kurt that Tom is really a good guy.* He watched Tom and Danny briefly. It was neat to see Danny so happy.

oh! Danny's narrative vanished from his consciousness. *I just realized something: there's no water polo today… Mark doesn't have anything to do… what if he went to the cabin?*

Julian's immediate impulse was to find an excuse to go to the Meadow—at once.

Hold on—his inner critic popped up suddenly: he had to keep dum-dum from doing something really stupid. *What would you do once you got there?*

Julian sat back. *you're right. what excuse is there?* Making stuff up was not something he knew how to do; he searched his mind for an idea—nothing. *besides, maybe Mark wants to rest or something.*

Yeah, that's right; he never gets any time alone, thanks to you.

Julian had a jab of guilty conscience. *I never thought about that... good point. someday, though... someday Mark will be expecting me.*

Sid's interest in Danny's exciting morning had faded. He was waiting for a chance to nudge Julian without being seen. *I better do it quick before Danny's done talking...* he inched his hand around behind.

Julian felt Sid's finger poke his left cheek. He turned his head. Sid had a huge smile on his face. Julian stifled his urge to laugh. *too bad we can't talk about it.* He gave Sid a wink and a nod.

Sid nodded his head, satisfied. He pretended to pay attention to Danny's tale. *we can talk later.*

Julian looked over to the F dock. *Nick is still talking to Kurt.* He glanced at Sid. *I wonder if he knows what's going on. no matter. Nick will get it sorted out.*

Leonard was keeping track of water activities as usual; the attendance was still relatively light today. This allowed him to pay special attention to the small group out on the platform. *these 10 x 50 binoculars are ideal... one day I'll learn how to read lips.* A small cluster of scouts from Tom's troop had taken over the space. Leonard had developed a keen interest in that particular bunch. *hmm... Tom and Nick are back on the platform... no, Nick's out on the top branch of the F dock. He and Kurt are talking. what can they be up to? very intriguing.* "More mystery in Troop 9." *oh-oh—here comes more after church crowd—back to work, Leonard.*

Geoff had followed the scoutmaster from the service at a distance... he did not want to be detected. But he had to know more about this guy, especially places or times that he might be vulnerable to an "attack." The problem was, the trail to Barr's Meadow was brushed back so well that he had to hang back a hundred feet or so to avoid being noticed. A few times he'd stopped to "tie his shoe," to avoid a face-to-face encounter with a scout going toward the lake. When he saw Danny approaching full speed ahead, he was able to duck behind a large red oak just in time. He jogged rapidly to catch up—just in time to see the scoutmaster step into the cabin.

He noticed that the Troop flag had been leaned against the cabin wall instead of being returned to its mounting bracket in the Flaming Arrow camp. A closed door: a great unknown, and a great possibility: lots of fun could be had behind a closed door... he licked his lips. *getting in there without being seen, there's the challenge.* Hastily, he found a place across the trail to sit while he studied this. If he had to, he could duck behind the tree. He didn't dare prowl around. Troop members could pop up any minute. They had all taken off running to camp after being dismissed, for some reason.

I don't know the routines here... the man could come back out any minute, or a scout could come to the cabin—anything was possible. *it's an hour before lunch, at least.* More could be heading for the lake... *don't want to get spotted by them either.* He was tempted to walk up to the door right this minute and... *no. this man is not an easy mark like Leonard... this one requires some serious research... and planning.*

Thanks to the daily delivery assignment, he knew this trail well by now; however, he hadn't scoped out the side entrance potential. *hum... could there be an old trail between here and my camp? Tom said something about that on the way to the poker game. hmm.* Finding that would be a better use of time; there's no way to get close to the cabin in daylight. *some dodo cleared away most of the trees years ago. all the curtains are open... if I poked my head up to take a peek he'd probably spot me.*

Movement in one of the patrol camps off to the left caught his eye... likely some guys were about to go to the lake. *pointless to stay here any longer... time to exit and explore; I'll start from my supply tent. the woods are fairly open up there.* If there was a direct route from Hawk Camp to this perfect love nest, it would improve his prospects considerably. *I have Sarge's map in my tent! I'll check that first.*

Quickly, Geoff retreated back toward HQ. *I need to get clear as fast as I can... I don't want to be noticed.* He picked up his pace to a rapid jog. Being seen at my own camp before lunch might be a good idea, anyway.

if I don't find it right off, I'm free after the supply route with Danny ... no Canoeing class today. that's a thought: maybe Sarge has an older map that shows something.

—⚏—

The curtains of the south window were partially closed; Mark spread them wide and opened the window; he checked to see if anyone was in the Flaming Arrow camp. *no... at the lake, undoubtedly. I would be, if I was still a scout. all righty, then...* Working on tomorrow's schedule didn't appeal... *not enough time to take a run... might as well just relax—take a short rest before the formal dinner. I'm not particularly tired, but a bit of quiet time might be nice.*

He took off his long pants... no point in getting any wrinkles. *I'll be wearing shorts to lunch. I'll relax until it's time to dress up again.* He stretched out on the bed, hands behind his head.

the boys did very well this morning... not taking along the patrol flags was the right call. I'll include them for the banquet. Mark took a couple of deep breaths; he focused on relaxing, releasing the tension in his various muscle groups.

The sounds of the meadow were so faint it took a while to notice them. *sound must be muffled by the walls... in a tent I'd be listening to the sound of the spring, the breeze... maybe a bird. odd. aha, that's it: I'm so used to having Julian around I had forgotten about this quiet... last year this was a refuge of sorts. this year I don't feel the need for that. interesting.*

His thoughts went to Julian, as they were like to do these days. *he was up and at 'em early again today.* He smiled, remembering Julian's stealthy exit yesterday. He was very good at it, too. *plotting some kind of surprise up at the Flaming Arrow.* From the top secret attitude, Mark presumed it was probably one of those no adults welcome things. He hoped so, actually. *I can see so much growth and independence. what a difference in a single week. his self-confidence has always been high, but it's on a new level entirely. I haven't seen him staring at me either— he seems to have gotten past that. that is a huge relief.*

Mark thought a minute about the portrait Julian drew last night. *I'd like to look at that again. The clock ran out before I could examine it closely.   I'll ask about it tonight.   I wonder if he wants to add anything... shoulders, arms... I don't know what that kind of drawing usually includes.   he was sure all business last night.   the result was proof positive of that.   maybe he's over the crush.   found a playmate his own age.   let's hope so.*

it's so quiet here...   he gazed at the ceiling. The open beam construction was interesting. When was this built? Thirty years ago, probably—between the wars. A small breeze found its way to the bed. *should I open the cabin up?* The mid day temperature inside had started to rise, but it wasn't uncomfortably warm. He decided to leave the other windows as is; in an hour or so he'd just have to close them up again. Leaving them open when no one was here was unwise—birds flew in, squirrels... no telling what kind of critter might come sniffing around.

His gaze returned to the ceiling... had it been treated with anything? The wood didn't look freshly planed, but it didn't look thirty odd years old either. *no direct sun—makes a difference.*

After a while, the knots in the ceiling boards fuzzed...

Julian let himself lag behind Nick and Tom on purpose. He wanted to give them space to be together, but he also wanted to watch them. They had something he longed to have and would have one day. He'd begun to understand a lot more about it thanks to them. He was extremely grateful for that, and figured that he had lots more to learn before he was truly worthy and qualified to make his move on Mark. *boy I am so lucky I didn't do what I was planning. it was embarrassing to think about, actually.   Mark would have sent me back to the Wolf patrol so fast...   and I would have ruined any chance of fixing it later, too.*

There—Tom gave Nick another bump. Julian felt so warm inside when he saw things like that. They were getting better at being cool, too. He kept an eye out to see Nick return the gesture... *hee-hee!*

See how Nick waited? Julian's inside partner was good at pointing things out. *It's the time between that makes it look accidental.*

right. I'll remember that when the time comes.

What a wonderful day this had been. Everything was perfect. Leonard was super today, too. Something about him intrigued Julian. *he's sort of mysterious, but that isn't it. maybe he's like an older brother or an uncle—I never had either one. he makes me feel good; special or something.*

Up ahead of Tom and Nick, Danny cut left—*going to the latrine probably. boy am I glad I don't have to do that. we'll be in camp in a minute.* Julian looked behind. There were several others, but they were back a ways. *I lost track of Sid and Kurt. I'm so happy about that. I wonder if they'll get serious, like Tom and Nick. doubt it... but, you never know, I guess.*

Julian approached the cabin at last; he watched Nick and Tom head up slope to the Flaming Arrow camp. He turned toward the cabin landing and stopped. The troop flag was propped up against the wall by the door. *why did Danny leave that here?* He stepped up as if to enter, but hesitated... what if... he went to the left edge of the landing and leaned out. Holding on to the wall, he stood tippy toe to peek through the window. *Mark is asleep! ooo.* He stood away from the opening and thought about this. He needed a better viewpoint. The window was too far away... he stepped off the landing and stood directly in front of the window so that he could stand upright and secure. This was a rare opportunity—one that might never happen again.

He looked carefully... *Mark's prone body—hands are behind his head. he might not be asleep... might just be relaxing. but he's in his skivvies, so...* Julian's artist eye was analyzing the subject, as usual. But his other eye was looking as well; no tingle below yet, but it would show up if he stood here very long.

Be good, now.

okay... just another second, okay?

All right, but only a second.

Julian took five seconds. He had to show who was boss, for one thing. *now then: how should I go in? super quiet? if he is asleep, why spoil things?* He turned the knob quietly and stepped inside. *goody. didn't make any noise.* Mark didn't move. He closed the door silently and stood, waiting... watching.

He tiptoed over to his cot. He wasn't sure what to do.

A small breeze caught the curtain above the table. It was silent, but Mark felt it land on his bare thighs. He scratched his chin briefly. He realized that he had probably dozed off for a minute... *unusual.* He sensed something... *something's different. oho! the little devil.* He smiled. He couldn't help it.

Julian saw the smile and giggled.

Mark opened his eyes. "Hello there."

"I didn't mean to wake you up." Julian had started to study Mark's mid section; he had a T-shirt on, unfortunately, or he would have gotten a good look at Mark's bare chest. That was still missing in his mental picture gallery. But looking at the skivvies was always satisfying. *too bad I didn't walk over closer.*

Mark noticed Julian's rumpled hair... still damp from the lake. "What time is it?"

Julian looked at the clock. "Five minutes to twelve."

"Just right. Plenty of time to put on my lunch clothes." Mark swung around and sat on the edge of the bed. *I feel really refreshed. I should grab a catnap more often.*

Julian stopped staring. He stepped over to his footlocker and took off his T-shirt. He needed to get his long socks and put on his dress shirt for the fancy lunch. "How was the service?"

"Boring."

Julian giggled. *Mark is so cool.*

26   *formal lunch*

"I must say, John, I don't recall anything quite like it, ever." Dr. Frank Martens had not recovered yet from having been so closely attended by an audience composed entirely of young boys. He stood at the window that looked out over the entrance. The lake was to the left... it looked handsomely pastoral in the noonday sun. *what a charming place.* Hands clasped behind, he bounced briefly on his toes. The breeze coming in the window was pleasant enough. He was growing quite hungry, however; the aromas from the kitchen below were crowding his thoughts. He patted his stomach unconsciously with the fingertips of his two hands, as if it were a small bongo drum. He turned and wandered closer to the doorway so the aromas could be better appreciated. He was oblivious to the impression the sound had made on the small gathering. He was startled slightly himself, in fact: his tummy sounded strangely liquid just now, not empty; he should have heard an echo; instead, it was more of a robust, honeydew melon tone. He sniffed again, briefly. *yea, verily: his mouth did water.*

Martens had fully expected this morning's service to be a challenge—something of a trial, even. Instead, he was all puffed up about the apparent success of his delivery. *I must have done an unusually good job this morning.* He looked over at his companion, the music director. "Were you able to see, Darren? Many of them were actually writing down things I said!"

"I saw some of that, yes." He hadn't, but he knew when to be an echo. Darren Dow was generally satisfied with the service; they had done the same program dozens of times in various locations, so it was largely automatic. The upright spinet piano was seriously out of tune, which was unfortunate. His gospel quartet had sounded a shade sour as a result. Still, that was preferable to enduring a ragged and pale sing-

Camp Walker HQ Second Floor

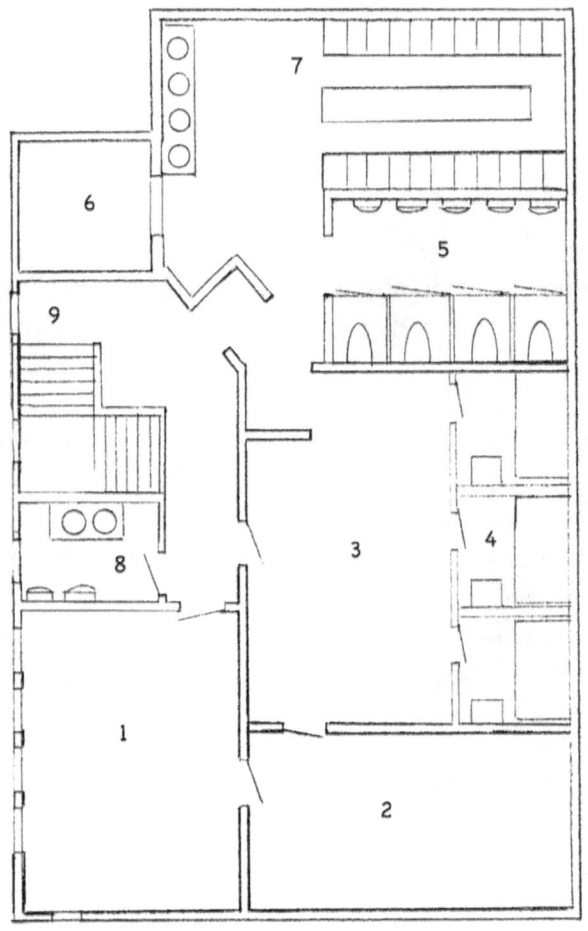

Second Floor

1 Conference Room
2 Storage
3 Staff/Counselor Lounge
4 Rest/Nap Room
5 Rest Room
6 Showers
7 Lockers
8 Lavatory
9 Stairway Down

along from a bunch of untrained boys. He hadn't really paid close attention to what happened out in the house; it wasn't something he usually did. He regarded his fingernails briefly. He needed to file them again—it annoyed him when one or more of them struck the white keys. He wondered where the quartet had wandered. He looked at his watch. *good... lunch is in ten minutes. it certainly smells like it will be ready in time. the quartet is likely close by.* He hoped they would get on the road as soon as possible. Frank's enthusiasm was a good thing; *it will make for a more pleasant trip back.* Darren was happy for him… as long as it didn't mean extending their stay. *these chairs are too Spartan by half.*

Camp Director Jorgensen was amused more than pleased. It was Mark's boys that had made this impression, not Martens' superior delivery. He was curious himself about what was going on. Admittedly, he had only paid token attention to the event—he was not particularly impressed by what he heard. The singing was… well, it would be best not to offer a comment on that. Troop 44 had a much better sounding group at the opening assembly. The homilies and exhortations were textbook and boilerplate. However, it wouldn't hurt to have this man report to the Council execs that all is well at Camp Walker.

Jorgensen sat up in his chair. In the distance the Troop Nine patrols were chanting their marching calls. He turned his head so that he could see them clearly as they approached. He'd been waiting for this.

Martens wondered if the walk into the camp this morning was what had made the difference. It was a bracing experience, in fact… not something he was used to. He was a little surprised they hadn't arranged to have his entourage driven in, but now he saw its value. *it was cleansing, wasn't it? yes, that must be part of it, surely.* It had certainly enhanced his interest in having lunch.

The chant of some scouts howling like a wolf startled him. "Whatever is that?"

"Come back over to the window, and you'll see. This is one of our troops arriving for dinner. They put on quite a show." Jorgensen was pleased that he had the guests upstairs where they could see this. He looked forward to seeing it again himself. He was expecting a few others to show up… some of them needed to. The chants grew louder as they approached; Jorgensen was delighted that he'd be able to see the entire entrance this time.

Mark led the troop up to the HQ entrance much as he had this morning, except that Danny was directly behind him with the flag, and Tom was in the rear. This morning had been an excellent rehearsal for the troop. The drill today was similar to the entrance they had made a week ago at the beginning of camp. They had an audience today, however... many more were probably inside already. He reached his stop position and performed a sharp left face. He took five steps, halted and did another left face. He observed the patrols take their positions; he detected no flaws. He enjoyed the reaction he saw on the faces of random groups that had stopped to watch.

Danny went twelve paces past Mark and stopped at the same spot he had this morning. He did an about face and stood with the flag directly in front of him. The troop filed into parade position and marched in place. Tom stopped directly in front of Mark and did a sharp right face.

"Troop 9, Halt!" Tom ordered. "Left Face!" He raised his arms into the V, counted to five, and dropped his arms sharply.

"Nine!" The troop shouted in unison.

Tom did an about face and saluted Mark. "The troop is ready, sir."

Mark answered his salute. "Have the troop stand at Parade Rest while I go inside. I will return presently."

Tom did an about face. "Troop 9: Parade Rest!"

Mark went in to reconnoiter.

Soames and Taylor had come into the room just as the Zebras gave their whinny. They stood with their hands on their hips, watching closely.

"He makes it look so effortless." Taylor shook his head... he had tried all year to little avail. His boys couldn't seem to get into it, for some reason.

Soames smiled grimly. "I really hate to say this. That at-ease was the best trim I have ever seen."

Martens looked at the two scoutmasters with curiosity. He did not know what they were so interested in. He didn't want to ask, so he gave his best please-fill-me-in look to Jorgensen.

"These boys could compete with a military school, if they had an occasion," Jorgensen explained. "What you are seeing is not typical. It's admirable, of course, but not many troops have this kind of polish." He was really glad Soames had made it upstairs. He's the Doubting Thomas of the bunch.

"I see." Martens just realized that he had seen only one other troop come marching in as a group. He was just as glad things weren't too militaristic.

"Gentlemen," Jorgensen spoke to the guests. "We might as well go down and be seated. I think Pièrre will be serving us in a few minutes." He gestured to the door, and let them pass into the hallway. He looked at Soames and Taylor. They were clearly going to stay and see Mark's boys file in from up here. He stepped into the hall. "If you'll just follow along…" he led them toward the stairway. Seeing the grand entrance of Troop 9 from the head table was going to be a delight.

—⚍—

Mark stepped back outside and spoke to Tom quietly. "We're in luck. It's just as I expected. No one wants to sit in front: the tables are all open. We will fill from the east side, and take the front half of the first seven rows, one table per patrol. The troop flag should be placed in the south aisle, right by the Panthers."

"Are you up at the head table again?"

"Yes. There are place cards, so I can't control anything. Once we're in, you're in charge." He paused. "They may have the guest give a blessing before the meal. We'll have to play it by ear, but I think that remaining seated will be in order, unless the Camp Director has everyone stand."

"Will you lead us in, then?"

"Yes, but I'll peel off and go to the head table to find my place card. You will take over at that point and direct the seating. At the end of the meal, I'll give the regular sign for you to begin the table policing." Mark thought briefly. "I don't know about the exit. I may have to hang around. If that's the case, you and Danny can lead the exit. Make it clean and crisp."

"What about the Patrol and Troop Calls?"

"If I give a thumb up, do them as you leave. Wait until the entire line is clear of the building. Danny should still be in front with the flag. If I come out in time, I'll take the rear position. If not, Nick can handle that."

Soames had his hands cupped behind his ears. He couldn't make out a word of what was being said below. He saw a couple of hand signals; the thumb up he recognized. He looked at Taylor.

Taylor shook his head. He couldn't hear anything either. He saw Mark nod, and the JA called the troop to attention. Taylor headed for the door—he wanted to see them enter this time. He had already seated his troop in a perfect block. That had to be worth twenty-five, at least.

Geoff brought up the rear of Troop 419 for a change, as he was ordered. His scoutmaster was leading them to the banquet. He had tried to get everyone into some semblance of a line, but they had no experience at this. They had never marched anywhere, as far as he knew. Evidently the scoutmasters had met this morning after the service, and Geoff's scoutmaster had got it into his head to impress somebody, or something. He had an idea about that: Danny's outfit this morning. *first there was that **HOT** scoutmaster—that hot, **overdressed** scoutmaster— and then there was the marching! it looked like they were from West Point or something.*

The unexpected benefit was being plopped at the back of the line, where he was free to think about his new quest. He had scouted for a trail downhill behind the supply tent for twenty minutes. It was so open that he couldn't tell if there was a trail or not. At least it wasn't choked with undergrowth. Without a compass, going any farther was too chancy. *maybe I can borrow one from Sarge after lunch.*

uh-oh. why are we stopped? we're almost there. Geoff went around the right side to see what the problem was. *maybe a twisted ankle or something.*

ohmygosh! they're at it again! Geoff was amazed—Danny was standing in front, holding the Troop 9 flag. Tom was facing the troop.

they're just standing there! they have their hands behind their backs. what are they waiting for? His troop had stopped to watch, along with a bunch of others. *oh! here comes the scoutmaster! he's wearing his shorts now. well, that's an improvement.*

"Troop 9: Attention!" Tom commanded.

Geoff couldn't believe his eyes. *look at Tom, would you!* His spine tingled. *that was Tom! just like Danny, this morning! only this time they're in a formation, not a line. with flags!*

"Right Face!" Tom ordered. He waited for Mark to step into the lead position. He nodded to Danny, who moved in front of Mark with the Flag. He stepped behind Mark and raised his arm. "Ready, sir," he said quietly. Danny heard, and started into the doorway. Tom dropped his arm and said, "Forward." The troop filed in.

Geoff dashed over to his scoutmaster. "Sir, can we sit next to them?" He wanted to sit where he could keep the Troop 9 scoutmaster in view.

Scott Olson had no problem with that. "Quite a show," he nodded. "Go ahead, take the boys on in right behind, if you like. Maybe some of this will rub off." He wasn't too worried about that. He had to admire this, all the same. The flags dipping down to clear the door opening was a surprise. *what are they going to do with those?*

Geoff moved a few feet in front of his troop and watched Troop 9 parade by. *they're like marionettes!* They looked a lot different from this angle: twice as impressive. *there's one of the poker players! he looks like a different person. are these guys hypnotized, or something? what do you know—the last two are Julian and Nick!* He waved at them like he was a movie fan. *hah!* All they did was wink back. *man, this is something.* Geoff stepped forward a few feet—it put him behind Nick, who was last in the Troop 9 line. He gestured frantically to his Senior Patrol Leader to follow along.

Lance jumped to his side. "What are we supposed to do?" Geoff wasn't exactly famous for letting him in on things like that.

"Have the guys sit next to this troop as best they can. I know some of them." Geoff looked at him in the face. "This is Troop 9!" He saw the surprised look. "Maybe they'll shed a few points our way, or something."

Just as long as he got to scope out that scoutmaster. He scurried forward—he didn't want anybody to crowd in.

—ɯ—

Henderson was at his place at the head table. He watched Mark's entrance. Schaefer had everything but a brass fanfare! They were in step this time. The general room noise went to a lull as the sound of the cadence drew everyone's eyes. The entrance was fairly rapid, but it seemed to last forever because it was so elegant and precise. They weren't stomping, but the uniform footsteps were like a chorus of muted snare drums. The indoor acoustic amplified the effect. He was pleased with himself for being here early enough to see the entire thing. *good grief! they're going to sit right up here in front. of course—Mark is shrewd. their performance will be right in the judges' laps. Scotty, you will just have to make sure your boys do that at the final assembly. Mark is never the first to arrive. well, I'll just move right into that first row on the last day.* He watched the troop sit as a unit without a verbal command. Suddenly, they became random, just like all the other scouts, as if someone had waved a magic wand. *incredible.*

"Howdy." Mark pulled out his chair and sat down. "I see they've put me here today." He placed his hat in front of his plate. "Somebody's going to make a mint if they invent a way to deal with these things. They take up half the table."

"Hi Mark. I didn't see you, I was so busy watching your boys. Nice work, by the way." He reached over to shake hands.

"Thanks, Scotty. We don't get a chance to strut that often. It's a lot of fun. The boy's favorite is the parade on the Fourth. We're sort of getting in shape for that." He glanced again at the place cards. Good news: he was seated between two Scotts. The one to his right was yet to arrive; he was grateful that he didn't have to sit next to the guest speaker. He looked out at the crowded room. It was filling up fast. The space behind his troop was almost gone already. He had a good line of sight to Tom. The patrol flags dressed up things nicely… each was clipped onto the front edge of a table. He relaxed… things were going perfectly.

—m—

Geoff had followed as closely as he dared, and he couldn't believe his luck: the table was half empty! He was able to sit down right next to Danny, who was directly across the table from Julian. Nick was next to him on the end, facing Tom. He was tickled to be right here with intimate friends who just happened to be big stars! *I might as well be a member of their patrol...* all of them except Julian had a Flaming Arrow on their right shoulder. Julian had a Wolf. *hmm. I'll ask about that later. not a perfect seat... third one in from the end.* Tom was on the end, where he would have preferred to be. The object he wanted to study was closer to the center of the head table than he liked. At least he would be able to see his quest without having to turn around or attract any attention.

"Hi." Julian spoke to the scout next to him. *somebody ought to say something.* "I'm Julian."

"Hi. I'm Willy. Troop 419." *what a cute kid... friendly, too.*

"We're from Troop 9," Julian gestured to his left. "This is Nick, our Scribe. I'm his assistant. I've met Jeff before." He nodded across the table. He nudged Nick. "This is Willy. He's in Jeff's troop."

Nick reached over to shake Willy's hand. "Hi." He wondered whether Geoff's talents were known to his troop members. He doubted it... only to the big ones, probably. Willy didn't seem to be one of those... nor the other one, next to him.

"Hi," Willy nodded toward Lance, directly across, and next to Geoff. "This is Lance. He's our Senior Patrol Leader." He looked at Lance. "This is Nick and Julian. They're from Troop 9!" Impressed, he raised his eyebrows... he didn't expect these guys to be so nice.

Lance reached over to shake Nick's hand. He noticed the scribe patch.

"Hi," Nick saw his leader patch. "Oh. You'll have to compare notes with Danny," Nick pointed. "He's our Senior Patrol Leader—just next to Geoff."

Danny was watching the head table, waiting to see if either he or Tom were supposed to do anything; he figured an order could come at any time. When he heard his name he turned his head. "Hm?"

Nick pointed: "This is Lance. He's a Senior Patrol Leader too."

"Oh. Hi," Danny reached in front of Geoff to shake hands. "What troop?"

"419. Same as Geoff, here." He nodded to his right.

Wow. Danny hadn't noticed that Geoff had sat down right beside him! "Hey, Geoff!" He wondered if... *hmm.* There was no way to ask about that... at least not here. He was sort of hoping Geoff was free this afternoon, but he didn't want to say anything out loud.

Geoff looked down at the arms stretched across his lap with a frown: *what's all this business with the handshakes!?* Geoff was trying to maximize his view of the crotch that had totally preoccupied him, seated now at the head table. He looked at Lance and Danny as they shook hands. *are they all settled now? or, maybe Danny would like to trade places? what brought all this on?* He smiled vacuously and returned his attention to the head table. *sitting by Danny was a bit of luck: maybe I can find out something useful. Nick didn't have much to say the other morning at the water polo tryouts.*

Tom was mildly annoyed. He wanted Nick to be sitting next to him, but Danny's rank required that he be sitting next in line. He was right across from Nick, but out of touching range—*these tables are too wide. well, I need to be on the job anyway. I have a good angle on Mark; I'll see all his hand signals, no problem.*

Geoff was delighted that the dignitaries were raised up on a platform. What he wanted to study wasn't precisely at eye level, but it was elevated enough to assist visibility... ambient light crept in from the lakeside bank of windows and highlighted things nicely. *footlights would have been nicer, of course... well, I can't have everything. hmm... would my super E.S.P. waves work any better from a front angle? maybe I could make those legs move, or shift to the left once in a while. He was truly grateful that those were short pants... mmm. long socks, unfortunately... superb knees...*

—⟋⟍—

The platform gave slightly as Scott Olson walked along the back edge to find his seat. *a little precarious back here.* He pulled his chair out and sat. His girth taxed the chair some, and it creaked as he scooted himself into place. He plopped his hat next to Mark's.

Mark felt crowded suddenly. *this other Scott is a wide load.* He nodded a salutation, and reached for his water glass. They had not met before; Mark had seen him at meetings. He shifted to the left to make room.

"Say," Olson leaned close to Mark. "Your boys do a pretty good job." He thought it only right to be neighborly.

Mark looked at Olson. *my boys, pretty good? hmm.* Mark was less than impressed: at least forty pounds overweight; he needs to get his clothes let out again or buy larger ones. The Friar Tuck hairline made him look comical without his hat. *well, I'll hold my tongue. getting touchy is pointless.* Mark noticed the 419 on his shoulder; not a familiar number. He extended his hand. "Mark Schaefer." He smiled perfunctorily. "I don't recall your outfit, I'm sorry to say."

"No reason you should," Olson shrugged. "We couldn't get plugged into the Atlanta camps this year, so John found us a place here." It was a little more Andy Jackson than he liked personally, but his boys were happy. Olson inhaled audibly through his nose. He was ready to tie on the feedbag. He reached for his napkin.

Mark had exhausted his supply of small talk topics. He took another sip of water. He was eager to be served for another reason entirely: getting this over with. *please, don't make me stay afterward.* He wanted to be down on the main floor with his boys. He looked at them proudly. They always exceeded his expectations. How lucky that the front had been wide open like that. He could see the very top of Julian's head over near Tom. *here's hoping I can get away without another meeting.*

At last: the yellow crew was approaching the table with salad plates in hand.

27 letters home

Dear Mom, Julian wrote. He sat back and looked at the empty sheet. He had never written a letter before. *boy. what should I put down?* He felt a little guilty all of a sudden. He hadn't even thought about his mom until Mark said he should write this letter. He'd been so busy and having such a great time and everything, it just had not occurred to him.

How are you? He was curious about that, come to think about it. He assumed she was just fine. Why wouldn't she be?

I hope you're okay. Have you been having any fun? Maybe she had, maybe not. Julian realized that he didn't really know what she might be doing. He was usually so wrapped up in what he was interested in, he didn't pay much mind to what she did—she read a lot of books and magazines. She didn't have any hobbies. *she's always reading up on houses and neighborhoods.* It was part of her job.

Julian frowned momentarily... *why am I so inconsiderate and self centered? Mom probably has other interests—her whole life doesn't center around me*—she was always interested, of course, but she didn't hover or cling or fuss over him, like some moms he had seen. She must have something besides Geraldine and the real estate office. *hmm. when I get home, I'll pay some attention to that...* Maybe there was something he should be doing for her. It was time for him to assume some responsibility... picking up his room and helping with the dishes was about all he ever did. Mowing the lawn... *yes.* His mom deserved to have some fun. Seeing to that just got put onto his list. *about time, too.*

How's Hazel been? She was the chatty neighbor lady that always came over to yak about this and that. She had funny stringy hair and always wore baggy dresses and frizzy sweaters that buttoned down the front, but were never buttoned. There was always a wadded up Kleenex in the little pocket. *she's ancient, too. real nice, though. her cookies are outstanding.*

Tell her I really miss her cookies. The ones here have mostly been... Julian needed a word here. *hmm...* **pretty boring.**

He sat back at read what he had written. There's a lot of blank paper left. *boy. how should I do this? drawing pictures is sure a lot easier than this!* He stared at the page. *if only I could think of a way to get started.* His mind wandered a little, remembering the fancy lunch. The jolly cook standing there with his tall white hat, carving slices of ham and roast beef... he was interesting. *hmm.* A sketch came into his head. He drew a quick cartoon version on the right side of the sheet. The mustache was important here. He had a funny kind of nose, too. His eyes were kind. He sampled his work too much, though. He had a small pot belly.

Next to the cartoon cook he wrote: **This is the camp cook. He made us a great Sunday dinner today. Usually he just cooks for the Counselors and Lifeguards. His lasagna wasn't that great. He almost never makes his own cookies; they are all the supermarket kind. I get to help Danny fix breakfasts every day. I know how to do scrambled eggs now, and my pancakes are real good too.**

what else could I write about? hmm.

—ᴡ—

Justin wrote,

Dear Mom and Dad—

We went to a special Sunday service today. It was okay. This is now beginning our second week. My merit badges are going well. I study Forestry with Julian, and Indian Lore with Freddy Scott. You probably don't know him. My swimming is coming along fine. I can go greater distances here, since it is a big lake.

I am getting used to it now, but it is so crowded at times. It's a lot of fun. We have a campfire most nights and do skits and sing songs and stuff. We sleep on cots. They aren't very comfortable, but you get used to them, I guess.

We come home on Saturday. See you then.

Love, Justin.

Justin looked at what he had written. It wasn't very long. Well, he didn't want to bore them or anything... usually when he started to tell about scout stuff they sort of... well, they didn't go to sleep, but he could tell they weren't that interested. Besides, Meg would probably make fun of it, anyway. *oh. better say something to Meg or she'll crab at me even more...*

p.s: say hello to Meg. She wouldn't like it here. There are no girls at all.

— ᨓ —

Bruce wrote,

Dad:

Well, I did it. I qualified for my distance swimming and I'll get my First Class by the end of camp! It was real hard, but thanks to my new friend Julian, I practiced and

247

practiced until I could do it. They won't let us take any pictures at the lake, or I'd take some for you to see. It's quite a place, and there are hundreds of scouts here.

I met Julian because we both volunteered to be rescued by these guys that were working on their Lifesaving Merit Badge. I learned a lot from that. I'm going to work on that next year, if I get to come here again.

I'm in a skit my patrol is doing. They have me playing Sheriff Dillon. It's pretty silly, but fun anyway.

Bruce reviewed his letter. *should I tell about my tent?* He was sort of in charge of the two Tenderfoot scouts… he didn't have much to do there. He could talk about the food, of course. He was learning to cook, which was really great. *hmm.* Maybe better not bring that up… there weren't any scales around here; he doubted if he'd lost any pounds. *nope. this is enough. Besides, I'll be back home soon, anyway.*

Well, so long for now.

Bruce

—∭—

Sid was in a fabulous mood. As soon as he finished this he would be off to the canoe dock. He wrote:

Dear Mom and Dad:

We're at the halfway point, and it seems like we just got here! It is the best of the best. Boy, I sure appreciate having that air mattress! I feel sorry for the scouts that don't have one. These canvas cots are narrow and hard.

I have met a new friend, and he is showing me how to operate a canoe. I'm getting real good at it. I think I'll sign up for the merit badge next year.

If anyone gets a snake bite or gets cut badly, I know how to fix you up good, now. We'll do broken arms next. That's my favorite badge to work on. Basketry is okay, I guess. Mostly I have fun at the lake; we get to swim every day. They have lifeguards every five feet, practically, and count heads every fifteen minutes. Nobody's going to drown around here, that's for sure.

We cook our own meals, mostly, except lunch. They have a famous cook that comes in the summer. He cooks for the counselors mostly, but he put out a fancy Sunday dinner for the whole camp. It was really something. We could have either roast beef or ham. (I managed to get some of each; you know me!)

I get to see Julian a lot, even though he got promoted to the Flaming Arrow Patrol. That's the bigwig patrol. Wouldn't you know it. So we're down to six scouts in the Wolf Lair.

Well, it's time to go swimming! I'll see you Saturday night,

Sid

p.s. thanks again for that air mattress!

Sid folded up the letter and inserted into the envelope. He placed his letter on the small pile in the middle of the table—everyone was finished except Jeremy. *Jeremy's writing a book, looks like.* Sid shook his head. *it figures; Jeremy was annoyed that there were no classes today. honestly. well, I have a latrine stop to make before heading to the lake. it was really good planning to have the stationery already here—Mark's always organized. time to jet...*

—m—

Alex wrote:

Dear LuAnne:

It's midway through camp, and we're supposed to write home. I don't know if the Major is around this week or not—but a letter from me would probably make things worse, if that's possible. So I'm writing to you instead. I hope that's okay.

No point in asking any questions... *I'll be home in a week; besides, they don't have a mailbag delivery here...*

How's it going with Jeff these days?

His sister had a huge crush on Jeff Baker. *he's okay... snobby, but...*

I think the Major likes him, so that helps some.

Alex tapped the table with his pencil eraser. He debated with himself about the last comment—he never could tell if it was smart to talk about his father. Certainly not if there was a chance he'd find out... sometimes LuAnne left things lying around... *better not say anything else.*

Camp is great this year, as usual. They have this guy teaching us about reptiles that is really fun. He must have connections, because he brings in these live examples to watch and study. We've learned about frogs, turtles, snakes and alligators—we even saw an alligator gulp down a live rat. It was pretty scary.

what can I write about? His sister didn't care about scout activities.

They changed me to a different three-man tent. They want me to sort of help out a Tenderfoot named Sandy. You know, show him the ropes, day to day. I'm glad to do it, but he'd rather spend time with the other Tenderfoots. The other guy in the tent is named Paul. He's sort of hard to figure out.

That was a huge fib. *Paul's a self centered braggart and showoff.* Paul was a year older; technically, as a Life scout, he outranked Alex too. But Alex was number **three** in the patrol rating, just behind Gary and Max. That promotion was what set off the argument with the Major last month. *man... he had really counted on the Major being proud of his achievement... he'd jumped ahead of two other guys, both a rank higher.* He'd worked hard on that. But the Major gave him a dressing down for being a brag, being too big for his britches... nothing seemed to please.

Alex tried to bring his attention back to the task at hand... Not easy with Paul rummaging around in his footlocker. *probably looking for that stopwatch... what's with that, anyway? maybe he's about to leave... it's usually a relief when Paul takes off. he's pals with that guy over in the Panthers.*

Personally, Alex thought Paul was some kind of sex fiend... *he always has a big one showing. hum... today he looks pretty normal.* There were times when he was afraid Paul might try to jump him or something; the way Paul looked at him at times was really weird... as if he was supposed to do something. Something wrong. A few years back the Major had warned him about guys like Paul.

well, it doesn't look like he's going to come over and write a letter, at least. He tapped his pencil again... *I need to concentrate on this.* He couldn't talk to LuAnne about these things. Or about his own problems... his temptations. What would he do if Paul actually... well...

blast! Alex felt that swelling sensation again. He glanced carefully over at Sandy... *he's busy thinking.* He didn't want Sandy to notice his growing problem. This happened more and more lately... he didn't know what to do about it. He didn't know whom he could ask about it, even. He had to think about something else, that's all... another trip down the hill wouldn't look very good... new topic. How about swimming... he slid his left arm across his lap; *I'll be covered if Sandy glances this way.*

The lake is just like last year except that they added another cubbyhole cabinet.

that was a stupid thing to mention. Alex shook his head in disgust. He checked on Sandy... *hm? he's just sitting there.* Alex turned toward him and smiled. The kid was stuck, his eyes sort of blurry, frowning a little. Sandy needs help.

"This is hard." Sandy noticed Alex was looking at him. He had been trying, but the only time he had written a letter was two years ago, when his mom made him write that thank you letter to Grandma Phelps. She'd pretty much told him what to say.

"Whom are you writing to?"

"Whom?" That sounded funny. *why didn't Alex say who, like everyone else?*

"Yes... your mom, or your dad? Or is it to both? Sometimes whom you write to makes a difference in what you write about." Alex had to go on theory here... he had no experience writing to either one.

"My mom, I guess..." *she would probably like what I write more... Dad could be pretty picky sometimes.*

"Okay, then start by writing "Dear Mom." Alex watched Sandy write the opening. "Good. What do you think she would like to hear you say? Or talk about? What do you think she is expecting, or maybe worried about?" Moms were supposed to worry a lot, weren't they? Alex had never known his mother, but he'd seen a few.

Sandy thought about that. "She was afraid I'd run out of clean clothes..." *that's an odd thing to write about, though.*

"You could tell about your merit badge classes. Is there something interesting or funny to tell about?" Alex would like to share lots of things, really... but no one he knew would find them interesting.

"Ooo, yeah!" Sandy sat up brightly. He could tell about woodcarving—he finished making the raccoon. She'd like that. He started to write:

Dear Mom—

Guess what I did this week? I carved a figure of a raccoon in the merit badge class. Scoutmaster Unger said it was a real good job. Now I'm working on a mother bear

and her cub. They have these really neat knives to work
with...

Alex watched Sandy's sudden change. He felt a small rush... he'd
actually helped the kid get started. It wasn't that big a deal, but it made
him feel good. He looked back at his own letter. He read what he had
written. *hmm. a waste of paper. maybe I should take my own advice:
I'll pretend LuAnne is interested in Indian Legends.*   Mr. Simmons
knows how to spin a yarn pretty well. *The Major would probably give
one of his dark looks if I even mention the subject, but LuAnne might be
interested in how these hills came to be so rugged... yes.* Maybe paying
attention to that would help calm things down below, too. Paul's gone
at last; that helps...

—w—

Julian did a line drawing of the gate at the lake with Leonard
seated at the table; a long thin horizontal shape. *hmm. I might do a real
one of this later.* He wrote,

We swim every day. Leonard is the man in charge
and keeps track of everybody. He's real nice. He knows
who everyone is. He must be pretty smart. He won't let you
in if you don't have a Buddy along. Nobody gets in the
swimming area all by themselves.

what else should I say? oh! silly—I haven't even mentioned Mark.

They have Mark real busy all the time. He is one of the
new Water Polo coaches. He helps at the rifle range, the
ropes, the archery, and I don't know what all. He
transferred me to the Flaming Arrow patrol, so I'm not a
Wolf any more. Boy, those guys in the Flaming Arrow are
sure smart. I get to be the Assistant Scribe now, mostly
because of my drawing. I get to work with a guy named
Nick. You'll really like him.

Oh… just remembered. He drew a bow across the page.

This is what I use in Archery. It is the smallest sized one. Did you know that you don't shoot arrows? You loose them. It seemed funny, but Mr. Samuels is real fussy about it. He said that you shoot a gun, but an arrow is let loose after you pull the string. I was sore for a long time, but I can do it okay now. My arms are kind of weak, I guess. Nick says I need to use some weights to fix that.

He drew another long narrow line sketch that showed the tents and cabin. He made a teeny flagpole with the Troop 9 flag.

We stay in these square tents. Each patrol has three tents and a picnic table in the center. We have to cook on camp stoves because they don't want a campfire to get out of control. They say the fire danger is really high, so everyone is very careful.

Julian read through what he had written. It didn't seem to be enough, but he didn't know what to add next. *well, I'll be back home in a week, after all…* He could show her all the drawings he had done for the scrapbook. Right now, he didn't want camp to end, ever. He couldn't tell his mom that, though.

This camp is just about the most fun thing I have ever done. Thank you for letting me come. I've kept good care of my clothes. We will come home on Sat. night. To be honest, I'm going to miss this place a lot.

Hugs and kisses,

Julian

He read through it again. He felt a little guilty. *if I didn't have the sketches it would hardly fill a single page. I should have asked Nick for some ideas. he knows how to write stuff.*

Mark should be back pretty soon. he's going around the camps collecting letters. he wants every scout to write home or else. maybe he has some ideas about what else I could write... I'll do some detail work on the portrait while I wait. the eyes need attention, especially.

—m—

Tom watched Danny and Nick scribbling away like mad. if only I was as good at this. Mark wasn't about to let him off the hook, so he had to produce something. He'd already decided what to write and who to. The envelope was addressed and ready. That was the easy part. Now for the hard part. He wrote:

Hey, Charlie—

I'm at summer camp and Mark is requiring everyone to write home, as usual. I'm writing to you instead. I'll be back home next week anyway, so I figured this was a better idea.

Nothing is wrong, so don't worry about that. Just the opposite. I had some really good luck last week, and you're about the only person I know who can understand it.

Tom paused. Writing letters was a chore. He hated it when he couldn't find the right word or remember how to spell. And anything he wrote to Charlie had to be perfect. Or as good as he could do, anyway. He had to do this on his own, too. He'd only written to Charlie once before.

I thought about you yesterday, which is why I'm writing, really. Do you remember Nick? I think you met him once when you and Buz were visiting from college. I think it was spring vacation. Well, anyway I thought about that a lot. Now, Nick is like Buz.

hmm.   that's not exactly right... Nick is more like Charlie; I'm more like Buz. well, no need to get too technical. He continued:

Sort of, that is. What I mean is that I think Nick and I are like you and Buz. I think that's about as lucky a thing as I could ever have."

man, this is hard to get right.

Anyway, I figure I owe you for this. Seeing you and Buz is what helped me figure this out. I might have gone nuts or something if I didn't have that. It was pretty confusing at first.

It was scary, actually. *no need to tell that part... better finish this before I mess it up.*

So thanks a lot. Maybe sometime we can all of us get together. Go bowling or something. I want you to meet Nick. He's...

Boy. Putting this into words was about as hard a thing as Tom had ever tried. He hated to be corny or mushy.

... just right. Hello to Buz. I don't know if he remembers me or not.

Tom read over what he'd written. *geez. pretty slim. maybe I should talk about some camp stuff.* Charlie would know all about that, being the all time top scout here himself once. Maybe he'd think all that was kid stuff now. The truth was, Tom had no practice at writing letters... Especially important letters.

"You about ready?" Nick stood up from the Flaming Arrow table and plopped his envelope in the center.

Tom was startled. "Uh, yeah. I'm about done." He signed and folded the letter quickly. *Nick doesn't need to know who I was writing to.   Mark will be by to snag this in a few minutes.* He tucked his envelope under Nick's and stood up.

He had mixed feelings about swimming this afternoon. Writing that letter had got him out of the mood. He shrugged. *might as well... nothing else to do.   it will make Nick happy; that's enough.* He hopped over and gave Nick a good bump. "Wanna race?" He took off running.

—∿—

Justin was the only one left in the Zebra camp. Everyone else had run down to the lake. He sort of wanted to go, but writing that letter had made him sort of miss things at home. He wasn't sure why that was so. It wasn't as bad as the first two days, at least. He was real homesick then. He couldn't understand why he would feel that way. He was pretty sure they didn't miss him any. It was so hard sometimes there to count for anything. His dad didn't care much about what he did or didn't do. His mom did, some, but she always did whatever Meg wanted. Meg never forgave him for being the oldest.

So when he got to join the scouts, things started to look up. Nobody made fun of him, and people like Julian cared what he did and gave him a pat on the back, even. They got to do lots of interesting things, too. Meg wouldn't like them, probably. *even though I'm one of the smaller kids in Troop 9, I'm just about the fastest swimmer.   of course, I'm the only one that knows that.   well, that's no big deal; there isn't a merit badge for fast swimming.*

Sometimes Justin wondered if Max knew what things were like for him, because the boy in Max's skit was like him in some ways. Sometimes he wondered if he got lost or wandered off if anybody would notice. He doubted if he could do any heroic rescues though, like the boy in the skit.

His mind wandered to that day on the platform when everyone was sitting in that circle. He put his head down on the table and squeezed his eyes shut real tight. He still cringed when he thought about that stuff. He didn't understand it. He wanted it to go away and leave him alone. Why couldn't he just do his plants and his Indians and his swimming and not be bothered by that other stuff? He fanned his legs in frustration. He stamped his feet and clenched his fists. No good... he kept seeing those things again and again, no matter how hard he tried to distract himself. He'd start to swell and feel that odd sensation between his legs sometimes too, and that made it worse. He hated the fact that it felt good.

He couldn't forget the time when he was a lot younger, and Meg made fun of him for having a pee-pee. She told him it was ugly and he should get rid of it. She pointed at it and laughed. He was only four or five years old. Why did that still bother him? For a long time he felt bad about it, because no matter what, Meg wouldn't accept him. He tried and tried, but nothing made her think he was worth a hoot. That's what she always said. "You're not worth a hoot."

Justin stifled a sniffle. He took off his glasses and wiped his eyes. He thought briefly of Jeremy again. He had started doing that. Jeremy had looked at him on the platform that day. *he seems to be sort of like me, somehow. at least Jeremy looked at me as if we were friends...* Justin didn't know how to express what he saw in that. It popped into his head once in a while. He never got to see Jeremy. *he's a Wolf. their camp is clear the other side of the creek past the Badgers.* He didn't know if he should ask Kurt about him... they're in the Canoe merit badge together. *Kurt's a nice enough guy. it's just that I never learned how to start a talk. I'm pretty good at answering.* The trouble was, most of the time no one said anything to him. Except Julian, of course.

"Why so glum, chum?" Mark sat down beside Justin. He put his arm on Justin's shoulder. The rest of the patrol was gone—to the lake, no doubt.

"Oh! Hi, Mark!" *wow. it's Mark, in person!* Justin turned red all over.

"Is that your letter?" Mark was a little concerned. This is the first sad face he had seen this summer.

"Yeah." Justin smiled. He was glad to see Mark.

"So what can we do to cheer you up?" Julian has not reported lately on Justin.

"Gosh, I don't know." Justin was embarrassed. "I'm okay."

Doubtful. A scout all alone in his camp, on a sunny afternoon, when everyone else is splashing in the lake? "How about giving me a hand? I need to make a list."

"List?" Justin sat up, eager.

"I need to make a list of scouts that haven't written their letter home yet." Mark was collecting them from all the camps. The Zebras were the last stop. "Are these the other Zebra letters?"

"Yeah. Tad hasn't finished his yet, I don't think."

Mark flipped through the small pile. "I don't see Clint's either."

"Oh. I saw him writing it." He stood up. "Let me check his tent." Justin ran over to the end tent. The letter was on Clint's sleeping bag. He grabbed it and ran back over to Mark. "Here it is!"

The smile looked a lot better on Justin. "How about it? Have you got the time to spare?" He wagged his list of names.

"Sure!" Justin was thrilled.

"Okay. This may get you a few points, too. Your patrol wouldn't mind that, would they?" Mark got such a kick out of seeing a happy face.

"Yeah!" Justin bounced up and down on the bench. "What do I do?"

"Just put a check mark by the names as I read them." Mark lifted his satchel onto the table and emptied the letters into a pile in the center.

"Jones." He thought about Justin as he read the names off the envelopes. *here's someone who needs a buddy. I thought that had been taken care of. hmm. well, to be fair, I have given Julian a lot of new responsibilities. I can't fault him any.*

"Dawson."

Justin found the name on the list. He was so happy all of a sudden. The clouds had vanished from his head and the sun was out. *wow. look at all these names! I've never seen all these before. how many of these guys have I actually seen? there's a lot of them! I've never heard of some of these guys, even.*

"Thomas." *when I'm through with the tally, we'll see if there isn't a change in Justin's outlook. he's just a little lonely. shy ones always have that burden, don't they?* "Jensen."

wow. I know who that is! he's a Panther!

"Radcliffe."   *I'll escort Justin down to the lake when we finish. Leonard will help link him with someone.   Leonard knows everyone.* Mark was pleased by Justin's enthusiasm… his problem had nearly faded away.

28   *opening day on South Ridge*

Andy had the clipboard and the "targets" under his arm. Fourteen of the contestants were here at the east end of the Archery Range, waiting for Freddy to arrive. He was slightly concerned because, technically, only the lake was open this afternoon. If they were spotted by the wrong person, the entire operation would be ruined.

Tony wasn't worried; if asked, he was on his way to the lake. Meanwhile, he was not so subtly checking out the contestants. He sat cross-legged and leaned back on his palms, admiring the random shifting from one leg to the other. *this low angle is ooo so nice!* There wasn't a whole lot of conversation. He wondered if these guys were even acquainted with each other. *it was brilliant of Andy to get into this operation.* Now the afternoons would have something to look forward to. *how did that Freddy guy get all these guys to join up? some of them are hot.*

"Hey, Andy! Up here." Freddy waved from just above the trail entrance.

Andy looked up the hill. *whoa... that's a surprise.* "Okay guys, here we go." He pointed up the hill. "Time to hurry, hurry, hurry!" The quotation from Max's skit was lost on this bunch, but he was amused anyway. He ran up the trail, beckoning the rest to follow.

Tony waited to "bring up the rear." That way he could do sort of a quick review as they passed by. No telling what gems might be waiting to be discovered by an enterprising person such as himself.

Andy was a little annoyed by Freddy's quick pace... he was way up there already. He didn't expect his phrase to be taken so literally... he hurried to catch up. "We're short one guy," he called out. Freddy had disappeared around a bend... *did he hear?* Andy put on some steam... *why the big rush?* "Wait up, will ya?" *this trail is steep.*

Freddy beckoned for Andy to hurry... he wanted the string of contestants to be out of sight from below as quickly as possible.

"Man, why..." Andy was short of breath... he caught up to Freddy, who was hurrying around another switchback. "I tried to tell you... we're short one guy."

"He's already there." Freddy came to a sudden stop where the trail crossed over to the south side if the ridge. He turned around.

"What's wrong?"

"Nothing... we're here." Freddy pointed to the right. "Turn off here and go behind that clump of ash."

"Oh." Andy had presumed it would be farther. *okay.* He stepped carefully—*a freshly beaten path might not be too good a thing.* He led the line of contestants toward the hidden clearing.

Freddy stood at the exit point and gave a personal sign of encouragement to each of his "contestants" as he directed them to turn off the trail. He was very pleased with himself. He would be uncovering a lot of new talent this afternoon. That is, they would be uncovering it themselves. He had a pretty good idea of what was coming, so to speak; he had confirmed each one at the lake while they were dressed in nature's own. Some of them were very nice. He followed the last one in. Freddy didn't recognize him. *must be the friend Andy spoke about. mmm... not bad, either.* What job could be found for him? *as long as he doesn't disrupt things, he'll be okay.*

Tony gave a polite nod as he passed Freddy—he had not been introduced. *looks like a secretary or something... not someone who would come up with a clever scheme like this. you never know.*

Andy stepped around the tangle of mountain ash saplings. Two guys were standing over by the far edge. *whoa...* he had no idea this would be so well conceived. It was all set up: three circles, each with five spokes. They looked like large wagon wheels without an outer rim. The spokes were strips from a paper towel roll; the ends were held in place at the center by a small metal hoop of some kind, about a foot in diameter. He saw instantly where Freddy wanted the saucers he had borrowed from his camp. He put them in place. *I have to hand it to Freddy... this looks like a good time already. helps explain all the mystery.*

"Okay, everyone," Freddy said loudly, "if you can look over here, please, I'll explain how this will go." He stood behind the three circles; a five foot space separated the circles, about six feet from the edge of a steep drop off. The archery and rifle ranges fifty feet below were obscured by trees and dense bramble.

"There are three circles, as you can see. You need to pick a circle. When everyone has found a position, I'll come around and give you a number. Andy here will write down your number on the blank playoff grid. Everything in the contest will refer to your number. Your names will never be used.

"You'll keep the same number until the very last day. Today, three guys will be eliminated: the worst shot in each circle will be out. Tomorrow, there will be four in each circle. Three a day will be eliminated until we're down to the final three. Every day the distance will be increased an inch and a half. We're starting at two feet even from the edge of the paper to the center of the saucer, which is the bull's-eye. The distance on the last day will be 30 inches." Freddy looked up to see if there was a question.

"Are there any special rules?" asked one.

"No, not really—unless you have one to suggest?"

"What about a time limit?" asked another.

"Hmm. I didn't think about that." Freddy scratched his head. "How many want a time limit?" He saw two hands raise, but they didn't seem to be that firm. "Okay, take as long as you need, I guess." He checked his watch. "We have seventy minutes left in the free swim period today, so we're okay. The other days will be shorter, of course." He looked for another question. There was none.

"All right then. We'll pass out numbers as soon as you have picked your spot." Freddy gestured to the spokes.

Andy was ready for this... he'd been checking out some of these guys. He wanted to lick his lips, but that would not be cool. He stepped over to Freddy. He was ready to write down the numbers on the master grid.

"Andy, this is Craig. He's the other assistant. Today, each of us will watch over a circle and decide who gets eliminated. Just keep track of where everyone hits." Freddy pointed to the first circle and indicated

Craig. Andy was assigned the center circle. "You get to decide who in your circle gets eliminated."

"Got it. This is Tony." Andy gestured to his friend. "He's the rally squad."

"Hey, come on! I was gonna be Howard Cosell!" He held up his hand as if it had a mike, and mimicked, **"Folks, you ain't gonna believe this one—it's ten inches if it's even one. This reportah has never seen anything like it! Take it from me, it's gonna smash all the reccahds!"**

Craig broke up, as did three contestants who had landed in the first circle.

Freddy was amused—he looked at Andy to see if this was his idea. "You do a good imitation!" He thought about it. *why not?* "Listen, I like the idea of having a good time here as well as... well, anyway: as long as nobody gets mad, or you don't spoil anyone's "shot," go ahead. Just back off if you make anybody go limp, okay?"

"Me? Cause a **limp** dick?! For shame!" Tony drifted to the side to think about how to frame his "opening" while the "officials" got everything underway.

Freddy started handing out the numbers. "Put this number on your lane where it can be seen clearly."

The numbers were large, written on a 3x5 card. Andy tagged along and entered the number next to the name on his list, and put the number on the first day's bracket. Each circle had its own page.

"Remember you guys, at the end today, you roll up your paper strip and take it along with you." Freddy had forgot to mention that earlier. That would reduce the cleanup requirements.

Tony wandered back... he nudged Craig. "They can decorate their tents with those strips as the week goes on. Tell them to be sure to autograph and date them. They'll bring loads at the auction next summer." He had discovered a six-inch pinecone: perfect for a microphone. He had his opening planned... *when should I start?*

Craig was delighted with Tony... *this is going to be fun after all.* He wasn't too thrilled to be a part of this, originally. But he owed Freddy; so here he was... *at least I didn't have to enter myself.*

"Okay, everyone," Freddy stood by circle three. "We're ready. I suggest you take your shorts off and put them behind you, or in a safe place over at the edge of the clearing." He'd love it if they took off shirts too, but he didn't think he could require it. He watched them undress. *good!* Several were stripping everything, clear to their shoes.

this is it: Tony strode across the clearing grandly, affecting a brisk eager Jim McKay voice: **"And now, WABS presents The Wild World of Spurts. Here is your special correspondent, Howie Cosell!"** He paused and did a mock crowd cheer, raising his arms up and down.

Andy joined the mock cheer briefly. *Tony is so good at these things! oop. time to be on the job.* He stepped closer to the center ring.

Craig was delighted… but he had to step over to his circle and become a judge.

Tony was in his element. He lifted the slender pinecone to his face and spoke in his best Howard Cosell twang: **"Thank you, Jim McKay! Yes, spurtsfans, we have excloosive coverage of the very fuhst Southeast Splat Tournament. It's opening day, folks, and all the champions ah heah. I've nevah seen anything like it. Theyah's Bigus Twelve ovah theyah, just itching to get it up!"**

Several guys looked at Tony in surprise. A few laughed, recognizing the voice.

"Tell me, Dead-Eye Six," Tony pushed his pinecone into an unsuspecting face. "Is it tah-rue that you can hit a foah inch tahget at three feet while yoah jumping in mid ayah?" He tried to affect a Cosell head duck, awaiting a reply.

Hank Sours blushed. He didn't know what to make of this. *how did he know my number is 6? oh… he saw my card.*

"Sorry… didn't mean to spook you. I'm just clowning around. Go ahead and get it up. Don't mind me." Tony winked suggestively and moved on. *I better back off a little.* He scanned the circles for another interview opportunity… *I have to be quiet once things are underway.*

Freddy saw that everyone was at the end of his paper strip. "Is everyone happy with their number?"

"What's the difference?" Number 7 asked.

"Some guys have lucky numbers, some don't. If anyone wants to swap numbers and places, now is your chance."

"Could I trade 11 for 9?" It meant trading circles.

Nine looked over at the other circle. Hmm... he liked a couple of those. "Sure." He traded places.

excellent! The new 9 was happy... he now had his lucky number, and a perfect view of Number 7. He'd been watching him all morning. *he is hot.*

Andy did a quick revision on his list of names.

"Anybody else?" Clearly this contest needed to get underway. Several erections were beginning. "Okay! Get ready, get set, go!"

Tony spoke low, cupping his hand over the pinecone as if he were on a putting green trying not to disturb a golfer's concentration. **"Thayah stahted, folks... this repoatah is going to let the camera do the talking foah now... he'll be back with an intahvu aftah these messages..."** Tony flashed his eyes at Andy and turned off his pinecone mike. He had some serious viewing to do. *look at all this meat!* He was starting to get a rise himself, here. How to get the most out of this... get systematic and survey each circle for sizes, first. *will anyone be as big as Tom? doubtful... I've seen several of these guys in the lake; amazing how much better they look up here on dry land.*

Freddy had assigned himself to the third circle on purpose. There were a couple of guys there that really turned him on. He walked around the circle slowly. He looked at each contestant briefly... he was drawn to 13... or possibly 10: either was his idea of where he'd like to end up by the last day of camp.

Andy noticed that Freddy was systematically circling his group. That made sense; good way to check them all out. *there are some good times standing here; how to get signed up, that's the question.* He did a first pass. *too bad I can only keep track of five, though. maybe tomorrow I can trade with Craig.*

Craig experienced a little unexpected discomfort down below... he was surprised at how hot the view was, now that it was here. All these vibrating cheeks! *man alive: Number 4 has the lowest hanging balls I've ever seen. he'd better not sit down on his bicycle too fast.* Craig wasn't sure where he should stand, exactly.

Tony spotted a nice one in Craig's circle. It was long and had a unique bend or curve to the right at the very end. The size was its greatest recommendation—it looked about eight inches—but the curve might just be fun, too. *Mister Curvy... yes.* He wasn't blind to nice buns, of course... as long as the front side looked real tasty—six and a half inches uncircumcised was the minimum there. *there are several... decisions, decisions.*

Number 11, the new one, was getting pretty hot watching 15. He put his imagination on active duty. He grabbed his balls with his left hand and filled his right palm with saliva. He reversed his hand and brought his fingers up underneath around the right side of his shaft, and pumped slowly. His imagination had placed his cock into 15's puckering butt and his mouth around the delicious cock he was watching having such a nice time. *mmm. this is very nice. it's weird standing up, though.*

Number 7 was conflicted. He wanted to know what that yummy guy that was wandering around with all his clothes on looked like. *why isn't he in the contest? why is he carrying around a pinecone?* what a waste. He could see the guy's hard-on, clear as day... *very nice.* Better than anyone in the circle. *the new 9 is okay, too.* Seven dipped his knees a little as he pumped. It helped him get a rhythm going.

Number 3 didn't like to stand. It made getting good and hard difficult. *they said there were no rules, didn't they?* He sat on his heels. *there... now I don't have to worry about my balance so much... I can shoot just as well on my knees.* He glanced at the others in the circle. He wasn't particularly turned on by any of them. His memory bank was all he needed for this job... he was counting the days until he got back home. Steven was waiting there; he has to work this summer. Steven is all that Number 3 wanted in life right now. Joining this tournament was a way to pass the time.

Freddy could kick himself for overlooking what was going to happen between his legs as he watched this... he was as hard as a rock and he couldn't do a thing about it. Is there a way he could justify whipping it out and letting go? *not a chance.* Besides... with his modest endowment, he might turn off the ones he was planning to... that he was hoping to get friendly with. He adjusted himself as best he could.

Andy had found a very nice set of buns. They were on Number 7. *yes, indeedy. so firm, so well formed. they look like they should be used as a model for one of those statues in the museum... like that one where the person or god was putting an arrow into his bow. these buns are yummy like those. you wanted to go right up there with your tongue and get to work.* He had to fix himself... he wanted to join in right about now. He checked to see if anybody was verging... *nope. that's okay. no hurry; take all the time you need, men! but Tony better be ready for an after game party!*

Craig was as hard as a rock. He had not expected this to be such a turn on. It was embarrassing. He was never comfortable being public about his personal preferences. Freddy is one of the only people clued in to that. It was exciting to see this—he had never imagined anything like it; his fantasy life had been transformed forever. *wow... what would it be like to taste Number 3?* Craig wanted to sit down right next to him. *boy, he looks yummy.*

Tony's hand found its way into his shorts; he was in danger of doing more than making an adjustment. He checked: *yep, wet and slippery... thought so. I could probably sneak one, but it would be stupid. plenty of time after this to jump Andy's bones. we can have a nice quick one before supper!* He removed his hand, and patted himself through the layer of cloth. Sometimes he could actually use good judgment. He never got enough credit for that. *right. well, let's get a Cosell line or two ready for the end of the Great Jackoff Tournament. which one should I interview...*

Number 12 was getting close... would it be smart to go first? He looked at the saucer. He had never tried to hit anything before; he usually did this on his back. It sometimes went pretty high up in the air—one time he had almost got himself in the eye. So he figured the two feet was no big deal. If he could aim right, that is. He started down the stretch. His thighs were hard to manage... *oh, oh!* Shot one went high... *it's inside the ring! missed the saucer though.* Shot two... *oof! short of the ring.* Shot three... *six inches. uh!* He squeezed out the last drop. *well, I was the first. is there a consolation prize?* His shots were all on the paper towel, at least. He sat down on his heels... *that was work. time for a rest.*

Number 6 felt the telltale verge right behind the tip. *this is such a blast, standing up.* He pumped his hand fast—he had gone the whole distance dry. *there's my first drop...* He leaned forward and bent over slightly to maintain his balance. He made sure he was lined up. "Nnnn!" he uttered softly, and shot.

> > *spling!* < <

It hit right in the center! *look at that!* He grinned wide. *how did I do that?* He giggled happily and looked around as he returned to his rapid arm movement. He shot again. It was short, but inside the ring. His third was a sputter, a three-inch arc. He squeezed, but there was no more. He spread his legs apart and relaxed. He appreciated Andy's admiring thumbs up. *who can I tell about this? a perfect shot!*

Number 4 had been watching Number 3 with a mounting degree of hunger. Ever since 3 had sat down, 4 could see his own cock just to the left, and he had synchronized his stroke to match. Watching them move together fed a momentary fantasy, and it brought him down the road to orgasm faster than he planned. He wanted to keep his eyes on that beauteous cock, but he had to look away and aim at that blasted saucer!

Number 9 couldn't stand it any longer: he reached out his left hand and grabbed the right bun of Number 10, who was standing at his left. *oh! yes, that helps.* **"nnnn…"** I'm verging… verging… He shot!

> > *whsst!* < <

It struck just past the center and slid off the far side of the saucer. The second struck soon after.

> > *tinng!* < <

It barely nicked the near side. The third was ten inches out, the fourth two inches. **"hoh!"** He grinned at Number 10. "Thanks." *for the feel and hitting the target.*

Number 10 was thrilled by the sensation of Number 9's hand grabbing his right cheek; he clenched to grab those fingers tight, and did a slow pump. *yes! 9 was staying with him… nearly there…* "whum!" He shot a graceful arc down the paper strip. It was a long stream, very thin, and left a five-inch long deposit that began just at the edge of the ring and ended right at the lip of the saucer. He looked at Nine and smiled. "Ditto."

Freddy made some notations; three of his had finished. The last two included one of his choice ones, thankfully. It was no strain at all to watch **him** finish.

Andy appreciated the quick grab ass that 9 and 10 had enjoyed. He was down to his final contestant; unless he fired super bad, 8 would be his washout—he was the short but thick one, one of the strangest cocks he had ever seen. *ah, there he goes now: Number 7, the one that does the ballet moves with the dipping knees and hot cheeks.*

> > *tlang.* < <

Number 7 made a perfect bull's-eye in the center circle. He made eye contact with Tony, who had been enjoying his performance. Number 7 enjoyed being appreciated—it had helped him make this perfect shot. He dipped his knees and aimed again.

> > *tkt.* < <

It also hit the saucer, but at the rim. He was amazed at his skill and his evident talent. He did a third and final dip. The shot went a respectable 18 inches and landed in the center of the paper strip.

Tony caught Andy's smile and returned it with a swipe of his tongue. They were in clear agreement about this one. He was a thoroughbred, all right. He sent Andy a pucker—code for "as soon as we can."

Craig was sorry for Number 2. He was sort of deformed, and his shots had veered to the right. He hadn't compensated for the way his cock bent, and all but one shot landed off his strip of paper. One of them would have been a bull's-eye for length—if only it had been aimed right. *Number 1 is the last one. he's working real hard... maybe he already got one off today and hasn't built up a charge yet. he's the only one still going in my group. everyone is watching him... poor guy.*

Tony realized this was his moment. He sauntered over to Freddy's circle and held his pinecone up. He spoke softly. **"Well, folks, we have seen history made today. It's all but ovah, and the contestants ah waiting for the judges final repo-at. Some ah starting to shrink afterwahds, as you would expect. Howevah, this repoatah wouldn't be surprised to see an encoah oah two. It looks like moah than one of these very talented boys ah ready to go again, even now."** He stepped over beside Number 12, who was fully erect, sitting on his heels. **"We ah heah with an exclusive inta-vue with Numbah 12."** Tony bent down and put the pinecone up to his face.

Number 12 stood, smiling awkwardly. He was not sure what he was supposed to do, or say. He folded his arms and looked at Tony.

"Can you tell the fans what is was like, being a paht of the fuhst splat contest of this season?" Tony flashed his eyebrows like Groucho, and ran his left hand down 12's nicely shaped right bun.

Freddy's favorite finished at last. He got on his knees and looked closely at a couple of globs. He shook his head… easy to see which one fared the worst. He stood up and looked at 12 sadly. He was glad Tony had him entertained. He stepped over to consult with Andy.

Number 12 blushed and giggled. He recognized the gag voice, and he really enjoyed the sensation of Tony's hand. He decided to play along. "I was the first to fire in my circle." *I'm probably the one who'll get cut.*

Tony was pleased that his hand was welcome. He squeezed gently. **"A sign of great powah and talent,"** Tony winked. **"Is it possible that yoah fans will get to see anothah one fire from that mastahpiece that seems to be pulsing so eagahly?"** Tony tucked his middle finger between 12's cheeks and gave a small poke. It caused his cock to wag automatically.

wow. That felt very nice. Number 12 blushed again. Nobody had ever done that to him. Maybe Tony would keep that up.

Number 1 fired at last, and Craig knelt down to verify what he knew was going to be the result. He stepped over to Freddy and reported that 2 was the loser in his group.

"Okay, guys…" Freddy checked to see that all the contestants were paying attention. "The results are in. First, though, about tomorrow: the circles will be the same, only with four spokes. Gather at the foot of the trail again at the beginning of the afternoon free period. The idea is to look like you're part of the group waiting a turn at the Archery Range. The guys that got eliminated today are welcome to watch. Remember, you can bring one friend, as long as they're sworn to secrecy." He looked around to see if there were any questions. "Remember to take your towel strips, please." He cleared his throat. "Oh: leave the number cards; I'll hand those back tomorrow. Sorry… but 2, 8, and 12 are the first to be eliminated. Good work, everyone. See you tomorrow!"

It was an awkward and abrupt ending. There was uncertainty; a few stooped to roll up their paper towels, and the others followed. They spoke quietly, some in pairs. They weren't in a hurry to go anywhere. There was a half hour before the free period was over. Some, like 12, didn't want to leave just yet.

Number 12 wanted that guy's hand back, for one thing. *shucks... he went over to the guy with the clipboard.* 12 looked around... *is anyone else hard?* Some were going down very slowly, at least.

"Got a place in mind?" Tony asked Andy, who was doing a semi-squat to free up a pinched scrotum.

"No, I don't. Maybe we can just sort of be the last ones to leave, or something." Andy looked at his watch. "There's plenty of time left, if we don't have to hike anywhere." He surveyed the clearing. Why not here?

Tony looked over his shoulder at 12. "What about a 3 way?" It just hit him that 12 was a good prospect.

Andy's eyes opened wide. "Who?"

"Mister Early Bird." Tony pointed over to 12, who had just stood back up with his roll of paper. His mast was up to the max.

"I'm game. He's cute. Yeah! I think a consolation is in order." Andy licked his lips and spoke softly: "You're better at making arrangements like this—proceed at once." He stepped over to Craig and Freddy. "So, do we leave things here, or what?" He gestured to the hoops and saucers.

"Hmm. Good question." Freddy looked around. "Let's stash them in that foliage." No one knew about this place, but it was best to be cautious; he had no way of guaranteeing that all the contestants would keep the place secret or stay away until tomorrow.

Andy glanced at the lingering crowd. "Too bad we don't have a second activity, or something." *a lot of potential is putting their shorts back on... a shame to see them just wander off.* The afternoon seemed sort of unfinished.

Freddy looked at Craig, who blushed. They had just made "arrangements." Their shorts were close to being shed—as soon as this place was clear.

Tony waltzed up to Number 12. "Are you in a hurry to go anyplace?"

Twelve looked up and grinned wide—he was surprised and delighted that he had come back. "Uh... no, I guess not." He could tell that Tony was sort of flirting. It made him blush.

"Yay!" Tony tossed the pinecone to the side. "I'm Tony." He flashed his eyes.

"I'm Mike." He realized suddenly that he was still undressed. *Tony is flirting!* His eyes dropped so that he could verify what he had noticed earlier. *ohboy... a very tantalizing bulge.*

"I'd like you to meet Andy." Tony pointed to Andy, who was helping Freddy and Craig stash the hoops and saucers. "We thought... well, that maybe you'd like to play around a little... you know, until we have to get back to our camps." He looked around. The contestants had begun to depart; some were introducing themselves and getting acquainted as they walked out.

Mike looked over at Andy and gave a positive nod. *how did I luck out like this? these two guys are really hot!* He had a problem, though. He didn't know how to tell Tony that he was not exactly experienced.

Andy looked at Freddy. *he's strangely silent... I'll go for it anyway.* "How secure is this place?"

The tone of voice alerted Freddy. He was afraid his plan was about to be ruined. He looked at Craig, worried.

Andy realized instantly what Freddy was trying to keep secret. "Listen," he said, softly. "There's plenty of space. Tony and I want to have a quickie with that yummy over there. We can go way down to the far end. You two can play right here. I promise not to watch, even." He elbowed Craig.

Craig looked at Andy. He wanted to swap him for Freddy, actually. That nudge was electric.

Freddy hadn't thought of such a thing; he'd never been to an orgy before. Well, this wasn't exactly going to be that, but... he looked at Craig to see what he thought. *he isn't having a panic attack.* "What do you think?"

Craig blushed and shrugged. This was all very scary and exciting. He was afraid to say yes, but he didn't want to say no, either. He nodded his approval. He glanced over to Tony—Number 12 was standing there, stark and hard. *wow. they're really going to!*

"Fab!" Andy hugged them together and smiled. "Just don't whoop too loud, okay?" He winked at them and hustled over to Tony.

Tony and Mike watched him skip over. His grin was infectious.

"We get the far end!" Andy said happily.

"This is Mike. He wants you to remove those things fast; he's been in agony waiting all this time." Tony reached over and gave Andy's shorts a tug.

Mike's jaw dropped and he blushed.

"Hi, Mike. I'm Andy." He reached over and shook Mike's cock, as if it were extended for a handshake. He looked at Tony. "So round, so firm…"

"So fully packed!" Tony finished the refrain. They all broke up laughing.

"Let me grab my stuff! You guys pick the spot." Mike ran over and grabbed his shirt and shorts. *this is going to be fun as well as hot!*

"Flip you for bottom."

Andy pondered. He remembered the time in the Forestry clearing with Tom, and Tony's mouth. *I had to pull it out before finishing…* He wanted the whole thing, which he had not gotten around to yet. "How about you be the front door, and let me back on the way you did? That way you and Mike can do a double!"

Tony looked at Mike as he ran back with his clothes. "I like it. Besides, he is so deserving." *and, he's about seven and a half inches.* He put one arm behind Mike's butt and the other behind Andy's, and headed them to the east end of the clearing. He felt the tube in Andy's pocket. *Andy is such a good boy scout.*

—⌇—

29   *Geoff goes exploring*

Geoff sat down to rest. He needed to get his bearings again. He didn't want to stray off south the way he had this morning. This time he had the compass old Sarge lent him, along with the map they used with

From Hawk Camp to Barr's Meadow

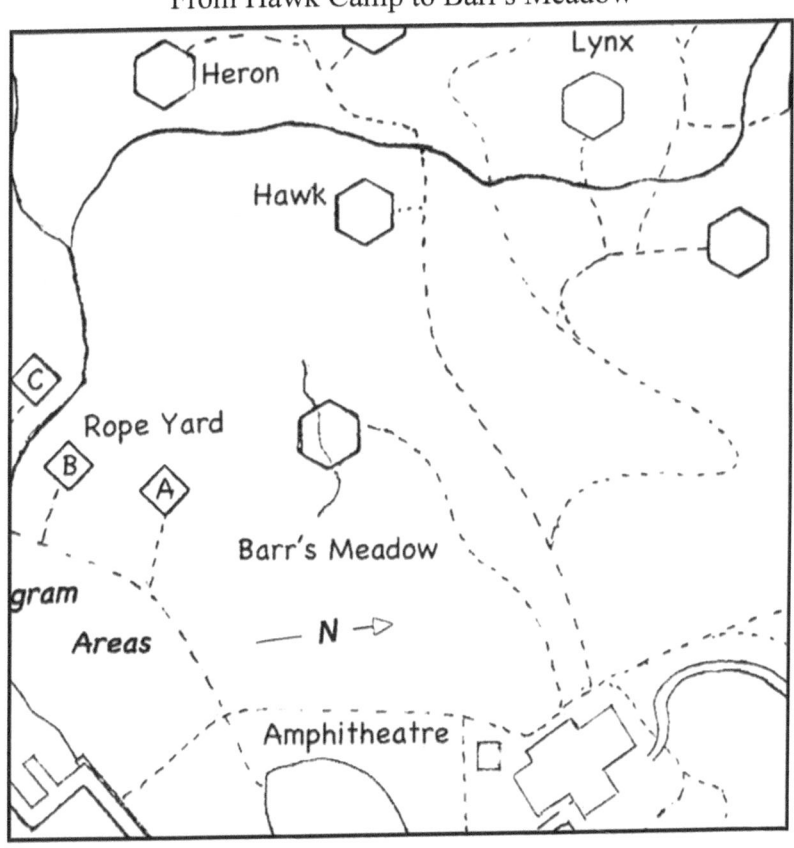

the supply cart. He just knew finding a back trail to Barr's Meadow was possible. Too many places looked like a trail had been there... too many to be an accident. However... it had been so long since he had used a compass.

these woods are very different from the Sierras... half or more are broadleaf trees... the undergrowth is completely different. I haven't seen a single paintbrush or poppy or purple lupin, either. maybe it's too humid here for those. underbrush is hardy... abrasive against bare legs. It reminded him of the coastal brush along the Pacific. He didn't want to snag his long socks, so he had put on his short gym socks. *what I need is a pair of jeans.* Luckily, there was more open ground than not; a lot of grass tufts and sandy soil, too. It isn't jagged and volcanic—the geology is unfamiliar. *real easy to head in the wrong direction and get confused.*

The lunch had cinched it for Geoff; no less than **three** Troop 9 scouts had stepped up and spoken to the guest speaker—what about was anybody's guess. But it seemed to give their scoutmaster a charge, because it made him fan his legs unconsciously. He was thrilled by whatever it was his scouts were saying. That, after a fabulous open leg slouch, had Geoff nearly going crazy. He could hug his own scoutmaster for sitting down where he had—it forced this Apollo to shift in his chair just right. The entire banquet was a voyeur's joy.

Then, miracle of miracles, the scoutmaster came over to the table to talk to Tom! He had to stay for some kind of meeting, and he was giving Tom last minute orders about how to lead the troop out without him. Geoff was nearly in a trance—he didn't pay much attention to what they said because he couldn't get his eyes off that basket! It was so tantalizing! The short pant legs flared out just enough at the bottom to enhance the contour of the thigh. It was probably lucky that he wasn't sitting at the end of the table... his hand would have explored.

Geoff shook his head. He needed to get back on task. He looked at the odd slope just ahead. *yes: I remember now... this morning I went to the right because it seemed like that's where the trail, or former trail, went.* He might have just discovered his mistake. Going to the left seemed awkward and pinched, but it would go more toward that cabin. *there must have been a slide along here... I need to veer more to the east. with any luck, I'll pick up the old trail again farther down... better leave a marker so that I can be sure to head back the same way.* He dug a direction arrow in the slope with his boot sole… hopefully that would do it. His watch said he had forty minutes left… *it's my turn to cook tonight, too. blast.*

30   *after the first round*

"I hafta stop a sec, okay?" Craig put his hands on Freddy's shoulder to signal a stop. He was about to shoot, and he didn't want to yet. He wanted to delay it mainly because what he was watching was so hot.

"Sure…" *what's the matter? am I doing it wrong?* He looked up at Craig.

"I was real close… I didn't know if you wanted me to shoot into your mouth, or not." He glanced back at the spectacle across the clearing. *wow is that hot… I sure wish we could watch up close.*

Freddy turned around to see what Craig was looking at. His jaw dropped. He looked at Craig. *wow.* He was about to say he wanted to take it in the mouth… *but this is something else!*

Craig whispered, "Is there any way we could watch closer up?" Craig had never seen anybody fuck before—or get fucked. He had never considered it a possibility, even.

Freddy agreed completely with the sentiment. He always wanted to try this, but never had the chance. "I don't know." He heard Andy moan with pleasure. He looked at Craig. "Let's crawl over slow and quiet. I don't think they'll mind, as long as we don't make any noise." He looked for agreement.

Craig nodded. They pulled their pants up enough to gain mobility, and crawled as fast as they dared, as quietly as they could.

Mike was in a glorious state of ecstasy. This was his first ever time to fuck anyone. That it would be the super hot Tony was a miracle! Not only that, he got to watch Andy back up and put his cock into Tony's mouth at the same time—*Tony's getting it at both ends! boy, am I ever glad these guys showed me how to do this...*

He wanted to suck some more, but it was impossible to suck and fuck at the same time... physically impossible. So he had to alternate. *if only I could be sucking when I shoot. no way, unless I pull out and jack off at the finish... don't want to do that.* He wasn't sure what he was going to do when the time came... *should I go first, or let Tony? mmm! it's so hot when Tony pushes his hips up like that! it means he wants me to suck some more...* He licked his lips and bent down again...

Andy was getting close. If there was one thing Tony did well, it was use that tongue! He slowed his pumping deliberately. He wanted to extend a little, and he needed to signal Tony that the end was near. They hadn't planned a precise sequence. Once Mike was shown what to do and had gotten underway, they had just started going at it. They were so horny that they hadn't stopped. He massaged Tony's ears, he fondled his hair... he just decided: *I'll come first, then pull out and kiss Tony until he comes.* He wasn't too sure what Mike was doing, but it set a good rhythm. They had been using it as the base.

Tony preferred the fucking to the sucking—but he wanted Mike well versed in both. *you never know when you might want to party... when Mike focuses on his fucking again I'll use my hand.* He could tell Andy was just about ready—he'd been tasting pre-cum for a while now. He squeezed his lips to signal that he was ready for Andy to fire at will. He reached up and held Andy's buns. He was getting close himself. If Mike would stop sucking... *there! I can delay, now, until Andy starts...* He squeezed Andy's buns.

Freddy and Craig were agape, only four feet away, laying flat on their stomachs; they didn't want to be noticed. The sounds! The spectacle amazed and delighted. It was obvious that these three were having a fabulous time. It was so gymnastic!

Andy moaned softly and pulled back. He held a second, then drove in, firmly, clenching his buns tight. Tony had brought his right forefinger around and inserted it—perfect timing. Andy's sphincter grabbed as he shot into Tony's mouth. "Uhhmm." He hummed deeply, tossing his head back. He did four more of these deliberately slow pumps... *Tony knows just what to do. oh! ...exquisite.*

Craig and Freddy looked at each other, mouths open wide in amazement—then watched again.

When he opened his eyes, Mike realized that Andy was coming. The view of his clenched straining buns was incredible. He slowed pumping to watch. Tony's hands were very instructive again... he massaged and poked in time with Andy's thrusts.

Andy pulled out of Tony's mouth and scooted back so that he could kiss. He pressed himself hard against Tony's torso and they worked their mouths and tongues. They did a humming duet; mellow, yet intense.

Mike sensed that he needed to move again—*wow!* Tony began to tighten himself—Mike's thrusts were forced to get stronger and deeper. He could tell he was hitting that spot inside because of the way Tony jerked. Getting very close now... he sensed he was supposed to go all the way. He joined the humming. His chest bumped against Andy's butt as he drove.

Tony reached around Andy's back and pulled him down tighter to increase the pressure on his slippery pumping. Andy's legs ran flat along Mike's calves.

Tony alternated his pumps with Mike's thrusts, and let the friction against Andy's chest be his release channel. He shot his first while pulling back—this greased his run for the next four. He could feel Mike filling him at the same time.

Mike had never felt anything as intense as this. Tony's insides grabbed at him and almost sucked the cum out. "Mmm-mm." Five thrusts, five shots. That was all he had. Tony had stopped too.

The three held their places a moment. Andy pushed up and smiled. "Very nice." He gave Tony a small kiss and swung around and sat on his heels, his eyes closed. He wanted to rest a second before letting the real world back in.

Mike looked down briefly at his cock, still inside Tony. He wanted to remember this picture. He pulled it out, slowly. He was still hard.

Tony was satisfied. It was nice to have a good student. This one had proven himself. *I'll have to plan a second lesson. Mike needs to know the other side of this—a two way would be best. mmm... the afterbuzz is excellent this time.* He heard a faint sound and glanced to his left.

A few seconds later, Andy and Mike opened their eyes. They glanced at Tony at about the same time; he was smiling strangely. They followed his gaze and saw the amazed faces of Freddy and Craig. They broke up, rolling on their backs.

Craig turned very red. He felt like he had been caught stealing or something. He went limp suddenly—his balls were aching. He studied the ground under his nose.

Freddy snickered. "Well, what do you expect!" he protested self-righteously. *boy, do I need to finish up.* He sat up and looked over at Craig. He poked him softly... he should sit up, at least.

Tony looked over at them again. He saw Freddy's hard one poking out. "You didn't shoot yet?"

Both Craig and Freddy shook their heads.

Tony looked at Andy. Instantly, they knew the solution to the problem they had caused—they had a responsibility! They crawled over on their knees at once. Tony went down on Freddy where he sat. *Mister Minimus! smallish, but tasty enough.*

Andy took Craig's left arm, and, as if he were rescuing him in the lake, pulled him over onto his back. He spread the fly open and drew the limp cock into his mouth. It revived in seconds. *yum!*

Mike watched in wonder. *these guys!*

Tony reached up and pressed Freddy's chest... he wanted him on his back. Freddy figured it out. It was awkward, but he managed to get his legs around in front. Tony pushed again, and as Freddy flattened, Tony tugged his shorts down... *gotta play with the balls too.*

Freddy had never been in such a whirlwind! *I'm getting close, too.* He didn't see how he could draw this out. He felt Tony's finger exploring underneath his balls. *ooo!* He shot. That finger made him fire even harder! That was the quickest and best shot he had ever had.

Andy pulled down Craig's foreskin and bathed the back of his cock with his pressing tongue. As he crossed the head, Craig bucked reflexively. Andy did that a second time, and Craig fired. "Ah!" He had three big shots. He had instinctively put his hands on Andy's back, and he caressed the shoulder blades as he gently tossed his head from side to side. *this is incredible... unique...* the best ever shot in his life.

Almost to the second, Tony and Andy sat back. Tony turned and beckoned the amazed Mike to scoot over between them. "Cluster hug!"

The five stood awkwardly and hugged. Tony and Andy grabbed cheeks on each side and squeezed. Everyone was half hard.

Tony broke the trance. "Thanks for the dessert," he winked at Freddy.

Andy giggled. He reached over and squeezed Craig. "Me too."

The group broke apart, laughing. Craig and Freddy looked at each other, nervously. The afternoon had gone differently than either one had expected. They needed to have a talk.

Tony wagged his butt on his way over to dress. He was surprised a little; Mike was a good deal smaller than Tom, but he felt satisfied. *hmm. maybe I should figure a way for this Shooting Gallery program to have a second part every time...* Seeing all those yummies leave earlier didn't strike him as a good way to finish the party at all. Several might just be a real good time. Nothing against Mike, of course, but why not sample another one tomorrow? *it's Freddy's show, but he probably won't mind.* Tony consulted his watch. *oh-oh.* "Guys... I have to be cook in my patrol in less than thirty minutes. Gotta run!"

Andy had finished dressing; he tapped Mike on the arm. "Thanks. Sorry you were eliminated, by the way." He took off after Tony. *food sounds like just the thing.*

Mike had forgotten about the fact that he'd washed out on the first round of the Shooting Gallery. Well, he'd won a terrific consolation prize! Maybe he'd see these guys around. *boy am I hungry. the hike up to Shawnee Camp will double my appetite.*

Freddy watched the Troop Nine duo skip up past the clump of mountain ash and out of sight. "See ya tomorrow," he called after them. He shook his head. He had no idea what he was getting when he recruited Andy to help out. *man.*

31   *without permission*

It was quieter than usual tonight in the meadow; Robin could only hear three crickets. He hadn't paid that much attention to them before now. There used to be a lot more. *yeah—some nights it sounded like hundreds were out there. not tonight.* But waiting for Jason to fall asleep took longer than he had planned. Isolating the crickets had been the perfect task to help him stay awake. Maybe if the breeze were from the southwest more of their sounds would carry this way. *they all seem to be between here and the Panther Camp tonight. do crickets take the night off sometimes?*

The time had come. This was the wildest thing he had ever *thought* about doing; incredibly, he was about to go through with it. He lifted his head slowly and gazed over at Jason's cot. *outstanding! his back is turned. must be trying to avoid the light.* The nearly full moon cast a bright swath across that side of the tent. *good.* Robin flipped back his blanket.

He sat up carefully, pivoted and stood. Everything was ready. He was able to prepare his pack after the campfire while everyone was racing down to the latrine. Luck prevailed there, too. He'd just finished tucking his pack under the cot when the guys started to return. It seemed like forever, waiting for the lights out call. He'd crawled under his cover blanket without undressing. Jason hadn't noticed anything. He wasn't chatty last night either, which helped. *Jason is a good tent partner—I lucked out there. last summer I had to put up with Paul. no thanks.*

He sat on the ground and put on his sneakers. He wouldn't need boots. Carefully, he pulled the pack out from under his cot. He rotated onto his knees and arranged the blanket to look like he'd be right back from a trip downhill. Jason wouldn't wake up anyway, probably, *but it's best to play it safe.*   He put the pack on. His sleeping bag and a towel was all it contained. *Jack's bringing everything else.*

He was ready... he stood. *now then... are the rest of the Lynx asleep? no reason to think otherwise, but with the moon this bright I'll be spotted at once.* He didn't have a watch, but his sense of time was pretty reliable. *I'll risk it. luckily my tent is closest to the trail... I'll be out of sight in seconds.* He stepped out into the moonlight. He glanced up—*it's full all right, or almost.*

brrr... chilly tonight. surprising. too bad all I have is short pants. once my blood gets circulating I'll be fine... there's the junction. He turned east and headed down toward the latrine. *no one will see me now. unless they're up to something.   not likely—even Tony wouldn't do anything as crazy as this.*

He was tempted to cut across the bottom of the meadow and take the shortcut below the Tiger camp. *I'd get there in half the time, but the risk is too great.* He'd be exposed for a fair distance, and someone from either the Panther or Tiger camp could spot him very easily. *even on the regular trail I'll get there before Jack anyway. Jack has twice the distance to cover.   oh—I forgot my flashlight.   will we need one? probably not, with this moon.   maybe Jack will bring his.*

Robin crossed in front of the latrine booths and headed for the main trail. The Barr's Meadow trail was practically a freeway, as trails go. *so far, so good. I'll be at the amphitheater in fifteen minutes—twenty, tops.*

An owl hooted. *second one tonight.   maybe it's an all-clear signal or something.   I'd like to think that the owls are on my side.* Jack sat up slowly and glanced at the cot on the other side of the tent. Conrad's shoulder moved slightly in a regular rhythm. *excellent: sound asleep. with any luck, everyone else in Eagle camp is in dreamland too.* He glanced at his watch: ten thirty. *boy.   a little risky, this early.*

go for it, Jack.   you have a major challenge ahead.   a few minutes early will be very helpful.   take a lesson from Geoff—press forward like it's an assignment from the scoutmaster.   Geoff always gets away with things just because he barges in like he's in charge. confidence, that's what it is. self-confidence. okay: he swung his right leg out of his sleeping bag with determination.

> > *whack!* < <

ow!   Instant sharp pain—he had just banged his toe on the footlocker.   *damn...* not hollering out loud took all his strength—it smarted something awful. He froze in place... *is Conrad still asleep?* He didn't turn over to look, or anything... *must be all right. swing over the other leg, Jack. be careful this time. cripes. after a week here you'd think you'd be able to get out of bed without raising the dead.* He sat on the edge of the cot and felt his toe carefully—no blood.

He opened the footlocker and pulled out a pair of socks. All he had to do was get dressed. Carefully he slid a sock over his right foot... *man, does that sting. feels like I smashed it with a hammer.* He shook his head, disgusted with himself. *at least my pack is ready to go.* He'd been able to get that squared away earlier, after supper. He had his canteen, a towel, flashlight, first aid kit, four candy bars—oh, and a small Kleenex pak. He slipped on his scout shorts and stood. He zipped up quietly and tightened his belt. *all ready now.*

what else will we need? He thought for a sec. *nothing. after all, I'll be back by sunup. oh—pillow. Robin's bringing his sleeping bag.* He lifted the flap and tucked his pillow down into the pack. *hmm... better put this on after I'm outside. no more banging things, please.* He stepped out of the tent. He looked to his right. All the other tents were in that direction, fortunately. He and Conrad had been assigned the two-man at the lower end. Only four other tents were line of sight visible. *the trees are my allies tonight.*

Jack watched his feet as he stepped toward the trail. The ground was uneven enough to cause trouble. His toe was still complaining. *the moon is a big help, but it's deceptive. the trail is dappled more than lit.* The broadleaf canopy fractured the light into bright spots and dark shadows... *interesting patterns.* He stopped for a moment to put the pack on—he was well away from camp now. *wait—just had a thought.* He took the pack off again and fished down for the flashlight. Smart to have that in hand in case any part of the trail was too hard to make out.

Amazing how different this looked at night. *good thing I know the trail... it's uneven and a little rocky until the creek crossing.* He clicked on the flashlight. Good idea: it spoiled the nifty patterns of light and dark, *but the trail bumps show up nice and clear. it pays to be careful— I have zero hours of night hiking experience.*

Jack was having second thoughts about Conrad... *hmm. maybe I should have told him what I was going to do. if he should wake up and discover the empty cot... what will he do? it isn't likely... or is it? I have no idea if he ever wakes up in the night or not. hmm. well, Conrad is pretty savvy about things. it's not as if he's tender and innocent. after all, he was in one of Brian's poker games last winter. but he doesn't know about Robin—no one knows about Robin.* He was not ready to let that be known; it was too powerful, too important.

here comes the creek. this bridge is sure deluxe. it's wide enough for the supply and maintenance vehicles. this camp isn't really very primitive. With hundreds of Tenderfoot scouts around, it made sense. The tough trail stuff was reserved for the merit badge crowd. *at least these trails aren't paved; you can pretend you're out in the wild.*

>> *whump... whump-***crack!** <<

The sudden sound was loud, violent.

"Wha—" Jack froze, scared stiff.

> > *whump...* **crack***—swish...* **crack!** *whump... whump... whump* <<

what's that?! He aimed his flashlight over to the right, down the slope. The sound receded down the hill. *whoa.* His heart was beating a mile a minute... his legs were shaking. He had frightened off some sort of animal. *must have been a deer. sure was loud enough... cleared away a few branches just now, whatever it was.*

He took a deep breath and continued on. *are there any bears around? hmm. I don't know what there is around here, actually. big cats? no one gave us any kind of warning about that... it must be safe enough. turkeys, squirrels, owls, cardinals... I've seen or heard those. and deer, now. that has to be what it was. wow.* At least he didn't get a pair of eyes reflected back when he passed the flashlight beam down there. *man alive—what if there had been a pair staring back? I don't want to think about that one much...* Jack's bravery was somewhat skin deep. Warding off nocturnal beasts wasn't a part of his training. He was an Eagle, but a city Eagle. *in Atlanta, the big animals are strictly zoo residents.*

Mr. Simmons told us once on a hike that the dangerous predators were the ones you didn't hear. most of them were more afraid of man than the other way around. he said they heard or smelled man coming and got out of the way, usually. still, you had to be careful, if they were super hungry. hmm... maybe I should make a little noise or something, scare them off in advance as I go along.

"Ahem..." he cleared his throat... did a cough. "Coming through..." *oh... maybe talking or whistling isn't a very good idea— somebody might hear. how far does sound carry in the woods? I am off limits, after all. the woods belong to the critters at night.*

The trail was too soft—walking didn't make any racket. *it's wide and clear from here on. the moon is brighter along this stretch; I'll keep the flashlight going anyway—wave it around some. The batteries rattle a little... that might help. I'll be there soon. maybe I should pick up the pace.*

Robin was comfy, all things considered. His pack made a good seatback. At first he waited by the fire pit, but the charcoal smell wasn't very pleasant. Now, against the cottonwood tree he felt a little more secure and less out in the open. *no breeze here, so the night chill isn't a problem.* He'd been here a while—Jack should appear any minute. He could see partway up the trail by the HQ building. *speak of the devil!* A flashlight was just now visible, blinking as it moved down the trail. Robin stood up and stretched. *I am so looking forward to this!*

After he passed by the HQ building, Jack checked his watch again: *eleven thirty. not bad. not bad at all.* Soon he crested the west side of the amphitheater—he spotted Robin at once. What a thrill—he was walking slowly across the arena below. Jack felt a rush. This was like a movie scene—Robin and his moonshadow. He paused; he had to indulge himself... this was a mental snapshot to savor. *I'll want to remember this. tonight is an incredibly good idea.*

Robin had expected Jack to be here by now—he looked up. *hah. must be ESP or something... there he is. why is he just standing there?* Robin turned to face him and did a bow, arms extended outward.

Jack applauded at once. *this is perfect.* A fresh ripple of goose bumps raced down his back.

Robin stood tall, and transformed his open arms into an open gesture, inviting Jack to join him. *I'll hold them open until Jack steps into place. watching him approach... wow. right out of some movie.*

Jack peeled off his backpack on the way down the slope. He dropped it off just in time to embrace Robin and deliver a tender kiss.

"Why the flashlight? It's as bright as day almost." Robin focused on Jack's forehead. Its texture in the moonlight looked velvety.

"I had to scare off the wild animals along the way. Forgot to turn it off." Jack ran his right forefinger along Robin's upper lip. The fine hairs were like silk. *some day this will be a moustache.* He was in no hurry for that.

They weren't in the mood for a wild love scene just yet. They'd had a good time earlier today and weren't in any great need. They just had to be together, that's all.

"You want to stay here a while?"

Robin looked up at the amphitheater. "Seems a little public." Even empty, it looked too on display.

Jack looked up as well. "You're right... don't need to draw a crowd."

Robin turned and stepped back to the tree. He hoisted his pack onto his left shoulder. Jack snapped off the flashlight and tucked into the pack. He hoisted it up to his right shoulder and joined Robin. They headed down to the dock.

"What do you know! Leonard doesn't lock this." Robin opened the gate. "I thought we'd have to climb over."

"Leonard is a sweetheart." Jack had a gut feeling that Leonard would approve highly of this visit. He was tempted to leave a note. He followed Robin out to their favorite boat.

Robin kneeled on the dock and put his pack behind the bow bench of boat number five; he held his hand out.

Jack handed his pack over. "Let's not go just yet." He had a sudden urge. He took Robin by his right hand and led him out to the end of the dock. He gazed at the expansive lake, and the moon and the stars. It was perfect.

Robin tugged gently; they sat cross-legged. The dock was too close to the water surface to allow them to hang their legs off the edge. Soaked shoes wouldn't be much fun. They scooted back and leaned against the canoe rack, just under the lifesaver ring.

The breeze was so faint it was almost not there—the lake was like a giant mirror. They had to stay right here for a while. This had to be absorbed. They might never have this experience again. They squeezed their hands together gently once in a while… that was better than any words. There was no hurry. They had until dawn. Their heads leaned together. They'd row over to their private clearing in a minute or two. This was a perfect world right now.

Coming Next:

Thunder and Lightning:

Julian's Private Scrapbook, Book 4

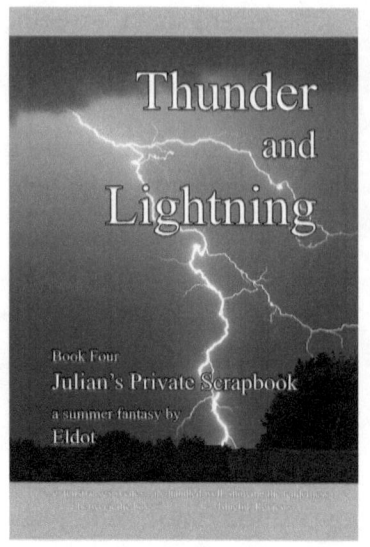

The ninth day at Camp Walker begins just after midnight. We are still at the lake. **Robin** and **Jack** complete their adventure, though not without a surprise. They are able to make it back to their camps undetected, but only just. They drift into the background while the focus returns to Geoff.

Geoff continues his quest to seduce scoutmaster **Mark**; will he succeed, or settle for his pursuit of Leonard? Will Danny's plans for Julian proceed smoothly? Will Tom and Nick's Love Palace remain undiscovered? Will **Freddy** and **Andy's** "tournament" be a success? And will **Kurt** remain satisfied with Sid? Will Julian remain focused and patient in his personal goal to gain Mark's affection? Does he suspect what Geoff is plotting? Mark continues to flourish, but is uneasy about his relationship with the other scoutmasters. He seeks to improve that, unaware of the other forces lining up against him.

The second fun filled week at camp continues with surprises, challenges, successes and a few disappointments. There are romances, and there are lots of extra-curricular activities. **Tony** in particular has a good time.

The weather springs a surprise on Wednesday, and an accident at the lake brings unexpected opportunities. Camp approaches its final days—an unwelcome prospect for some, a relief for others.

a word from Eldot about the style...

For readers new to the Julian series, here's a heads up about an unusual device employed in the revised version. The goal is to maximize the reader's ability to get inside the characters while retaining the advantage of being an observer outside.

Standard narrative practice is to place the reader either inside or out, not both: inside means using the **first person,** seeing only what the character sees—usually a single character. Outside means using the **third person** point of view, seeing the character and the world of the story from outside, akin to watching a film.

The original version employed an experimental style that intermingled first and third person usage; getting an inside-the-character perspective while retaining the advantages of seeing the character from other perspectives was the plan. The device was not a complete success—it was awkward in places and to some readers, somewhat annoying.

The revision has dealt with that problem directly by employing visual clues instead. All first person point of view elements are in *italics*. No other use of italics is permitted. If italics would usually be employed to express emphasis or stress, **boldface** is used instead.

Here's a sample quoted from chapter 7:

> "Let's head in. I want to get caught up on the newsletter." They had a little more than half an hour left, which should be just about right. Nick had been going over things in his mind; he had it figured out, pretty much. *if only I had a little more confidence.*
>
> Julian felt really good today. Nick's help had made a huge difference. *boy, having a real watch is something: a second is a long time! I'm tired...* It was a happy tired. He went to his cubbyhole while Nick returned the stopwatch to Leonard. *boy am I lucky to know Nick... I*

have a new sketch to show him. will he like it? it's a little different. he'll probly guess what it is real quick. Julian wrapped his towel around his neck and took his Buddy Badge off the swim hook. He stepped over to Leonard's desk to wait.

"Do you have to sit there all day?" Leonard must get pretty bored.

"It must seem that way. Only during the free swimming periods." Leonard looked at Julian fondly. *what a gem. they'll be chasing after this one soon.* "Thanks for asking." He noticed the sketch tablet. "Can I peek at your work?"

"Sure!" Julian was delighted that Leonard was interested. He handed the sketch tablet over. *I like Leonard's face. hmm. yes...* he formed a picture in his mind... *I'd like to draw that face... distinctive nose; lips sharply defined.*

"My, Julian..." Leonard was impressed. "What are these for, may I ask?"

"The Troop 9 Scrapbook, mostly. Maybe the newsletter, I'm not too sure yet about that... if Nick wants to use any." Leonard's positive reaction gave him a nice feeling. He was the first person to see these.

Nick dried himself off systematically, but roughly... he was eager to get going. The wild morning with Geoff was threatening to intrude into his thoughts again... that he did not need. He had to get this matter of Julian's cooperation taken care of. He wouldn't get a better shot at it than now. He had been trying all afternoon to figure out how to get started. *how much information can Julian handle? he's barely into puberty, to look at him. here goes; I'll figure something out on the way.*

"What do you think of my Assistant Scribe's work?" He patted Julian's shoulder.

Leonard looked up. "I have to say I've never seen its equal." Leonard closed the tablet and handed it back. "I hope you'll let me look at these again, Julian. I'm quite impressed."

Julian blushed. "Sure." *maybe next free swim. hmm. that way I can figure a way to put Leonard in one, too. narrow wrists, elongated. interesting.*

"See you later." Nick held the gate open. "We're off to an editorial meeting."

Julian followed Nick out and turned to look at Leonard with a smile; he waved as he hung his badge on the inactive Buddy Board. He did a skip and trotted on ahead. Leonard had given him quite a boost.

Leonard watched them walk up the trail... moments like this made his job the best in the world.

The third person-first person mix is easy to see; the goal is to enhance the reader's engagement with characters.

This technique has been utilized in varying degrees. In many places it is not used at all, in others it is extensive. Generally, the goal has been to get the reader into the character's perception while keeping the ability to see things the character doesn't. So when you run across this phenomenon, you'll know what's going on—I hope it makes the experience of Julian's Private Scrapbook even more fun.

Preface to the first edition, abridged

The most magical time in a boy's life is when he discovers who he is sexually. It can be scary, threatening, and it can be fun and exciting; it can be a mix of these things. At the end of the process, he is forever changed physically and psychologically. This story looks at that process in a way that is unusual, and perhaps unique. It is not a typical coming of age story, though that is central to the work.

Julian's Private Scrapbook makes an unusual underlying assumption. It departs from "accepted" mores of contemporary American society in a central way: it posits a society that is accepting and non-judgmental. Right and wrong still exist—but the puritan ethic and moral code are dispensed with, *as the norm.* Moralizers of the puritan sort remain—they are an archetype, after all. They may be problematic, but *they* are the aberration in this society. Sexual issues are no longer taboo. They are still complex, private, mysterious, and very special—but they are out from under the mindless repression we know so well.

Therefore, an individual is not faced with the "coming out" drama that preoccupies so much of our society; rather, he is faced with the process of "coming into." That, as the reader will see, is still a full time challenge.

The time selected to play in is the early 1960's, before the technical gadget revolution. The relative naiveté and general optimism of those years is a comfortable fit for the subject, and not so remote in time that it is unfamiliar—nor would the world of Camp Walker be preposterously utopian.

The story is meant to entertain, not preach or argue the underlying social issues. Nonetheless, the subject is sufficiently complex to make demands. Standard modern novel criteria cannot accommodate the matter satisfactorily and fully—space sufficient to remain honest to the material is not available. The solution has been to craft the story into a form that can satisfy both the contemporary rules of length, and the expectations of the subject: it is presented in a series of novels. They progress chronologically and grow in complexity. Each is a complete segment, but the combination as a whole is greater than the parts, allowing the subject to be fully addressed. So this is a hybrid of sorts in structure, somewhere between a Dickens doorstop tome and a modern adventure series.

Readers of these books will be subjected to humor, titillation, and naughty behavior. Any two-week stay at a boy scout camp would have to have that as a minimum. You should expect to have a good time and feel elevated as a human being. This is, above all, a celebration of who we are. You will have to do your own lesson drawing and moralizing, however. And be warned: if you are a puritan at heart, you will not be pleased.

The first novel was introductory, as one would expect. We witnessed the sudden flowering of two very different romances. Julian, the talented young artist, was engaged in a quest to land his dream love, Mark the scoutmaster. How and why this love story began is the basis and core of all the books in this series. As a counterbalance, another story runs parallel. Nick, the assistant to the Assistant, succeeded in his plan to turn the tables on Tom, long his object of devotion. Tom's complacency was shattered, and he is faced with the task of discovering what has happened and who he is.

The second novel took us through the fifth day of the two week camp. We witnessed the growth and progress of the two stories and discovered a good deal about several of the other players, especially the exotic Geoff.

The third novel completes the first week and takes our characters to a new level of development and prepares them for the second week. A new story emerges at the very end, daring and intense. It leaves us anticipating the outcome in the next segment.

Special Edition note

The pedantic urge to amplify this topic for the 2024 Special Edition was strong, but not sufficient to appear at the front of the book: the Preface is always best kept bare bones brief. But, for those interested in the rationale behind telling Julian's story, a few additional words may be of interest.

Before now, Society rarely allowed itself to look *through the eyes* of the adolescent at the needs and drives they feel. That perspective was outsourced to the clinical psychologists; society generally preferred to avoid dealing with it directly—simply wait it out and hope for the best. It's usually dealt with by phrases like "You'll grow out of this..." or "Take my word for it; one day you'll understand..." or "This is for your own good..."

Nothing is more annoying than being patronized. It is a form of cowardice; the personal offense it gives often neutralizes the good intent. The recipient, regardless of age, is ill served—and they realize that at some point. The unaddressed problem does not go away; for some it festered into something more difficult or impossible to manage.

Instead, too often the story that gets told is one of exploitation or perversion—the adolescent's needs are bypassed entirely. Often it is distorted into a morality story that seeks to manipulate society rather than help it become whole—or it's profiteering: manipulating sensational material to generate sales. Sometimes a memoir deals with the subject honestly; those can be tender and sympathetic. Perhaps that is because Memoirs are fact based, and not written to please those that feed on prurient material.

What lies *behind* the latest story of teen suicide? That question is never addressed—it too is largely a taboo area. Campaigns to deal with bullying are helpful—but are usually after the fact. They too sidestep the core issue of the Julian series: why has this youth fallen in love with the "wrong" person? That question is not allowed. How then, is it addressed? It never is—it gets sidestepped. Instead, the youth's object of affection is condemned outright without trial or chance to offer a defense. The pointed finger of blind prejudice controls the narrative.

Often the accused has done nothing at all; some have been falsely accused to save face. They are presumed guilty because they surely will be eventually. The doctrine of original sin has been applied sanctimoniously once again, without regulation or supervision. How they could have dealt with the situation is never seriously considered.

That is the challenge the Julian books dare to take on.

Synopsis of Books 1 and 2

This is a summary of the first six days of a two week stay at Camp Walker, its major characters and events. The order is largely as it was presented, though some summarizing and analysis is provided. The purpose is to provide a concise review for readers seeking background information about the characters and events of Book 3. Entries in the index and glossary provide additional information.

Book 1: Barr's Meadow

Germination

It is early June, 1960. In a small town in central North Carolina, Julian Forrest has just turned thirteen years old. He and his mother, single parent Francine Forrest, are formerly of Joliet, Illinois. Julian has just finished his first year of junior high school. Adolescence has taken him by storm, and he is in a hurry to grow up. His main focus has been Cub Scouts, and he has completed all the levels offered by the organization. His dream now is to become a boy scout.

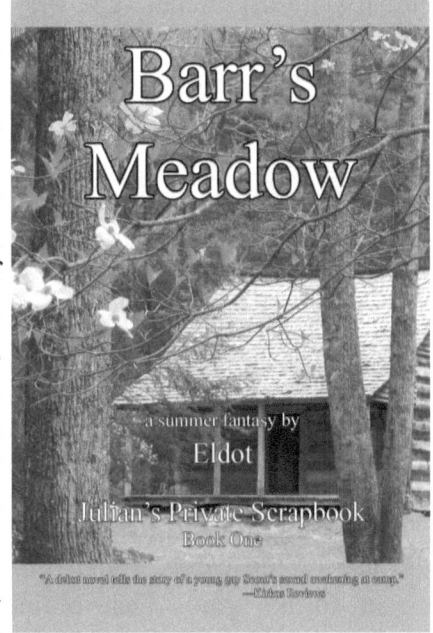

Their neighbor, **Mark** Schaefer is a manager in a locally owned department store. His wife of three years is a nurse who is studying to become a physician. Mark is scoutmaster of the Boy Scout troop sponsored by the same church that sponsors Julian's Cub Scout pack. He invites Julian to join Troop 9. This is a dream come true for Julian, who has long had a fixation on Mark.

Sunday, First Day

Julian has been in the Boy Scout troop for nearly two years. He has moved up in rank rapidly. He was recently promoted from Second to First Class, just in time for the annual summer camp. His new Troop 9 scrapbook has made him known in the troop. **Mark** has given him leadership opportunities, and he has handled them well.

The first day of summer camp begins with a long bus trip west. The drive provides a glimpse of what is to come in the next two weeks. The troop hikes to the camp and the scouts get set up in their tents at Barr's Meadow, the prize campsite. The first day is given to orientation and registration activity.

Several other scouts in the troop are introduced. Many will be important in the events of the next two weeks. **Sid** Thomas and **Jeremy** Baker are Julian's closest friends, and they are in his patrol. They moved up from the same Cub Scout pack. **Tom** Dawson, **Danny** Laskey and **Nick** Harrison are members of the Flaming Arrow, the exclusive troop leadership patrol.

The primary event takes place at the end of the day: the start of Julian's mentorship with Mark. Mark makes the decision to invite him to stay in the cabin, primarily as a shelter from extracurricular activity. Mark is astounded by the extent of Julian's naïveté. His is relieved to discover that his fears about Julian's predatory inclination were overblown. Julian is smart enough to proceed with his plan very cautiously.

Mark had planned for some time to promote Julian as an assistant to the troop scribe. He moves the timeline up, and Julian is transferred to the leadership patrol the first night. Mark lays down strict guidelines about the use of the cabin. Julian thinks Mark has inadvertently moved him closer to his goal. That remains to be seen. Julian is practiced at dissembling about his true feelings, and he has no ego need to boast or brag. His closest friends do not suspect and will never know his secret ambition.

Monday, Second Day

It is the first full day of regular camp activity. **Julian's** routine as a member of the leadership patrol is established. He gets to know each member of The Flaming Arrow. **Tom** Dawson, the Junior Assistant

Scoutmaster, is accustomed to being the kingpin. He spots Julian first thing and sets out to add him to his very long list of sexual initiates. **Nick** Harrison, the Troop Scribe, has been assigned to mentor Julian as a troop journalist. He is savvy about Tom and engineers escape plans without either Julian or Tom's becoming aware. **Danny** Laskey, the Senior Patrol Leader, is also new to the patrol; he is assigned to team with Julian in camp operations. He has a crush on Julian and lures him into a private space where he hopes to establish himself as Julian's steady boyfriend. His clumsiness and inexperience make it possible for Julian to turn the event into an exploratory game.

Leonard Stafford, the staff member in charge at the lake is introduced. The lake is a major center of what happens at the camp—much of that is because of Leonard's efficient but benign rule.

Merit badge study is a major part of scout camp, and Julian attends his first class meetings. **Justin** Blake, a younger scout that Julian has been mentoring, is with him in Forestry, and Cory Summers, the scout with a water phobia, is Julian's Archery partner.

The highlight for Julian's day is helping Nick qualify for his Lifesaving merit badge. His pretend drowning fools everyone. He becomes friends with Nick, who makes a passing comment about Julian's derrière that preoccupies Julian for days. He has been oblivious to backsides until now, and sets out to study the phenomenon of Choice Buns.

The first Troop Nine campfire is held. The process of selecting a Troop Skit is begun. **Max** Webster's is the first to be presented. It is a fable that involves the entire troop. They are divided into small choral groups that punctuate the narrated story line similar in style to the ancient Greek chorus.

The major event of the day comes after lights out: the relationship between **Nick** and **Tom** is explored. Nick surprises Tom and himself with a sexual maneuver of his own. Neither had guessed that a familiar after hour activity could be so consequential. Nick succeeds in shattering Tom's shallow self indulgent frame of mind—sexual gratification as he has understood it is transformed.

Book 2: The Poker Club

Tuesday, Third Day

Mark rises early and takes a pre-breakfast run. **Julian** begins his study of backsides. Nick's comment has made him reflect on an area of anatomy that had escaped his notice. He decides that Mark's backside is perfect, but he is intrigued to learn more. His aesthetic sense is part of what drives his curiosity.

Tom has an embarrassing moment at breakfast—a result of the love-making session with **Nick**. Mark converts the moment to comic relief by announcing the installation of an official Farting Post.

Danny's haste to get a tan on the first day resulted in a nasty sunburn that threatens his plan to secure Julian's affections. However, he and Julian discover an unusual application for sun lotion. Julian's natural curiosity and naïveté play into Danny's plans a second time. Julian senses that he needs to be careful to keep Danny at a relative distance.

Introducing **Geoff** Staples, a west coast transplant. His British father and Cambodian mother have provided him with a unique background. He, **Jack** Haley and **Brian** Rogers are from the suburbs of Atlanta; their scout troops are at Camp Walker for the first time. They have **Tom** in their sights for a very special and exclusive club. Tom joins them for a game of strip poker—extreme strip poker. The event makes Tom at once enthusiastic and confused. His experience last night with Nick is still unprocessed in his mind. It troubles him more as the day goes on. One positive side effect is that his preference for young untouched backsides has vanished forever. It takes him some time to notice that. Tom is not an analytic person.

Introducing **Casey** Snyder and **Robin** Simmons from Troop 9. Like several others in the troop, they've had the dubious honor of being "broken in" by **Tom** Dawson. They are drawn into Tom's new poker club; a game is scheduled for tomorrow morning.

Julian befriends **Bruce** Ruggles, the seriously overweight Second Class scout. Bruce had been a fellow volunteer victim at the Lifesaving test. He is under orders from his father to earn his swim rating and lose weight—in that order.

Julian and **Nick** become closer both as friends and as journalistic partners. Julian works hard at improving his swimming skills.

Camp Director **John** Jorgensen pays a surprise visit to Barr's Meadow and observes the second Troop 9 campfire skit, a parody of *Gunsmoke*.

Julian and **Mark** have another brief conference; it is cut short because Mark has to install his featherbed mattresses before lights out.

Tom has agonized all day, unable to articulate his feelings about **Nick**. He takes the revolutionary step of insisting on an overnight sleeping session in the supply tent. He is compelled to figure it out, and he knows Nick is the key to that. Nick quickly understands what has happened; but he is patient and has the sense to let Tom discover for himself that he is in love. Nick will not put words in his mouth. Nick isn't sure he trusts yet what seems to have happened.

Wednesday, Fourth Day

The roles of protector and protected are unexpectedly reversed in the Flaming Arrow patrol. **Julian** and **Danny** find themselves cast as guardians. Nick and Tom have overslept and are discovered in the morning by a very surprised and envious Danny. The discovery is shared with Julian, who is sworn to secrecy.

The Poker Club's second game runs into an unexpected complication. **Geoff** abandons the game because of his plan to meet with Danny; he displays his skill as a comical impresario and drafts **Nick** to be his replacement. Nick is forced out of his back row comfort zone, and Tom discovers how awkward it is to not be in charge.

Danny takes his second major step in learning who he is and where he wants to go in life. His new assignment with **Geoff** to make deliveries to troop campsites provides an ideal opportunity to learn about the amorous arts from an expert. He rationalizes that it will serve him well in his designs to ensnare Julian.

Paul Harris and **Doug** Tucker are another pair of scouts from Troop 9 who were initiated by Tom in past years. They were not happy with that experience, and have struck out on their own. They have a stopwatch that serves as a timer for their hobby of exploring new venues and techniques for oral sex. For two days they have been testing the lake near the boat dock shallows.

Julian and **Sid** discover Doug and Paul's secret activity. Sid cleverly gets Julian to join him in trying out what they saw Paul and Doug doing. Julian wisely suggests the privacy of the scoutmaster's cabin; their long friendship takes on a new dimension.

After hours in Barr's Meadow is special on Wednesday; relationships, perceptions develop and grow. **Tom** insists that the joint sleeping arrangement be permanent for the rest of camp. **Danny** agrees to serve as a sentinel. Tom declares his love. **Nick** makes it mutual.

Mark and Julian have a major conference to get caught up with a host of things. **Julian** learns about boundaries that must be respected. Mark gets a reminder of what a scout's eye view was like. He instructs Julian on the importance of discretion.

Thursday, Fifth Day

Water Polo teams are formed, allowing **Tom** to engage and lead in his favorite sport. **Mark** is selected to be one of the coaches. The opportunity is just what Mark has needed, professionally. At last he is an underdog, a challenge he finds invigorating.

Geoff had such a good time teasing Nick on Wednesday before the poker game that he jumps at the chance to have some more fun. **Nick** surprises both Geoff and himself in his ability to engage in repartee. We learn the back story of Nick and Tom's romance.

During a Forestry class field exercise, **Julian** and **Justin** come across a pair of scouts enjoying themselves in a secret clearing. They are astounded by the very advanced "do-the-dog" performance.

A new story emerges: **Robin** Simmons from Troop 9, and **Jack** Haley from Troop 152. By chance, they were put together in the second "layer" of yesterday's Poker game. Robin is one of Tom's "initiates;" Jack is one of the original Poker Club members from Atlanta. Some special unexpected magic from that second game follows.

Troop Nine has a barbecue; it's the social event of the summer. The menu of beans, franks, and potato salad are a combination that causes flatulence for many. Brad, in the Tiger patrol, sees to it that the meal is enhanced with quantities of chopped sweet onion. His patrol in particular is primed, and ends the evening with a merry time torching farts.

Mark and **Julian** have another major conference—it helps offset the handicap Julian has always had of not having a father around. The merriment Julian hears in the distance makes him reflect on no longer being one of the gang. Julian is learning about life and himself at a fast pace. He understands and is grateful to have the advantage of Mark's knowledge and wisdom. He also resolves to move forward on another program he has devised: learning lovemaking techniques in preparation for the time he will need them—when he is ready to make his move to conquer Mark, he wants to be fully prepared.

Site descriptions

Barr's Meadow

Barr's Meadow was used year around. It featured a small one-room cabin with an indoor bathroom. There were four campsites with a cabin in Camp Walker, but this one was the best. It had its own well, electric pump, and water heater. The site was a favorite during the winter and outside groups paid a premium to use it. The small fireplace on the west wall was for wintertime use only.

A system of paths and carefully fashioned water access points were designed to keep the meadow as natural as possible. Campers were expected to use the trails and paths at all times. The latrine was down slope of the campsite string, near the entrance trail. It had a set of six stalls next to a urinal trough. It was maintained by Camp Walker, not the client campers. No individual camp facilities were permitted, but each camp had a waste disposal bin. Refuse had to be packed out weekly to a central collection area at HQ by each camp. Patrol Leaders generally assigned this duty to scouts needing to erase Demerit Points. No burning or burial pits were permitted. A shower platform for general use was near the latrine. It had two separate shower spaces, supplied with cold water from an overhead tank. Scouts wanting to shower worked the built in hand pump to fill the tank. No laundry facilities were available in the camps. Each troop had a two-hour block reserved in the HQ laundry room at the end of the first week. The troop campfire assembly area was on the other side of the trail, farther uphill.

South of the cabin, each patrol had a campsite that consisted of three tents grouped around a picnic table and cooking area. A network of footpaths connected the individual campsites to each other, the latrine, and to the main trail. Thirty to forty feet of meadow separated the camps from each other. All scouts were assigned to a two or three man wall tent. Each person was supplied a folding canvas cot and a footlocker for clothes and personal belongings. No camps were located closer than twenty feet from the spring fed creek. The meadow was open except for a few yellow birch trees and some scrub pine. A small marshy zone above the latrine had dried up years ago. All the other campsites at Walker were in forest locations.

Barr's Meadow

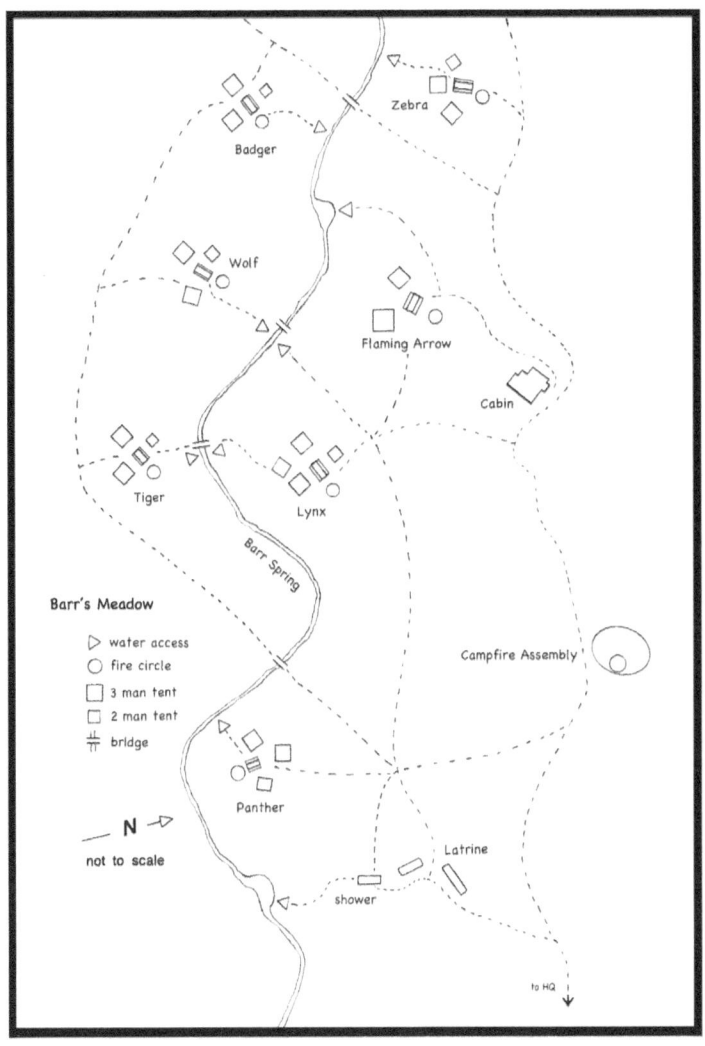

Zebra

Badger

Wolf

Flaming Arrow

Cabin

Tiger

Lynx

Barr Spring

Barr's Meadow

▷ water access
○ fire circle
☐ 3 man tent
▢ 2 man tent
╪ bridge

Campfire Assembly

Panther

Latrine

N ⇾

not to scale

shower

to HQ

Camp Walker Headquarters Building

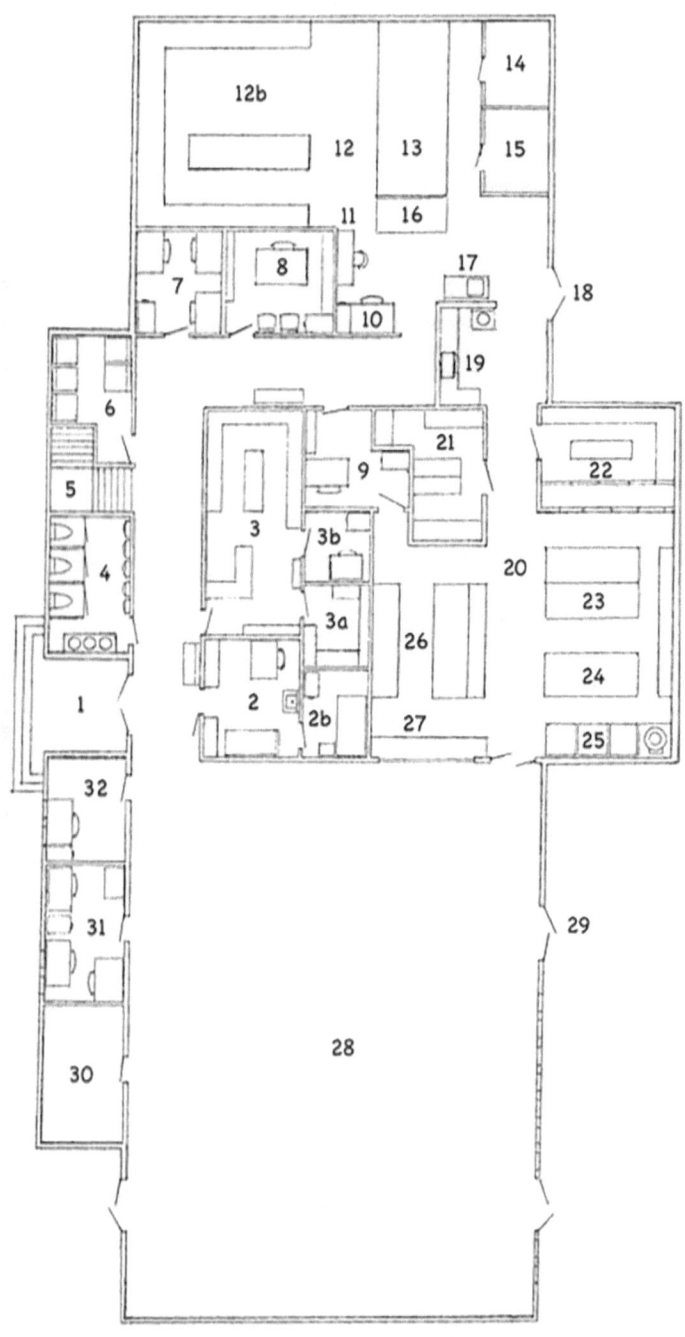

Camp Walker Headquarters

1	Main Entrance	15	Pillows, Blankets, Tarps
2	First Aid	16	Moveable Worktable
2b	Recovery	17	Sink
3	Trading Post	18	Delivery Entrance
3b	Supply Room	19	Dishwashing
3c	Office/Security	20	Kitchen
4	Rest Room	21	Dry good Stores
5	Stairway up	22	Walk-in Cooler/Freezer
6	Laundry	23	Prep Tables
7	Instructor's Office	24	Grills
8	Camp Director Office	25	Ovens
9	Foods Office	26	Food Assembly
10	Camp Ranger's Office	27	Pass Through
11	Workbench	28	Assembly/Dining Hall
12	Supplies and Equipment Warehouse	29	Safety Exit
12b	Hand Carts	30	Table Storage
13	Tool Cage	31	Waterfront Director
14	Featherbed Storage	32	Activity Director

Camp Walker

Camp Walker is in the Blue Ridge Mountains near the Nantahala National Forest in western North Carolina and the Chattahoochee National Forest in northern Georgia. The extensive acreage has areas for a variety of activity, large and small. Each troop in the Council has a reserved campsite for the two weeks. Trails to the sites radiate out from the central headquarters buildings. A separate permanent village serves the counselors and staff. Each camp session averages between five and eight hundred scouts, or up to seventeen troops. Nearly a hundred miles of internal trails connect the camps and provide for training and hiking activity. South of the HQ are areas for large multi-troop assemblies, recreational fields, and over 200 feet of lakeshore. When not in use by the Scouts, parts of the facility are leased to outside groups.

Prior to Affirmative Action in 1970, the camp observed the late nineteenth and early twentieth century custom of nude swimming at segregated sites. Women were not allowed in camp.

Glossary for terms in Julian's Private Scrapbook, Book Three

Bears: Second year Cub Scout level.

Beefcake: On Tuesday, Julian saw Brian Rogers at the lake; in jest, Nick called him a Beefcake. Brian was an all-state wrestler at the time.

Blue Ridge Mountains: the eastern portion of the Appalachian Mountain Range that extends between Georgia in the south and Pennsylvania in the north. The highest point is Mt. Mitchell, North Carolina [6,684 feet].

Buddy system: Primarily a safety structure that requires all scouts to remain with another scout at all times when outdoors in the wild. It has broadened to an expedient in organizing and monitoring progress in many program areas. In Camp Walker, special Buddy Badges were given to each scout. It showed their swimming proficiency and was required to be presented at the gate prior to lake access. A red top half meant restricted to the shallow training area. A blue bottom half meant the scout was proficient and was free to use the entire facility.

Chattahoochee National Forest takes its name from the river that has its headwaters in the north Georgia Mountains. The name originated with the Cherokee and Creek Indians native to the area. It borders the Nantahala National Forest in North Carolina.

Cherokee Double Wall: The most intricate Cherokee baskets are made from river cane, which can be woven in both single and double layer designs. Cherokee basket makers also use materials such as white oak and honeysuckle to execute their distinctive basketry traditions. The process of making a basket, from finding good materials to weaving a complex geometric design, takes skill, concentration and a great deal of time.

Farting Post: On Tuesday morning Tom accidentally broke wind at the breakfast table. Mark diffused the embarrassment by announcing that he would install an official farting post at a safe distance downwind. He selected a branch from the firewood stash.

Flaming Arrow: The leadership patrol, an executive council. Includes the Junior Assistant Scoutmaster, Senior Patrol Leader, Scribe and Bugler.

Gold, Silver, Bronze Palm: Palm branch badges are awarded to Eagle scouts who continue to earn merit badges.

Green stool: Julian made a stool his first year in Cub Scouts. He used it routinely to compensate for being short.

Hayden Park: A nature reserve near the high school in Troop 9's town. Hiking trails, park benches and picnic areas make the five acre park a favorite. This was where Tom frequently took his new recruits to be initiated.

Howard Cosell: Famed sportscaster for ABC radio and television. He was new and controversial when he began to seen nationally in 1961, the time of this story.

Hurry, hurry, hurry: A refrain in Max's skit.

Jack Spratt: refers to a nursery rhyme character who could eat no fat, and whose wife who could eat no lean. Together, they licked the platter clean.

Joliet, Illinois: a community near Chicago. Julian's childhood home. His mother leaves because she wants to raise her son in a smaller community, well away from urban influences.

Life rank: between Star and Eagle.

Lynx wash station: At the beginning of Camp, the central wash station for the entire Barr's Meadow was assigned to the Lynx patrol. It was against Camp Walker regulations to do any washing directly in the spring.

Max's skit: in Book One, Max Webster presented his proposed skit for the troop to perform at the closing assembly. It was a spoken choral parable about courage. Each patrol repeated selected words and phrases in unison.

MG: Ronnie owned a sports car produced by MG division of the British Motor Corporation from 1955 to 1962. The MGA replaced the older T-type cars and represented a complete styling break, the "first  of a new line" to quote the advertising. The MGA had no exterior door handles.

Nantahala National Forest: Located in the mountains and valleys of western North Carolina. The terrain varies in elevation from 5,800 feet to 1,200 feet (along the Hiwassee River below the Appalachian Dam). It is the home of many waterfalls. It borders the Chattahoochee Forest in Northern Georgia.

Pershing hat: worn by scoutmasters and scout executives. It is a wide flat disc with four ridges forming a point at the top of the crown. Also called a Campaign hat; made familiar by Army General John Pershing during World War I. It is also used by several State Police and the Canadian Mounted Police. A smaller, modified version was the standard hat for all scouts prior to WW II.

Second layer: Geoff's innovative addition to the Poker Club. A euphemism for a second round of sexual activity.

Secret drawings: During his first year in scouts Julian had begun to do study sketches of Mark from memory; the sketches were in the middle of the sketchbook where he thought them safe from being seen by others. Mark caught a brief glimpse on the bus coming to camp.

So round, so firm, so fully packed: this slogan was used extensively by the Lucky Strike cigarette commercials and became a widely used slang expression. It originated in a 1947 Merle Travis song.

Star rank: The next advancement in rank after First Class.

S.D.H: Abbreviation acronym for Shit Damn Hell, Julian's demerit free cussword. There was a 5 demerit penalty in Troop 9 for profanity or swearing, enforced by Patrol Leaders.

S.Y.I.T: Sweet young innocent thing.

Troop shake: The left-handed Scout handshake is made with the hand nearest the heart and is offered as a token of friendship. It is made firmly, without interlocking fingers. The "Solemn Version" in Troop 9 included interlocking fingers and two lateral twists followed by two vertical shakes.

Wolf Patrol: Julian's first home in Troop Nine. He was placed there with his friends Jeremy and Sid.

Zebra Patrol: Newly added to allow the Troop to grow in size. One of the West twins was made patrol leader because of his outstanding leadership ability. His brother is patrol leader of the Lynx patrol.

Index of Names in The Shooting Gallery

Dale Baker: Tiger Patrol Leader, Life scout. Strict and by the book; frequently awards demerits to Tony in particular.

Danny Laskey: Star scout, newly appointed Senior Patrol Leader of Troop 9. He bypassed several able scouts because Scoutmaster Mark sees him as the best potential leader to become Junior Assistant Scoutmaster. He has had a crush on Julian for a little more than a year. Though he lives across the fence, he and Julian have only had a nodding acquaintance prior to this camp. He is assigned to supervise Julian in the daily breakfast and camp inspections, and makes his first attempt to seduce Julian. Afterwards, he gets sunburned at the lake on the first day of camp. Drops his Backpacking class and is assigned to assist the camp Quartermaster. In Book 2 he was taught some advanced love-making techniques by Geoff. He agrees to provide cover for Tom and Nick's unauthorized sleeping arrangement in the supply tent. Takes it on himself to instruct Julian in the basics of sex play.

Darrell: Life scout, member of Troop 12; Shooting Gallery contestant #2 ("Mister Curvy").

Darren Dow: Guest piano accompanist and music director.

Don Felton: First Class scout in the Badger patrol (Fester in the Badger skit).

Doug Tucker: One of the "stopwatch duo." A First Class scout in the Panther patrol; he was introduced to sexual activity a year ago one day after school by Tom. He is self-indulgent and not interested in serving anyone else's needs. In Book 2 he and Paul are seen and imitated by Julian and Sid.

Dr. Frank Martens: Guest speaker for Sunday service.

Erik: Mark's first love, killed in an airplane crash when Mark was a college Junior. Until this year, that memory has been a protective shield against any intimate relationship.

Francine Forrest: Mother of Julian, daughter of Oscar and Elizabeth Mattson, deceased, of Joliet Illinois. Estranged and divorced from her husband while Julian was an infant, she has made a new life in a new state.

Freddy Scott: Tenderfoot scout in the Badger patrol. (Played Billy the Kid Jones in the patrol skit.)

Freddy: Star scout from Troop 118; devised the Shooting Gallery.

Gary West: Patrol Leader of the Lynx patrol, Life scout. Twin of Jim.

Geoff Staples: Junior Assistant Scoutmaster of Troop 419, Atlanta. Life scout, recently from Burbank California. English-Cambodian descent, poker club member, sophisticated and experienced. Danny's co-worker in the supply duty; tutored Danny in sexual techniques. Respects Nick's intellect and tutors him in the amorous arts as well.

Geraldine Smathers: Real Estate Agent, friend and employer of Francine Forrest.

Hank Sours: Shooting Gallery contestant #6. Makes first bull's eye.

Jack Haley: Junior Assistant Scoutmaster of Troop 152, Atlanta. Eagle scout, recruited by Geoff to join Brian's private poker game. On Wednesday, he and Robin were matched in the second poker game; they have been obsessed with each other since. They met the next day and found a private place to meet along the east lakeshore. Jack names it Whispering Oaks. It becomes their regular destination during the free periods.

Jason Jones: Second Class scout in the Lynx patrol; Robin's tent partner.

Jeremy Baker: Julian's friend, First Class scout in the Wolf patrol; was a Cub Scout with Julian. In Canoeing class with Kurt.

John Jorgensen: Serving his fifteenth year as Director of Camp Walker.

Johnny: Fictional character in Max Webster's skit.

Josh Green: Tenderfoot scout in the Badger patrol.

Julian Forrest: First Class scout, main protagonist. Unaware that he has inherited extraordinary artistic talent from his father, a Greenwich Village sculptor whom he has never known. Serious, single minded, and determined from an early age to spend his life with Mark, a close neighbor. The first night at camp, Mark invites him to stay in the cabin. It was not what he had hoped for. His talent for acting comes to the fore the next day when he takes part in the lifesaving class. He learns to experiment in sexplay with other scouts in Book 2. His goal is to earn Mark's affection and respect and eventually his love; he works hard to improve his swimming and drawing ability.

Justin Blake: First Class scout in the Zebra patrol. Julian's protégé and Forestry Buddy. In Book 2 he and Julian witness an advanced

have begun to sleep together in the camp supply tent. Earns his Lifesaving rating and coaches Julian in swimming. Befriended by Geoff.

Norman Miller: Star scout, assigned to help Julian on the first day at camp. Assistant Patrol Leader of the Wolf patrol.

Oscar Mattson: Julian's maternal grandfather.

Pat Schaefer: Wife of Mark; a Registered Nurse, studying to become an M.D.

Paul Harris: First Class scout in the Lynx patrol. One of the stopwatch duo.

Robin Simmons: Life scout in the Lynx patrol. He and Casey are invited by Tom to join the Poker Club. He falls in love with Jack on first sight. He is a skilled boatman, and takes Jack on a magical ride along the east shore where they finish what they had started after the poker game.

Ronnie: Surfer, Geoff's first love in California. He is extremely wealthy and twelve years older.

Sandy Smith: Tenderfoot, member of the Lynx patrol.

Sarge Oliver: Camp Ranger/Quartermaster, assigned to supervise Danny and Geoff as camp supply crewmen after they drop the Backpacking merit badge class.

Scott Henderson: Scoutmaster of Troop 7; Teaches Forestry merit badge. Julian is fascinated by his sash; it exhibits an impressive array of 37 badges.

Scott Olson: Scoutmaster of Troop 419, Atlanta. Teaches 2nd Class Rank to Tenderfoot scouts.

Scoutmaster Benson: Troop 14; Teaches Reptile merit badge. Not related to Tad, a member of the Zebra patrol.

Scoutmaster Samuels: Troop 12; Teaches Archery.

Scoutmaster Simmons: Troop 152; Teaches Indian Legends.

Scoutmaster Soames: Troop 6; Teaches First Aid merit badge. Annoyed by Mark's continued success.

Scoutmaster Taylor: Troop 2; Teaches Backpacking and Climbing merit badges.

Scoutmaster Unger: Troop 4; Teaches Wood Carving.

Sid Thomas: First Class scout in the Wolf patrol. Julian's friend from school and Cub Scouts. He is known for his prankster sense of humor and his extremely skinny physique. His mother bought him a new turquoise air mattress for camp. In Book 2 his snorkel became an unexpected enabler when Julian borrowed it to investigate Doug and Paul's underwater activity. Their friendship becomes more personal as a result.

Stan: Life scout from Troop 152; contestant #7 in the Shooting Gallery.

Stuart Walker: Wolf Patrol Leader, Life scout.

Tad Benson: Second Class scout in the Zebra patrol. A gifted runner.

Tom Dawson: Junior Assistant Scoutmaster of Troop 9 and Eagle scout. A star swimmer and football player. A secondary protagonist that relies heavily on the analytic ability of his protégé, Nick Harrison. He helps Julian at the first free swim at the lake as a ploy. But his plan to seduce Julian gets derailed by Nick. His whole sexual world gets turned upside down when he allows Nick to show him a new way to make love. Recruited into the Poker Club the next day. Outstanding leadership ability, his fetish for fresh adolescent backsides is quenched by the discovery that he is in love with Nick. He makes the decision to commandeer the troop supply tent to serve as a bedroom for himself and Nick for the remaining days at camp. Chosen to captain Mark's water polo team.

Tony Johnson: First Class scout in the Tiger patrol. Talented, comical, and usually in need of points. He tends to annoy his patrol leader, and is frequently penalized for simple infractions and oversights. He is the troop's most talented actor and clown.

Willy: First Class scout, member of Troop 419, Atlanta.

Troop 9   Mark Schaefer, Scoutmaster

1 Panthers

1 Nathan Jensen	[16] L
2 Charlie Larson	[16] L
3 Ryan Kruger	[16] S
4 Calvin Radcliffe	[15] 1st
5 Doug Tucker	[16] 1st
6 Ben Jasper	[14] 2nd
7 Don Bennett	[13] T

2 Tigers

1 Dale Baker	[16] L
2 Jay Porter	[16] L
3 Andy Ashbaugh	[16] L
4 Brad Fisher	[16] S
5 Chris Smith	[14] 2nd
6 Tony Johnson	[15] 1st
7 Shawn McGee	[13] T

3 Lynx

1 Gary West	[16] L
2 Max Webster	[15] L
3 Alex Trent	[15] S
4 Robin Simmons	[16] L
5 Paul Harris	[16] 1st
6 Jason Jones	[14] 2nd
7 Sandy Smith	[13] T

4 Wolves

1 Stuart Walker	[16] L
2 Norman Miller	[15] S
3 Casey Snyder	[15] S
4 Sid Thomas	[14] 1st
5 Jeremy Baker	[14] 1st
6 {Julian Forrest}	
7 Billy Bradford	[13] T

5 Badgers

1 Arnie Shaw	[16] L
2 Chuck Nelson	[16] L
3 Tommy Carlysle	[15] S
4 Don Felton	[15] 1st
5 Bruce Ruggles	[14] 2nd
6 Freddy Scott	[13] T
7 Josh Green	[13] T

6 Zebras

1 Jim West	[16] L
2 Kurt Davis	[15] S
3 Cory Summers	[15] 2nd
4 Justin Blake	[13] 1st
5 Tad Benson	[14] 2nd
6 Clint Walker	[14] 2nd
7 open	

Flaming Arrow

1 Tom Dawson	[17] E
2 Nick Harrison	[16] L
3 Danny Laskey	[15] S
4 Frank Ferris, bugler	[16] L
5 Julian Forrest	[14] 1st

Ranks

E=Eagle	(1)
L=Life	(14)
S=Star	(8)
1st=First Class	(9)
2nd=Second Class	(7)
T=Tenderfoot	(6)

Position

16 Patrol

1-7 Individual

chronological age in brackets [ ]

Camp Walker Staff   [June 1962]

Camp Director: **John Jorgensen**

Camp Ranger/Quartermaster: **"Sarge" Oliver**
> *Senior Counselors for camp deliveries and maintenance* [3]
> *Junior Counselors for camp deliveries and maintenance* [3]

Associate Ranger, Purchasing, Trading Post, Laundry: **Gerald Madsen**
> *Senior Counselors for Trading Post sales* [2]
> *Junior Counselors for Camp Laundry* [2]

Food Director: **Pierre Arsenault, Chef**
> *Senior Counselor assistant* [1]
> *Junior Counselor assistants* [5]

Medical Officer: **Harold Symonds**
> *Counselor Assistants assigned when needed*

Waterfront Director: **Leonard Stafford**
Senior Counselor Lifeguards [5] Billy, Joey, Ted, Ken, Lanny
> Adult Staff Instructors:
> Swimming 1: **Roy Franklin**, Advanced and Intermediate
> Swimming 2: **Matt Smith**, Beginning and Intermediate
> Rowing: **Phil Jensen**; *Senior Counselor* Beebe
> Canoeing: **Sam Brady**; *Senior Counselor* Walls

Program Director: **Fred Russell**
> *Special Assistant*:* Tom Dawson, JA, Troop 9
> *Senior Counselor Assistants*: [12]
> *Junior Counselor Assistants*: [18] Mason
> > Adult Advancement Instructors [2]*
> Harold Carter, Troop 2 (1st Class),
> Scott Olson, Troop 419 (2nd Class)
> Adult Merit Badge Instructors: [12]*
> Scott Henderson, Troop 7 (Forestry)
> Ed Taylor, Troop 29 (Backpacking/Climbing)
> Mike Fuller, Troop 8 (Basketry/Leatherwork)
> Archie Samuels, Troop 12 (Archery)
> Frank Thompson, Troop 17 (Pioneering)

Ted Soames, Troop 6 (First Aid)
Rick Strauss, Troop 13 (Marksmanship)
Frank Simmons, Troop 152 (Indian Legends)
Ron Benson, Troop 14 (Reptile Study)
Carl DeBeery, Troop 76 (Fishing)
Sedley Unger, Troop 4 (Wood Carving/Woodworking)
Donald Brimm, Troop 227 (Bird Study)

Recreational Director: **Benjamin Bradley**
  Special Adult Recreational Assistant:* Mark Schaefer, Troop 9
  Senior Counselor Assistants [6]
  Junior Counselor Assistants [6]
  Rope Yard: Adult Supervisor Volunteer* (rotating assignment)
  Rifle Range: Adult Supervisor Volunteer* (rotating assignment)
  Archery: Adult Supervisor Volunteer* (rotating assignment)
  Water Polo: Volunteer Coaches* Schaefer, Franklin, Smith,
Russell

  *   Drawn from Attending Scoutmasters and Scouts
  •   **Full Time Camp Employee in boldface**
  •   *Seasonal employee in italics*

a word about the author

Eldot is a simple cipher: the author's first initial spelled phonetically followed by a period [L. = Eldot] Why? When this novel was first published, the subject matter was more sensitive and controversial than it is today. Lest relatives, friends or former colleagues be inconvenienced or victimized, the nom de plume was adopted as a shield. Secondly, the author didn't want media opportunism to distort what the book was seeking to achieve. Media treatment of the subject was the major motivation to write Julian's side of the story in the first place.

All the Julian books received positive critical reviews. The potential for controversy still exists, but the extremist groups have lost their clout—society has evolved rapidly: social media and the cell phone have changed the landscape; the Julian novels are made more topical than ever. In 2018 the subject matter is relevant and openly discussed; a movie on the same theme is a contender for the 2018 Best Picture of the year. For this reason and to satisfy readers' response, the five books have been revised, updated, and re-issued as the five volume *Julian's Private Scrapbook* set.

Thus it's appropriate to let the reader get a peek behind the curtain. Eldot has lived in the Pacific Northwest for most of his life. In order to avoid the Viet Nam war, he took an occupational deferment to teach high school Drama and English. The interminable nature of the war and the draft lottery kept him in that occupation so long that the refuge morphed into a successful career. Why change a good thing? He became a local and state leader in his profession. After thirty terrific years as an educator, he retired. Now he's taken up writing. The novels are not autobiographical.

Leland Alan Hall

Publications:

1960: Emperor Commodus Prompt Book: Use of Masks in Drama
  [Honors Thesis, a translation from the Greek, housed at University of Oregon Library]
1979-81: Editorials, *Oregon Education*
2011: *Little J and Roger* [eBook only]
2012: *Barr's Meadow*
  The Poker Club
  The Shooting Gallery
  Thunder and Lightning
2013: *The Champions*
  Inside Eldot's World: a literary gazetteer [eBook only]
2015: *You're in High School Now*
2016: *'56 Scrapbook* [PDF and spiral bound]
2018-19: *Julian's Private Scrapbook, books 1 thru 5*
2020: *He's kinda tall: Julian's Sophomore Year, Part 2*
2022: *'56 Bookend* [PDF and spiral bound]
2024: The Julian Novels ATP Special Edition
2024: *Untitled: Julian's Sophomore Year. Part 3*

Author Website Link: http://www.diphra.com
      ATP website: eldotbooks.com
Facebook: https://www.facebook.com/AuthorEldot/
Twitter: https://twitter.com/AuthorEldot
Tumblr: https://authoreldot.tumblr.com/

Promos

Summer Camp!!!

Spring is here—get ready for a fun romp at Camp Walker.

Eldot presents his debut novel about coming of age. Comedy, Adventure, Action and Surprises— it's not to be missed.

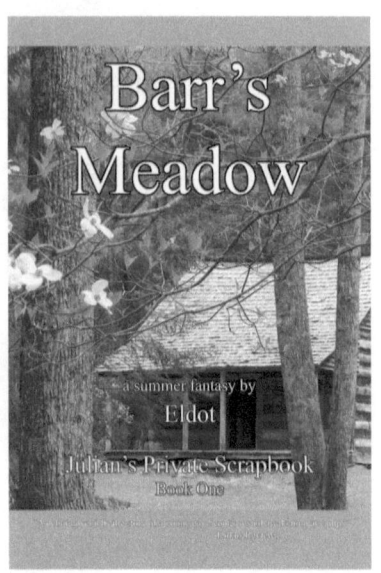

It's the early 1960's

Over 650 scouts are at the two week camp, and many of them have *plans*. This is one look at days past that goes beyond nostalgia. This is the camp you wish you'd gone to. Here's your chance at last.

This is the story of Julian's very first summer camp. His goal is to land the dream of his life, Mark. The endeavor begins in Barr's Meadow—he soon discovers that it will be a lot harder than he imagined.

Julian's Private Scrapbook is a series of five novels that explores many ways that boys discover themselves and others. Sensitive, thorough, and uncensored; you're sure to recognize more than one of these boys. Some are new at these things... others are highly skilled. Few return home unchanged.

available in e-Book format now at:

diphra.com

also at Amazon, Barnes & Noble, and most bookstores

For Mature readers

Published by Diphra Enterprises LLC

Last Man Standing…

A secret game room, a special deck of cards, a savvy crew from the city, an unsuspecting recruit:

Eldot continues his summer camp novel about coming of age with three days of activity and action— it's even more packed than the first installment.

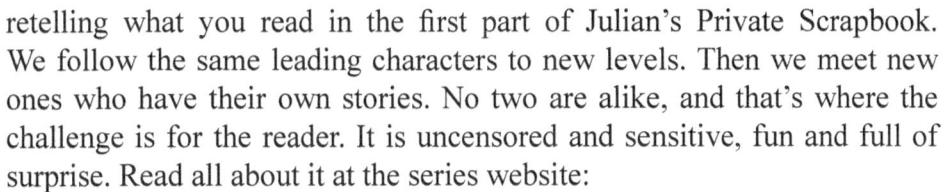

It's mid June, 1962

The sequel begins right where Barr's Meadow left off. No time is wasted retelling what you read in the first part of Julian's Private Scrapbook. We follow the same leading characters to new levels. Then we meet new ones who have their own stories. No two are alike, and that's where the challenge is for the reader. It is uncensored and sensitive, fun and full of surprise. Read all about it at the series website:

http:/www.diphra.com/ljrindex.html

available in e-Book format now at:
diphra.com

also at Amazon, Barnes & Noble,
and most bookstores

For Mature Readers

Published by Diphra Enterprises LLC

Review

Barr's Meadow: (Julian's Private Scrapbook: Part One)
Eldot
Xlibris, 248 pages, (paperback) $15.99, 978-1-4691-4512-9
(Reviewed: December 2013)

Pleasant, nostalgic and ingenuous, *Barr's Meadow* is set at a Boy Scout camp in the early '60s, the fictional story of a gay young man named Julian.

Julian, nearly 13, is handsome, enthusiastic and affable, as well as a skilled artist. Julian has a crush on Scoutmaster Mark. Mark — who, while married, has been open to same-gender sex in the past — has resolved to confront this with sensitivity and fraternal affection, realizing that Julian's trusting nature could make him the victim of more predatory scouts.

Author Eldot (who writes under one name) explores the daily activities of scout camp and the politics of sex between teenage boys. The author focuses mostly on the gay characters and Julian's sexual thoughts, but this is not really gay erotica (although the back cover warns: "Not for sale to persons under 18"). With the exception of two somewhat explicit (though not heightened) passages, it reflects on same-gender, male sexuality while generally avoiding the salacious.

Eldot gets inside the heads of the characters, including Julian and Mark, as in: "Mark stepped around to the other side of the bed and watched Julian hustle. He bounced on his toes unconsciously. He had faced the unknown here and it had gone very well. I was right about this."

Barr's Meadow is comparable to other teenage boy coming-of-age narratives, such as *The Last Picture Show*, minus the cynicism, sophistication or relative depth. This doesn't mean that it's poorly crafted; only that Eldot's prose is simple, direct and seeks to examine the lives and thoughts of guys who are only beginning to view the world with introspection. Eldot walks the precarious line between making the boys evolved and depicting them as saints. He allows them moments of tenderness and nurturing without suggesting their virility has been tainted.

Barr's Meadow, the first in a series, never breaks through to the transcendent realms of literary brilliance, but it is intelligent, moving, well-grounded and memorable.

KIRKUS
REVIEWS

TITLE INFORMATION

BARR'S MEADOW

Eldot

Diphra Enterprises LLC (283 pp.) ISBN: 978-0-9966325-5-3

BOOK REVIEW

A debut novel tells the story of a young gay Scout's sexual awakening at camp. Twelve-year-old Julian Forrest has been raised by his single mother, never knowing his father. He loves drawing and being a Cub Scout. He has even made a Scouting journal full of drawings of his activities. He has recently become aware of his sexual desire, which is wound up in his habit of watching a neighbor, the adult Mark Schaefer, come home from work every day. When Mark comes over to the house to invite Julian to join his Scouting troop, the youngster can barely contain his excitement—or hide his erection.

Two years later, Julian gets to attend the annual two-week Scouting summer camp at Walker Lake. By this point, Mark is aware of Julian's crush, though he is unsure how to proceed: "What bothered Mark—a little, not a lot—was that Julian had become a presence in his thoughts... *at this point it's only a presence... but it's something new...* it felt pleasant, it made him feel light." The first two days at Walker Lake will prove transformative for many people, including Nick Harrison and Tom Dawson, members of the troop's leadership patrol. In the all-male environment of a Scouting camp, Julian quickly discovers some of the rules of his new masculinity—and a few things about his burgeoning sexuality as well.

Set in the 1960s, this series opener deftly depicts feelings of childhood nostalgia, as evidenced in Eldot's wistful prose: "At last the sausage patties and pancakes were ready and waiting in the oven. Julian helped Danny put out the OJ and milk. *oh! a bubbling sound— the coffee!* He rushed over to the stove to watch." But the author dwells heavily on the sexual thoughts of several characters, including the teenage Julian. While these aren't necessarily erotic, there is an undeniable romanticism to them. This will likely make many readers decidedly uncomfortable, particularly those scenes that deal with the attraction between minors and adults. Eldot may argue that he's depicting an experience common to young gay men, but if this book isn't crossing a line, it's walking right up to it.

An uneven coming-of-age tale.

The Poker Club: Julian's Private Scrapbook, Book 2

Eldot

Diphra Enterprises [perfect bound] 15.95

106,286 words   350 pages

ISBN 978-0-9966325-6-0

Reviewed December, 2018

Quality Review Service

Second in Eldot's Julian's Private Scrapbook (a summer fantasy) series: *The Poker Club* details Julian's ongoing adventures during a two-week stay at Boy Scout Camp. Julian (like many teenage boys) lacks a father figure in his life, and has a mancrush on Mark, the scoutmaster who invites him to stay in his cabin at camp. Julian already knows Mark, they're neighbors back at home. Mark senses Julian's ache for the presence of a caring dad in his life, and is happy to provide that, as he can. Julian is an ingenue in the true sense of the word. He's guileless, gifted, sweet-natured, gung-ho and quick with a searching and curious mind. Like the older scouts, Mark feels very protective of Julian, and tries to acquaint him with the convivial (but sometimes risky) world of maleness, with its jovial mischief, code of behavior, and amped up libido that tortured us as adolescents. Mark tries to answer all Julian's questions about sex, with admirable frankness and discretion. Julian is somewhat overwhelmed by his feelings for Mark (it's all so much to process) but there's great warmth in their platonic connection.

Like the other scouts, Julian has his goals: learning new skills, earning merit badges, improving his swimming technique, depicting experiences in his artist's notebook. Julian's sophisticated technique is impressive and puts him much in demand. Other key characters include Danny, Tom, Nick, Geoff, Bruce and Sid. There are all kinds of activities to master. Archery, riflery, backpacking, planning skit night, to name a few. Lots of the boys enjoy swimming the cold, exhilarating lake, exploring underwater breathing, speed, rescue and distance. Like the YMCA and other all-male gatherings, they happily and casually swim naked, often without a second thought. This sets Julian's interests in motion, but no more so than other guys.

The Poker Game referenced in the title is a diversion for the older, more intrepid scouts (Tom, Geoff, Jack, Brian) where slyly introduced removal of clothing leads to avid sexual experimentation and fulfillment. This is 1962, and the world outside may not be quite so understanding of such behavior, so the guys must be discreet and careful. Eldot recognizes that teenage boys (consider *Spring Awakening*, *The Last Picture Show*) have an impetuous, profoundly intense need to actualize the rush of male hormones that runs through their veins. Not all the guys are headed for a life of same-gender coupling, but they want to express their manhood, and enjoy each other's company, in a zillion different ways. They are giddy, game and secretive, but never disrespectful or brutal. They are kind and gradual, never foisting themselves. Eldot imbues these passages with a kind of celebratory energy while avoiding hyperbole. Julian gladly helps his friend Danny by rubbing lotion on his painful, sunburned "buns". What follows is spontaneous, friendly, and mutually pleasurable.

I struggle to explain the balancing act that Eldot manages in Julian's Private Scrapbook series. Eroticism between guys is a part of the tapestry, to be sure. But by creating a rich, layered context of male companionship and clustering, it takes on a different hue. Eldot confides the goofy, ridiculous, sweet, hilarious, imperative and earnest world of boy scout camp with its all-male milieu. Julian's previous lack of closeness with other boys serves as a springboard for discovering what it means to connect and bond. Male Fart Culture, silly skits, learning to shoot dive, cook for the other guys, it's all in there. There's a kind of spirited, military feel, with none of the negative implications that so often accompany that experience. Erotic enjoyment is described in plain, forthright, unflinching language that is neither inflated or suffused with salacious intent. What makes *The Poker Club* so effective is Eldot's mastery at evincing that sexuality is simply one aspect of a vast, full, contented life. He convincingly shares the rowdy, raucous joys of maleness, in all its boisterous and sometimes nuanced mystery.

QRS Highest recommendation

The Poker Club: Julian's Private Scrapbook, Part Two
Eldot
Xlibris, 279 pages, (paperback) $15.99, 978-1-4771-1834-4
(Reviewed: March, 2014)

This unusual novel is sure to cause controversy for its subject matter. The second in a projected five-novel series, the book takes place at a scout camp during the summer of 1962, and follows several groups of boys as they form friendships, learn new skills, and fall in love. Much of the book concerns their various sexual explorations; indeed, the "Poker Club" of the title refers to one group's method of beginning such activities – and the author is careful to note on the back cover that the book "is meant for mature readers."

In between the sex, several plotlines start to form. Julian, who has a crush on his scoutmaster Mark, learns more about life matters while interacting with his fellow scouts. Tom, an older boy who has been with many other boys, finds himself falling for Nick, one of his earlier conquests and now a friend. Geoff, a co-founder of the Poker Club, recruits other scouts to join in the fun, including Tom and Nick.

While the extensive explicit sex scenes can feel somewhat exploitative, generally they are handled well, combining experience with innocence in an endearing way. Julian in particular, while certainly experienced in some sexual matters, still has much to learn. His sweet, innocent looks make Mark and the other scouts want to protect him from such things, so that, for instance, while a remark about "choice buns" makes Julian curious about what that means, he doesn't learn the answer until nearly the end of the book.

The developing relationship between Tom and Nick is also fascinating; in the previous book, Tom hoped to seduce Julian but now only wants to be with Nick and feels guilty for his earlier pursuits.

The author includes a summary of the first novel along with maps of all locations. If readers are open to the subject matter, they will find intriguing insights into the complex world of boys in this unique novel.

Also available in hardcover and ebook

Thunder and Lightning: Julian's Private Scrapbook, Part 4

Eldot

Xlibris, 327 pages, (paperback) $15.99, 978-1-4797-5684-1
(Reviewed: May 2014)

This unusual novel, the fourth in a five-part series, takes place at a scout camp during the summer of 1962 and follows several groups of boys as they form friendships, learn new skills, and fall in love. Much of the novel depicts their various sexual explorations, and the author clearly alerts readers to such content. "This series is meant for mature readers," he writes on the back cover. "…This book should be stored in a place not accessible by persons under 18."

In between the sex, several plotlines progress from the earlier books. Tom, an older boy who had been with many others before committing himself to Nick, makes amends for his past treatment of Kurt, an earlier partner. Nick advises Kurt on how to overcome his fear that his past with Tom will sabotage his relationship with his current partner Sid. Julian continues to improve his artistic skills, drawing beautiful portraits of the lifeguard Leonard and his scoutmaster Mark, while taking on further responsibilities in the campground. In a new development, Geoff, another older boy, becomes attracted to Mark and devises a plan for seducing the unwitting scoutmaster. Meanwhile, Mark begins to confront his past trauma.

While the extensive sex scenes may make some readers uncomfortable, they are handled well, showing the tenderness between the boys. Their relationships are fascinating to watch, as many are now committed couples, yet their emotional bonds are strong enough to allow them to learn new positions and techniques in sessions with more knowledgeable boys. Geoff's pursuit of Mark is handled humorously, leading to a situation where both attempt to conceal their erections. The author helpfully includes summaries of the previous novels, a glossary of terms and characters and more at book's end.

Thunder and Lightning is a charming read in spite of the controversial subject matter. As it shows further growth in the series' characters and their relationships, it sets the stage for the concluding tale.

Also available in hardcover and ebook.

The Champions: Julian's Private Scrapbook, Part Five
Eldot
Xlibris, 375 pages (paperback) $15.99, 978-1-4797-8041-9
(Reviewed: June 2014)

The conclusion to a sexually infused five-novel series, The Champions takes place during the last day of a scout camp during the summer of 1962 and follows several groups of boys as they deepen their relationships, build on new skills, and ponder life after camp. Much of the novel depicts their various intimate explorations, from a final ejaculation contest known as "the Shooting Gallery" to the couples pleasuring each other on the bus ride home. In between, several plots building during the previous books reach their end.

Geoff, one of the oldest scouts, makes his move — even with his injured foot — to seduce the scoutmaster, Mark, in the middle of the night. Julian, while working on his remarkable drawings, befriends Sarge, the camp's quartermaster, and draws out the gruff retired Army man's soft side, even calling him "Uncle Max." Tom, continuing his process of maturing, learns how to get out of uncomfortable situations without the help of his lover Nick, and even becomes a confidante to other scouts worried about their relationships.

Mark comes across as one of the strongest figures in this novel, encouraging all the scouts under his care to become the best that they can be. He makes plans for Julian to receive art lessons after camp, further developing his talent. He shows his tremendous strength, both physical and moral, during his late-night encounter with Geoff. It's no surprise that his troop wins all the prizes at the last day's competitions, or that Julian has a crush on the scoutmaster.

Charming and humorous, with sex scenes that are erotic without being over the top, the novel successfully ends the series, while leaving open the possibility of further adventures. The controversial subject matter may make some readers uncomfortable, but for those interested in a sexual adventure told from a gay perspective, this is a wonderful look at boys transitioning between childhood and adulthood.

Also available in hardcover and ebook.

You're in High School Now: Julian's Sophomore Year, Part 1
Eldot
One Spirit Press, 610 pages, (paperback) $15.99 978-1-893075-77-1
(Reviewed: June 2015)

This charming novel continues the story of Julian, from author Eldot's series Julian's Private Scrapbook. Set in the early 1960s, it follows Julian's coming of age as a gay man through the first half of his first year in high school, as he makes new friends, learns about girls, and navigates this strange but exciting new world.

The title refers to the refrain his mother and her friend continually use when explaining to Julian why he must pay attention to his clothes now and other new "rules." Julian's only real concern is his mother's interest that he take out a girl. Since he is only romantically interested in his scoutmaster Mark, that presents an obstacle. Fortunately, he attracts the attention of Rita, one of the school's prettiest girls, who invites him to the Sadie Hawkins dance. Julian's complete ignorance about Rita's intentions during the dance and the car ride afterwards (as well as his description to his mother later) provides some of the novel's funniest scenes."

Julian is certainly experienced when it comes to sex, however. He continues the explorations he discovered at scout camp the previous summer, both as an initiate in a secret society of like-minded boys, as well as with Randall, recently moved from Washington. Randall, a victim of bullying at his previous school, is instantly drawn to Julian when he sees him, and they form an immediate, deep friendship. Julian introduces Randall to his scouting troop and takes an interest in his photography, and Randall is deeply impressed by Julian's drawing skills. The two bring out the best in each other.

While not every reader will appreciate the sex scenes, they are sensitively drawn and important to the story. The only complaint this reader has is waiting for Part 2, where it seems the situation will become complicated. Well-written, with engaging, likable characters, this book skillfully presents the challenges and pleasures boys who love men face in growing up.

Also available in hardcover and ebook.

You're in *high school* now:

You're in *high school* now

a romantic comedy
by Eldot

Julian's Sophomore Year, Part 1

Julian's Sophomore Year: Part 1

Q Press, 626 pages (paperback), 978-1-893075-77-1
Reviewed: **October, 2015**

KIRKUS REVIEW

The life and times of an adventurous, gay high school sophomore.

In the latest installment featuring Julian, the affable lead in the Julian's Private Scrapbook YA series, author Eldot (*The Champions: Julian's Private Scrapbook*, 2013, etc.) re-creates the autumn of 1962 as Julian embarks upon another school year full of books and boys at Jackson High School. Amid a backdrop of artistic inclinations and first-day jitters, Julian's romantic feelings for Mark, his Scoutmaster at Camp Walker over the past summer, continue to simmer, with their exploratory fondling lingering in his memory. But his concerned mother, Francine, encourages him to show an interest in girls. When Rita, an attractive, mischievous schoolmate, asks Julian, aka "the blond masterpiece," to the Sadie Hawkins dance, the obvious awkward clashing of orientations ensues.

Humor is one of Eldot's strong suits; he has an impressive capacity for penning farcical, innocently disastrous moments. He also builds a good supporting cast, like Mark, who is in a heterosexual marriage of convenience after his longtime partner died seven years prior; and Randall, a gay virgin and recent arrival to Jackson High. Intimate shenanigans occur at a secret society campout for randy boys, but the author takes care to handle these moments with restraint. Structurally, however, Eldot fumbles a bit. He shifts perspective awkwardly and adds too many disclaimers, style notes, and end matter that are meant to illuminate Julian but result in informational overload. Still, Eldot successfully taps into the experiences of gay youth with a believable blend of engaging characterization, humor, pathos, back story, and teenage angst.

Fun, frolicsome series with good humor and a message of unity and equality; new readers may want to start at the beginning.

KIRKUS

You're in *high school* now

Julian's Sophomore Year, Part 1

Reviewed by Amanda Silva, July 23, 2015

You're in *high school* now

This YA romantic comedy reflects traditional coming-of-age themes, further complicated by issues of sexuality and identity.

Eldot's romantic comedy *You're in High School Now* follows Julian, a young gay man in who is getting to know himself while creating his place in the world. This particular world is high school in 1962, a microcosm fraught with prizes and pitfalls, where bullies abound and fitting in is a constant quest. This narrative reflects traditional coming-of-age themes, further complicated by issues of sexuality and identity.

a romantic comedy
by Eldot

Julian's Sophomore Year, Part 1
Second Edition

These are sensitive topics for many readers, regardless of age, but Eldot writes with an urgency to connect with those young adult readers for whom these issues might be especially difficult. This story is an extension of Eldot's earlier series, the Julian's Private Scrapbook novels, but can be read in isolation. Readers should be aware it contains sexual content and adult themes layered throughout.

Julian is a sympathetic character, thoughtful and comical in his observations about himself and those around him. His internal struggles and interactions with his peers will likely connect with young readers, regardless of gender or sexual orientation. Self-acceptance rings as a universal desire and pursuit throughout these pages.

Although the writing is clear, the structure is not. While it is admirable for an author to experiment with a new writing style, the clarity of the work can sometimes be compromised. Eldot eventually explains—but not until the end of the book—that the narrative intentionally combines first- and third-person points of view as a means of freeing both writer and reader from "cumbersome conventions" concerning paragraph structure and punctuation. Eldot is a teacher with more than thirty years of experience; his frustration, or perhaps boredom, with convention is understandable. However, the resulting lack of clarity ultimately detracts from his work.

And this is important work. At the very outset, Eldot writes: "The grand social purpose that motivated the *Julian's Private Scrapbook* series lurks in the background, unsolved as always: social change is never as rapid as one would like. There are still bullies … So it's worth the effort to add a positive chapter or two."

Eldot's message is, indeed, as important as ever. When it comes to sharing that message through mainstream media, however, revisions in defense of convention and organization would bring these already bright and positive chapters to greater light.

He's kinda tall

a romantic comedy
by Eldot

Julian's Sophomore Year, Part 2

Another memorable snapshot of LGBTQ+ high school life in a bygone era.

HE'S KINDA TALL

BY ELDOT · RELEASE DATE: N/A

The continuing saga of a resilient gay high schooler's adolescent adventures.

Prolific author Eldot picks up where You're in High School Now (2015) left off, with young North Carolina high school sophomore Julian Forrest facing new feelings and challenges in late 1962. The author again succeeds in establishing the era in which his protagonist's youth plays out amid themes of inclusivity, friendship, burgeoning sexuality, and the precarious state of race relations during the school desegregation movement of the mid-20th century. Eldot imparts many life lessons over the course of the narrative; the first is that focused dedication to one's schoolwork will not only garner one good grades, but also beneficial recognition from instructors when one least expects it. Julian's consistently pleasant demeanor, personal flair, and conscientious, hard work make his teachers think of him as a model student. His rare, enviable qualities draw the attention of several teachers who believe he would make an ideal helper for an incoming Black student named Kassa "Kasey" Wood. The son of a prominent Boston scientist, Kasey is a polite, friendly, and impressively talented young pianist who comes to appreciate the time that Julian devotes to helping him adjust to a new town, a new school, and new classmates; in a compelling sequence, Julian even insists on racial equality at a segregated "whites-only" diner. The relationship between these two characters would be sufficient to carry the entire novel, but Eldot has grander visions in mind, carried out by a parade of peripheral teenage characters who take their turns marching through the novel.

Their storylines—some fleeting, some with greater staying power—definitely add some panache to the tale and enliven what becomes a rather overlong tome, as it extends to nearly 600 pages in length. Readers will likely want Julian, a budding artist, and pianist extraordinaire Kasey to remain at center stage, and they often do. However, they're upstaged much too often by other scenes concerned with randy camping adventures, fart jokes, or extended family melodrama. The omniscient third-person narration is often dryly humorous, but the book also explores Julian and Kasey's friendship through the eyes of folks who know very little about them. This narrative twist affords readers a look at what it's like to be observed and blindly judged by casual strangers. As with the other books in this series, the author doesn't ever shy away from the nuances of sexual attraction, which plays a particularly substantial role in Julian's young life. The teens' flirtations and overt physical carnality are portrayed as unashamed and innocently exploratory; they show the characters to be primarily concerned with mutual, guiltless pleasure, but also fully aware of the necessity of social discretion in that time and place. Although the narrative does feel extravagantly expository at times, its overall sense of social consciousness is remarkable. A concluding, expansive glossary, filled with historical references to the 1960s, will be helpful for newcomers to the setting.

Another overly busy but nonetheless memorable snapshot of LGBTQ+ high school life in a bygone era.